This book is due for return on or before the last date shown
above; it may, subject to the book not being reserved by
another reader, be renewed by personal application, post, or
telephone, quoting this date and details of the book.

HAMPSHIRE COUNTY LIBRARY

2/11/90

SAINT—WITH RED HANDS?

SAINT—
WITH RED HANDS?

The Chronicle of a Great Crime

by

YSEULT BRIDGES

MACMILLAN

First published 1954

Reissued by Macmillan & Co. Ltd., 1970

This book is copyright in all countries which
are signatories to the Berne Convention

SBN boards: 333 11338 1

Printed in Great Britain by
LOWE AND BRYDONE (PRINTERS) LTD
London

TO MY DAUGHTERS
HALCYONE AND CHARMIAN

ACKNOWLEDGMENTS

I have to express my thanks to Mr. and Mrs. Greenhalgh of Langham House, Rode, for their courtesy and the help they gave me when I was beginning to write this book; to the Editors of the *Somerset Standard* and *Wiltshire Times* for allowing me access to their files; to the Chief Constables of Wiltshire and Somerset for their readiness to assist me; and to all who gave me information relating to the case either by word of mouth or in response to my letter in the *Somerset Standard*.

I am especially grateful to Mr. John Rhode, not only for his permission to quote from his book *The Case of Constance Kent* and from his essay on the crime in *The Anatomy of Murder*, but also for his interest and kindness, and for allowing me to reproduce his copy of Constance Kent's letter to Sir Peter Edlin.

My thanks are also due to Mr. A. Tilney Bassett for his help over the Gladstone Papers; to the Hon. Gilbert Coleridge,[1] son of the first Lord Coleridge, and to the present Lord Coleridge for permission to quote from the first Lord Coleridge's letter to Mr. Gladstone given in Appendix III; to Lord Harcourt for similar permission in the case of Sir William Harcourt's letter in Appendix IV; to Mr. Orlando H. Wagner and the Rev. A. N. Coombe in the case of the Rev. A. D. Wagner's letters; and to Mr. Charles A. Gladstone of Hawarden in the case of the letters of Mr. Gladstone himself.

I must also acknowledge my gratitude to Mr. H. Hamilton Maughan and the Coelian Press, Dublin, for permission to quote from that authoritative monograph *Wagner of Brighton*; and to the following publishing houses for similar permission in the case of the works given against their names:

[1] Mr. Coleridge, in a charming and lively letter, informed me that he was present in Court at the age of six when Constance Kent was tried at Salisbury in 1865. He died on 6th November 1953.

Messrs. Geoffrey Bles	*The Case of Constance Kent* (John Rhode)
Messrs. Constable & Co. Ltd.	*Murder and Murder Trials* (H. M. Walbrook)
Messrs. Chapman & Hall	*Memorials of Millbank* (A. Griffiths) *The Secrets of the Prison House* (A. Griffiths)
The Richards Press Ltd.	*The Road Murder* (J. B. Atlay)
John Lane, The Bodley Head	*The Anatomy of Murder*

And, finally, I wish to pay tribute to the unfailing efficiency and helpfulness of the East Sussex County Libraries.

CONTENTS

Book II

THE SEQUEL

ILLUSTRATIONS

PRINCIPAL CHARACTERS IN THE CASE

(The ages given are those at the time of the crime)

Members of the Family

Samuel Savile Kent, aged 59.

Mary Ann Kent, née Windus, 1st wife of S. S. Kent (died 1852,
   aged 44).

Mary Ann, aged 29
Elizabeth, aged 27
Edward Windus (died 1857, aged 22) } Children of the above.
Constance Emilie, aged 16
William Savile, aged 15

Mary Drew Kent, née Pratt, 2nd wife of S. S. Kent, aged 37.

Mary Amelia, aged 5
Francis Savile, aged 3 years 10 months } Children of the above.
Eveline, aged 20 months

A boy was born one month after the crime.

Indoor Servants

Elizabeth Gough, aged 21, nurse.

Sarah Kerslake, cook.

Sarah Cox, housemaid.

Emily Doel, nursery-maid. (Employed daily; lived in Road.)

Eliza Holcombe, charwoman. (Employed daily; lived in Lane Cottages, Road.)

Outdoor Servants

James Holcombe, groom-gardener. (Lived in Lane Cottages, Road.)

John Alloway, odd-job boy. (Lived at Beckington.)

Daniel Oliver, casual labourer. (Lived in Road.)

Esther Holley, washerwoman. (Lived in Lane Cottages, Road.)

Martha Holley, daughter of E. Holley. (Lived with mother.)

Police Officers

Captain Meredith, Chief Constable of Wiltshire, Devizes.

Superintendent Foley, Wilts County Constabulary, Trowbridge.

Superintendent Wolfe, Wilts County Constabulary, Devizes.

Superintendent Abbott, Wilts County Constabulary, Warminster.

P.C. Dallimore, Wilts County Constabulary, Trowbridge.
P.C. Heritage, Wilts County Constabulary, Southwick.
Superintendent Summers, Somerset County Constabulary, Frome.
Inspector Pitney, Somerset County Constabulary, Frome.
Sergeant Watts, Somerset County Constabulary, Frome.
P.C. Urch, Somerset County Constabulary, Road.
James Morgan, Parish Constable, Road.
Chief Inspector Whicher, Metropolitan Police, Scotland Yard.
Sergeant Williamson, Metropolitan Police, Scotland Yard.

Other Characters

Reverend Edward Peacock, Vicar of Road-hill, Road.
Joshua Parsons, M.C.S., Physician and Surgeon, Beckington.
Rowland Rodway, Solicitor to S. S. Kent, Trowbridge.
W. H. Dunn, Solicitor; replaced R. Rodway as solicitor to S. S. Kent after crime, Frome.
J. W. Stapleton, Certifying Surgeon to Board of Factory Commissioners, Trowbridge.
George Sylvester, Surgeon: Wiltshire County Coroner, Trowbridge.
William Nutt } Discovered body { Cobbler, Lane Cottages, Road.
Thomas Benger } { Smallholder, Road.
Eliza Dallimore, wife of P.C. Dallimore: Female Searcher.
James Fricker, Plumber and Glazier, Road.
Helen Moody } School-friends of Constance Kent.
Louisa Hatherall }
George Groser, Correspondent of the *Daily News*.
W. Slack, Solicitor, Bath.
T. B. Saunders, J.P., Retired Barrister-at-Law, Bradford-on-Avon.

Additional Characters in 1865

Reverend Arthur Douglas Wagner, Vicar of St. Paul's Church, Brighton.
Caroline Ann Greame, Lady Superior, St. Mary's Home, Brighton.
Chief Inspector Williamson, Metropolitan Police, Scotland Yard.
Sergeant Durkin, Metropolitan Police, Scotland Yard.
Sir Thomas Henry, Chief Magistrate, Bow Street.
Mr. Justice Willes, Assize Judge, Western Circuit.
Dr. Bucknill, Specialist in Mental Diseases, Rugby.

N.B. For the sake of brevity the *Trowbridge & North Wilts Advertiser* is referred to in the text as the *Advertiser*; and the *Somerset & Wilts Journal* as the *Journal*.

BOOK I

THE CRIME

CHAPTER ONE

PREVIEW

I

THE story which this book tells possesses all the ingredients of a Greek tragedy played out against the solid background of middle-class family life in mid-Victorian England. It is a story which not only exercises an unique fascination over the mind, but is in every respect unique in the annals of crime.

On 30th June, 1860, the whole country was shocked by the news that the little son of Mr. Samuel Savile Kent, of Road-hill House in Wiltshire, had been taken from his cot in the nursery during the previous night and brutally murdered in the garden. His nurse, whose bed was only nine feet from his own, swore that she had heard no sound during the night. His father and mother, sharing a room next door to the nursery, made similar statements, as did the six adults occupying the floor above. Yet, while it soon became obvious that the deed could only have been done by one or more of these nine persons, there appeared to be no motive and absolutely no clues.

The police of two counties and the most celebrated detective from Scotland Yard were engaged in attempts to solve the mystery; the Press devoted the closest attention to it, while amateur sleuths published hypotheses in the form of pamphlets which sold by the thousand.

Two men claimed, falsely, to have committed the crime; two young women were, successively, charged with it: Constance Kent, the child's half-sister, and Elizabeth Gough, his nurse. Neither was committed for trial.

The circumstances of the sequel, which occurred five years later, led to scenes of mob-violence and ended by determining once and for all an intricate point concerning the law in relation to the Church which had been in abeyance since the Reformation and which now leaped into prominence.

"The outcry," writes H. M. Walbrook, "with which the final revelation was received was almost drowned in another and entirely different wave of popular passion, half political and half religious. And to crown the singularity of the whole story, it is by no means certain today that the punishment which finally fell upon the criminal was not a miscarriage of justice almost as tragic as the original crime."[1]

2

The first book to be written on the case—*The Great Crime of 1860* by Dr. J. W. Stapleton—was published the following year. By then the authorities had abandoned their efforts to solve it, and it looked as though it would remain unsolved for ever.

Although Mr. Kent had never been charged with the crime, public opinion had openly asserted that he was the murderer of his son, and it was Dr. Stapleton's object to vindicate the man who had been his personal friend and official colleague, even at the cost of distorting evidence and casting suspicion upon innocent persons.

It seemed to me all too much that had been written on the subject since then was mere repetition, and that it must surely be possible to glean information on the spot which might shed new light on the many obscure features of an event which happened only ninety years ago.

I set out on my quest in the spring of 1950. It led me into Somerset, Wiltshire, Gloucester and Sussex, and was well rewarded. I visited the various places where the Kent family had lived. I was courteously received and conducted over Road-hill House by its present owners; I met and corresponded with a number of the immediate descendants of those whose lives had been caught up in the meshes of this most sensational case; and, finally, with some who had known Constance Kent in her later years—one intimately. All were glad to tell me what they knew.

I share the view of those writers who consider that the Road mystery consists not only of one but of two crimes, of which

[1] *Murder and Murder Trials*—H. M. Walbrook.

the second is the more insidious and dramatic; and the aim of this book is to provide a full account of the whole case from all the existing material. It is told in chronological order, and the conversations related are taken *verbatim* from the evidence given at various inquiries.

A brief account is included of the antecedents of Samuel Savile Kent—so far as they can now be known—for the very good reason that the clue to the whole mystery is to be found in his own life, *before* that June morning when the body of his little son was discovered with the throat cut and a vicious knife-thrust in the side.

That life can be divided into two distinct cycles, each set in motion by almost identical impulses, each closing in a sudden death, and each marked by a startling chronological similarity.

CHAPTER TWO

SAMUEL SAVILE KENT

I

As the eighteenth century had been the heyday of the aristocracy, so the nineteenth was that of the middle-classes to which Samuel Savile Kent—the son of a carpet manufacturer with a place of business at London Wall—belonged.

So paradoxical were the people of that century that, while they made us the richest nation in the world, yet they began the movement for the abolition of sweated labour from which that wealth was derived; while they boasted of national unity, yet they exercised the most rigid class distinctions; while they made a cult of sentimentality, yet they were often cruel past the limits of barbarism. It is not surprising that they earned us a reputation for hypocrisy.

With a queen on the throne, men were the dominant sex. They lived with gusto and had a religious respect for the liberty of the individual; yet they denied their wives and daughters any form of self-expression or independence. But while they straddled their hearths like colossi, out of that domestic limbo to which their wives and daughters were relegated as subjects of their will arose the movement for female emancipation and sprang such intrepid women as Mary Kingsley, Mary Slessor and, above all, Florence Nightingale; such outspoken writers as the Brontës and George Eliot.

Samuel Savile Kent, born in 1801, was a typical product of his class and century. He bore his second name with pride, for it was that of his mother's family who, as owners of property in Colchester, sprang from a "superior sphere of life" to that which his father, as a tradesman, occupied. Of the seven children of this marriage only himself and two sisters survived—for, although the population was increasing fourfold, infantile mortality in an age dependent upon the tender mercies of Sarah Gamps was appallingly high.

He received a good education, after which he entered his father's carpet factory, gaining experience which was to prove invaluable to him in his later career. But at twenty-five he secured a partnership in the large and thriving firm of North & Co., dry-salters, of Aldermanbury.

Hitherto his social contacts had been confined to a circle whose pursuits centred wholly upon trade, but now he gained the *entrée* into one where the acquisition of wealth was combined with wide literary and artistic interests and achievements.

Thomas Windus came of a family whose wealth was derived from established city concerns and whose way of life was characteristic of all that was best in the class now moving to its zenith. A scholar of distinction and a Fellow of the Royal Society of Antiquaries, he entertained some of the most distinguished figures in the contemporary world of art and letters at his house on Stamford Hill.

It was a novel atmosphere for Samuel Kent, but he possessed a rare ability for adapting himself with ease to his company and surroundings. Within the year he was paying court to Mary Ann, the eldest daughter, then seventeen. He had charm; he had a way with him which invited confidences and which most people found irresistible—and she fell deeply in love with him. But attractive and presentable though he might be, he had neither the position nor the expectations to commend him to Thomas Windus as the husband of his daughter, which may explain why their marriage did not take place until four years later, in 1829, when Mary Ann reached the age of twenty-one. It seems likely that she then inherited some money of her own, for they set up house in Artillery Place, Finsbury Square, then "a select residential neighbourhood" much favoured by business men because of its proximity to the city. They entertained considerably, and there was a constant interchange of visits between Stamford Hill and Artillery Place, for the Winduses were a united family.

She named her first child Thomas Windus after her father, and her second Mary Ann after her mother and herself. Her first grief—of a long succession—came with the little boy's death of convulsions when he was a year old. Another child, Elizabeth, was born at the end of 1833.

The following spring Samuel Kent caught a chill which settled on his lungs. Tuberculosis was the terror of the age, and he was hurried away from the fog and smoke of London to the Devon coast. Here his health improved rapidly, but it was decided that his constitution could not stand a return to office life in London: the partnership in North & Co. was disposed of and, through the influence of the Windus family, he obtained the post of Sub-inspector of Factories in the West of England under Lord Althorp's Factory Act of the previous year.

Hitherto children had been sent to the mills almost as soon as they could walk, and in rush seasons young women were kept at work, usually under the most unhygienic conditions, all day and half the night as well. The main purpose of the Factory Act of 1833—which not only the employers but the poverty-stricken workpeople themselves did their best to evade—was to prohibit the employment of children under nine years of age, to limit the hours of work and improve the conditions in the mills.

To enable the Inspectors to enforce the provisions of this Act powers similar to those of a magistrate were conferred upon them; and to obviate the dangers of corruption to which their powers exposed them Government took pains to select only men of integrity—which generally meant in those days men of assured social position.

Not only was it immensely gratifying to Samuel Kent's self-esteem to quit trade and mingle on terms of equality with the landed gentry and professional classes; not only did the experience gained in his father's carpet factory—experience which his colleagues had to acquire—hold out the promise of early promotion, first to a full inspectorship and ultimately to a seat on the Board of Factory Commissioners itself; but the peripatetic nature of his work and the fresh contacts it continually brought him exactly suited his energetic and gregarious disposition. By rail and post-chaise he was ceaselessly on tour over an area which covered large parts of Devon, Somerset, Wiltshire and Dorset.

2

Samuel Kent was the victim to that form of vanity which sacrifices everything to display. His clothes and his horses were the best that money could buy, he entertained his friends lavishly, and the houses he occupied were always larger than either his means or his requirements warranted. To offset these extravagances he became increasingly parsimonious over domestic expenses.

As he expanded in affability towards an ever-widening circle of friends his wife faded into the background. In the big house which he had taken at Sidmouth—and which he kept understaffed—Mrs. Kent found herself very much alone. Instead of the bustle and activity outside the windows of Artillery Place she now looked out over a limitless expanse of empty sea. Cut off from all that was familiar, from a life warmed by family affection and friendships, and stimulated with interests, she now existed in a state of domestic isolation punctuated only by her husband's constant departures and uncertain returns. Trained as women were in those days to suppress their feelings and accept their fate, she bore her tribulations uncomplainingly, and in this a deep religious instinct supported her.

She was pregnant, and Mr. Kent, preoccupied with his own concerns, failed to notice how thin and wan she had become until a harassing cough called his attention to her health. Dr. Gidley, the local practitioner, was summoned. He asked for a consultation with Dr. Blackell of Exeter, a lung specialist. No indications of phthisis were found, but it was advised that a mother's-help should be engaged to relieve Mrs. Kent of household cares until her confinement was over.

Whether Mr. Kent demurred at this additional expense, or whether she herself was reluctant to incur it, is not known, but the advice was disregarded, and the birth of Edward Windus in April 1835, after a protracted delivery, prostrated her with exhaustion.

Edward was a fine child and he throve, but the four babies who followed him between that date and April 1842 all died in early infancy. That post-natal incompetence was a contributory factor in their deaths seems probable, for when in 1843—after her return from a long visit to her people—Mrs. Kent again became pregnant, a nursemaid of better class and education than the average was engaged to look after the new baby—Constance Emilie—from birth and it survived and throve.

Mary Pratt was the daughter of a Tiverton greengrocer. She had received what was described as a "superior education", and, indeed, it was afterwards claimed that not only had she occupied a situation as governess before she came to the Kents but that she had actually entered their household in that capacity. But as the two eldest children, Mary Ann and Elizabeth, were at a boarding-school, and Edward, on the eve of departure to a preparatory school at Crewkerne, there was clearly no employment for a governess in the Kent family. Nor do governesses act as nurses to newly-born infants.

Dr. Stapleton says that she was recommended to the Kents by a neighbour, Dr. Walker, and also makes the curious assertion that Mr. Kent himself engaged her after going to see her parents. Another story alleges that she was a mill-girl, and yet another that Mr. Kent became acquainted with her during his wife's absence at Stamford Hill. But all agree that she was clever, and possessed, besides, good looks and vitality. Her age was twenty-one.

Constance Emilie was born in February 1844, and as soon as his wife's labour began Mr. Kent moved into his dressing-room, returning to the room they shared when she was convalescent. But at the birth of William Savile, rather less than a year later, he moved into a bedroom in another part of the house, and, as Dr. Bucknill afterwards wrote, "Mrs. Kent was left by her husband to live in the seclusion of her own room, while the management of the household was taken over the heads of grown-up daughters by a high-spirited young governess."[1]

With the entry of Mary Pratt into his household the first cycle in the life of Samuel Kent, which was to lead ultimately to the crime at Road-hill House, was set in motion.

[1] Dr. Bucknill, of Rugby, specialist in mental diseases.

CHAPTER THREE

THE FIRST CYCLE

I

MARY PRATT took over the management of the household gradually and circumspectly, and it was some time before the state of affairs within it became known. When it did, the need to move somewhere else grew imperative and Mr. Kent took a lease of Walton Manor, near Clevedon in Somerset, which, lying in a fold of the hills above the Bristol Channel, was effectively concealed from inquisitive eyes. Nevertheless, rumours as to the equivocal nature of the household soon got abroad, and the wives of the local gentry refrained from leaving their cards upon the tenants of the manor. These rumours, indeed, eventually reached the ears of the Board of Factory Commissioners, and Mr. Howell, one of its members—who was a personal friend of Mr. Kent as well as his official superior—approached him on the subject. The latter plausibly explained that since William's birth his wife had become an invalid—and surely the presence of his two grown-up daughters in the house should safeguard them all from malicious gossip?

But the gossip still persisted and grew more explicit. It declared that Mrs. Kent was kept a prisoner in her own room. This, probably, was an exaggeration. It seems more likely that she lived a secluded life in a separate part of the house. That she had her children constantly about her is borne out by the devotion she inspired in them and by the obvious signs of her influence upon them in their later years.

That she should have submitted at all to such humiliation may be inconceivable to the modern mind, but conditions in the mid-nineteenth century were different from what they are to-day. The only course open to her was to seek refuge with her family, but that would have entailed abandoning her children. In remaining where she was—apart from all question of the sanctity of marriage upon which she would have had unshakable convictions—she could at least protect them from the worst consequences of their father's infatuation. There was also the hope that the infatuation would exhaust itself, or else the realization of the damage he was doing to his career—if nothing else—would restore him to a sense of his responsibilities and he would rid himself of the woman.

2

Constance and William knew no other state of affairs than that which now existed in their home, and both appear to have been fond of Mary Pratt. Edward, on the other hand, had disliked her from the first and taken no pains to conceal it. Mary Ann and Elizabeth must have realized the truth, but appear to have been singularly ineffectual young women who remain strangely nebulous throughout everything. In contrast to them the characters of Edward and Constance stand out sharply defined. Both had inherited their mother's strain of mysticism. Both are described as being "talented and enterprising", as having "prepossessing manners" and a "high order of intelligence". Both were affectionate, forthright and self-reliant; both were amenable to discipline, but intolerant of tyranny; both had a capacity for suffering second only to remarkable powers of endurance. A deep attachment united them.

William, conceived when his mother was already aware of her husband's increasing indifference to her and born when she knew herself supplanted by Mary Pratt, was a hyper-sensitive boy, timid and diffident, who relied in all things upon Constance for moral support.

Insensitive and lacking in affection for his children, Mr. Kent exacted implicit obedience from them. Like the average Victorian father he made no allowance for individual temperaments, and any divergence from the code laid down for all was visited with sharp punishments. But in any case domesticity irked him. The restraint which his gentle, highly-civilized wife exercised over his rumbustious and primitive passions had grown increasingly tedious with the years. The young and vital Mary Pratt stimulated them. His character was essentially weak and hers essentially strong: she played upon his weaknesses and fed his vanity until she obsessed him; and she dominated him with a skill which kept him in ignorance of that domination.

3

In 1851 Edward, entering his third year at the naval school at Gosport, where he had done extremely well, spent, as usual, his summer holidays at Walton Manor, much in his mother's company. Before his return to Gosport she gave him her own Bible and obtained his promise that he would never be parted from it. At the same time she also arranged for the sum of £1,000 to be held in trust for Constance at the Bank of England until she reached the age of twenty-one.

Whether these actions were dictated by some premonition of impending calamity it is impossible to say, but there are indications that her husband's affairs were approaching a crisis. That spring another interview had taken place between himself and Mr. Howell at which it seems likely that he was given a hint that he must alter his domestic arrangements or resign his appointment. Then, in the middle of the autumn term, without warning or explanation, he removed Edward from the naval school and placed him as a permanent boarder in the "household of a private tutor at Bristol, from whose establishment it was now designed that he should enter the merchant service"[1]: a peremptory and tyrannical act which was not only a bitter blow to the boy but served to intensify the criticisms being levelled at his father.

Soon afterwards the latter was again house-hunting. His place of residence was largely controlled by the exigencies of his appointment; but Baynton House, in Wiltshire, of which he now took a lease, was the farthest point to which he could get from Walton Manor, and was singularly inconvenient for the performance of his duties, being six miles from the nearest railway station at Westbury. The move, which it was openly

[1] J. W. Stapleton.

said was made "to screen him from public censure as regard to his cruel indifference to her" (his wife) "and his misconduct in regard to the governess",[1] took place at the end of March 1852.

Where Walton Manor had been secluded Baynton House was isolated. Surrounded by close-growing plantations which effectively hid it from the hamlet of East Coulston, it lay, large and rambling, in a cleft of the Downs which arose steeply about it. To one side, beyond its lawns and across a rutted lane, was a tiny grey stone church among moss-grown tombstones leaning askew. A melancholy silence brooded over the whole, broken only by the hoarse cawing of rooks above the tree-tops and the murmur of a stream which fed a lake in the grounds.

Six weeks after their arrival Mary Pratt, "who had never been absent from her post for a single day, left on a visit to friends in Devonshire".[2] On the day after her departure— 2nd May—Mrs. Kent, "who had been in good health",[3] was attacked without warning symptoms by excruciating pains. The nearest doctor—a total stranger—was called in, but she died in great agony on the 5th. Mr. Kent was present in the house throughout her illness. Mary Pratt returned immediately.

The following lines are carved upon the stone which covers the grave:

"SACRED TO THE MEMORY OF MARY ANN
WIFE OF S. SAVILE KENT ESQUIRE OF BAYNTON HOUSE
DIED MAY 5TH 1852 AGED 44 YEARS."

And so the first cycle in the life of Samuel Kent was brought to a close.

---

[1] J. W. Stapleton.
[2] *Ibid.*
[3] *Ibid.*

4

When the news of Mrs. Kent's sudden death reached those places where she and her husband had previously lived, suspicion grew rife that he and Mary Pratt had "brought about her end". This allegation was revived eight years later, at the time of the crime, and hinted at in a Plymouth newspaper; but although it was quelled by a letter from the doctor who had attended her and who stated that she had died of "an obstruction of the bowels", the previous rumour that she had been kept a prisoner gained renewed prominence, and this Mr. Kent attempted to dispose of by asserting that she had been kept in seclusion because she was insane.

Since this charge, with all the appalling consequences it must have for her children, was to be disseminated by Dr. Stapleton—who had never even known her—and was finally to develop into a legend, it is necessary to consider it here.

Dr. Stapleton asserts that Mrs. Kent became insane as early as 1834, when she was pregnant with Edward; yet he is compelled to admit that she was carrying out her social and domestic duties in a normal manner up to the time of William's birth eleven years later, in 1845, while after this date she had the testamentary capacity to execute the Deed that placed £1,000 in trust for Constance, which of itself constitutes a rebuttal of the charge of insanity.

Apart from the fact that during this period when she was alleged to be insane Mr. Kent did not hesitate to beget six more children by her, it is inconceivable that he should have endured seven years of social ostracism and the displeasure of his official superiors over a matter which, if his wife had really been insane, was capable of so simple an explanation and would have won for him general sympathy and support.

Furthermore, at no time was any medical evidence of insanity produced. The whole allegation rests upon nothing more substantial than the fact that one of Mrs. Kent's brothers was mentally defective and upon two trivial incidents relating to herself which Dr. Stapleton quotes.

The first of these is that, one day at Sidmouth, Mrs. Kent took Mary Anne and Elizabeth for a walk and missed her way home: which proves nothing more than that, like thousands of other people, she possessed a poor bump of locality. The second relates how, also at Sidmouth, Mr. Kent once found his wife tearing out and destroying some illustrations from a book of prints. The nature of the illustrations, however, is not revealed, and it is easy to imagine that, if they were cartoons by Rowlandson, perhaps, or Cruikshank, Mrs. Kent was shocked by their coarseness.

CHAPTER FOUR

THE SECOND CYCLE

I

FOR the next fifteen months Mary Pratt continued to live at Baynton House as governess to Constance and William, now aged eight and seven respectively; then in August (1853), the period of mourning being over, the whole family went up to London, and, with Constance acting as bridesmaid, the marriage between Samuel Savile Kent and Mary Drew Pratt took place at Lewisham Church.

Edward was at sea. He had entered the Royal Mail Steam Packet Company and was completing a period of two years' service under sail which would qualify him to become an officer. When he landed in England some weeks later and proceeded to Baynton House he was ignorant that the nursemaid he so disliked had become his step-mother. In the shock of hearing the news his feelings overcame him and a furious scene ensued which involved the whole family and ended with his step-mother in hysterics and his father in a towering passion. He himself left the house and went straight back to Bristol.

The Crimean War had broken out and he immediately volunteered for service on one of his Company's ships which had been hired by Government as a transport, sailing almost at once for Balaclava as fifth officer of the *Kenilworth* without holding any further communication with his father.

The following May the second Mrs. Kent gave birth to a still-born child: she was no sooner convalescent than she was again pregnant.

Whatever may have been Mr. Kent's reasons for the move to Baynton House he now determined to dispose of the lease, and by October of that year (1854) he had taken one of Road-hill House. On the very eve of the move—in the middle of November—he received a notification that during a great storm on the

14th instant the *Kenilworth* had foundered with all hands off Balaclava.

His quarrel with Edward had been kept secret and the loss of his son brought him much sympathy; but only a day or two later, after they had moved to Road-hill House and as he and his wife were getting into their carriage to drive to Bath to buy mourning, the postman handed him a letter from "the son whom he had grieved for as dead".

Although this reads like an episode in one of the novels of the period, it is none the less true, and Edward's letter is quoted here in full partly because it is of some interest as a contemporary document and partly as a sidelight on his character. He makes no mention of injuries which he had received, nor does he allude to an incident which made a lasting impression upon him: before being cast into the sea he had managed to slip his mother's Bible into his pocket, and he believed that it preserved him from the fate which had overtaken all his brother officers.

> "R.M.S. *Trent*,
> at Balaclava.
> November 17th, 1854.

"My dear Papa,
          "I know you will be very glad to hear of my providential escape from shipwreck on 14th November. The *Kenilworth* was lying off Balaclava when a most fearful gale sprang up about 7 o'clock, and in an hour's time increased to a terrible hurricane. About 9:45 the *Kenilworth* parted from her anchors and was dashed to pieces on the rocks in the course of a very few minutes. Only myself and six of the crew were saved, and 23 lost. I am the only officer that is saved. Captain Ponsonby, of the R.M.S. *Trent*, when he heard that I was saved, sent for me, and, as there was an officer wanting on board the *Trent*, he made me acting fifth officer. I should think that the best thing that could be done now would be to write to the Directors, and try to get the appointment confirmed; as I suppose all further hopes of going in another sailing ship must be given up. I have lost everything but a shirt and trousers, and my watch, which

I had on me when cast ashore. Very fortunately for me the R.M.S. *Avon* was lying in Balaclava; and Mr. Langdon, the officer who was so kind to me on board the *Magdalena*, is on board her and he has given me some shirts and a suit of clothes, and lent me £4 to get what I wanted. Several other ships have met with the same fate as ours; and the loss of life has been most considerable. Captain Ponsonby is very kind to me. He is also very intimate with Mr. Arthur Windus, who always asks after me when he sees Captain Ponsonby; so the captain seems interested in my behalf. I must now conclude with love to you all. I remain, your affectionate son,

"Edward Kent."

With Edward's return to England the hatchet was buried, and both his father and his step-mother—who had given birth to a daughter, named Mary Amelia, earlier in the year—made his leave pleasant. The *Trent*, the flagship of the Company's passenger and mail service to the West Indies, was returned to her route, and Edward, his appointment confirmed, sailed in her as fifth officer. At the end of his voyages he paid visits to his family, but in the summer of 1855 he was transferred, with promotion as third officer, to the inter-colonial steamer which linked the smaller West Indian islands with the Ocean Mail at Barbados: an appointment which would entail an absence from England of at least two years.

Constance took his departure much to heart. She was now ten. Her eyes, deep-set under a wide, prominent forehead, were those of a thinker and a visionary. In repose her expression was grave, but her smile lit her face with radiance. Her single claim to beauty was her hair: chestnut-red, long, lustrous, and with a natural wave.

All England had been ringing with the name of Florence Nightingale, and Edward must have had many stories of her to tell—some perhaps from the lips of men whose lives had been saved by her devoted nursing. There can be little doubt that all that Constance learned of this remarkable woman made a deep and lasting impression upon her, and filled her with a longing to follow her example.

2

Even the most lenient of critics can find little good to say of the erstwhile Mary Pratt.

"She appears to have been a rather selfish woman," writes John Rhode, "the scope of whose affections was strictly limited. While she may, as a governess, have genuinely lavished affection upon Mr. Kent's children, no sooner had she become a mother herself than her affections were wholly centred upon her own children."[1]

Although the achievement of motherhood undoubtedly did monopolize her affections, the change which took place in her attitude towards her step-children was too radical to be accounted for by that alone. It is possible that the cause lay in that violent scene which had taken place at Baynton House when Edward had learned of her marriage to his father. Perhaps that scene had provoked a demonstration of family solidarity, and things had been said in the course of it which it was not in her nature to forget or forgive. She could when she chose conceal her feelings under an agreeable manner, as she had done when Edward was at home, and she knew how to make herself well-liked socially. But over-burdened with that domestic ambition which dominates women of her sort the very idea that she was disliked or unwanted increased her determination to exact an exaggerated obedience and respect, and kept her eternally on the look-out for slights. At the least incident, real or fancied, which impinged upon her authority, or tended to remind her of her former status, the jealousy and pique to which she was continually subject would flare into excessive rages. And in the consequences of these outbursts Mr. Kent invariably supported her.

She grudged every penny that could not be diverted to her own children. Mary Ann and Elizabeth had small incomes of their own, and were, besides, submissive to her will. But

[1] *The Case of Constance Kent*—John Rhode.

Constance and William she regarded as encumbrances: both went badly clothed and shod, and though now of school age she still taught them herself.

Dr. Stapleton, who knew her well, says, "Whether the governess possessed that experience, and tact and moral weight which fitted her for the responsibilities she had undertaken . . . are questions to which her memory and conscience alone can reply." He adds, "She ruled with a severe hand all beneath her sway," and goes on to relate how, to punish Constance and William, "she banished them into the hall at meal-times", "boxed their ears" and "confined them to their rooms".

William, who lacked his sister's stoicism, would sob out his contrition, but Constance endured these punishments without flinching—a trait which, in William, would have been regarded as a virtue, but which in her was looked upon as unfeminine and the expression of an "intractable disposition". Her fortitude made her step-mother all the more determined to break down her resistance, and when at last she discovered that she could make Constance wince by disparaging her dead mother, this became her favourite goad.

But matters did not reach this pitch until after Edward had taken up his appointment abroad. With him gone the only check upon Mrs. Kent's persecution of the younger children was removed, and under it Constance's health at last broke down. She was afflicted with "a painful malady of the legs". The family doctor, Dr. Parsons of Beckington, "forbade all exercise" and put her into "laced stockings".[1] When she grew worse he ordered a treatment at Bath: she was accordingly boarded at a school there and for some months had to be wheeled about in a Bath chair.

[1] J. W. Stapleton.

CHAPTER FIVE

FLIGHT

I

CONSTANCE had left Road-hill House sick in mind and body. At school she found those things of which she stood urgently in need: kindness and companionship, regular meals instead of semi-starvation, and the opportunity for learning at which she grasped eagerly. Here also the characteristic which distinguished her whole life, and to which all who knew her bore witness, was prominently revealed: "her extreme tenderness and devotion to little children". She "romped with them" and helped them with their lessons, tended bruised knees and comforted tearful faces. And they were drawn irresistibly to her and gave her their hearts.

After an absence of several months she went home for the summer holidays of 1857. She was thirteen, had developed mentally and physically and was now in good health. Her school reports had been excellent, and her mistresses expressed the hope that she would return.

She now possessed standards by which to measure her home, and the state of things she found at Road-hill House shocked and outraged her. Mary Ann and Elizabeth had degenerated into little more than the drudges of their step-mother; the servants—of whom there were only two: a cook-general and a housemaid—were chivvied and harried by their mistress in an attempt to make them do the work of four, and were in a perpetual state of smouldering resentment which frequently broke out in scenes that were always painful and sometimes violent.[1] William, in shabby suits which he had outgrown and clumsy boots which were all he was provided with, had been

[1] "Whether," writes Dr. Stapleton, "from their own misconduct or from domestic mismanagement, a constant and unvarying succession of female servants prevailed at Road-hill House." A contemporary estimate alleged that nearly two hundred came and went in the space of four years.

forced into a furtive back-stairs existence. Apart from the lessons his step-mother set him to do he was being given no education, and although he was now twelve, there seemed to be no intention on the part of his parents to send him to school. Constance, "whose passionate love for her brother William" was well known, alone had the temerity to take up his cause, and this brought down the full weight of Mrs. Kent's wrath upon the heads of them both, and one vindictive punishment followed another. They were "locked in their rooms for several days" with a minimum of food, and when liberated the whole household was ordered to ostracize them. As a final mark of her displeasure Mrs. Kent informed Constance, a few days before her new term began, that she would not be returning to school.

The children had absolutely no one to turn to for help or comfort. A thousand times they must have lamented Edward's absence, and at last in their acute misery they took a desperate decision. Constance cut off her long red hair and in an old suit of William's set out with him for Bristol, where they hoped to find a ship which would take them to Edward.

Footsore and hungry they reached Bath as night was falling. It was raining, and with exhaustion William's courage evaporated. Constance tried to rally him without avail. Summoning up all her own courage she asked for food and a room at the Greyhound Hotel, but her refusal to give any name brought immediate difficulties. The rest of the story can best be told in the words of the *Trowbridge and North Wilts Advertiser*.

"The landlord suspected that they were runaways and questioned them sharply. The elder boy said little, but the younger[1] told him to mind his own business, more than hinting that his conduct was impertinent. . . . He took the elder boy to the police station, thinking to terrify him into confession. The inspector on duty, however, . . . attempted to conquer by kindness and succeeded. He desired to go to sea, he said, and his companion, his sister, had dressed herself in his clothes and cut her hair short. . . . All the money they had was one-and-sixpence, but neither lack of cash nor

[1] I.e. Constance: the *Advertiser* was mistaken as to the respective ages of the children.

distance had been able to overcome the boy's determination,
or his sister's affection. The girl, we are told, acted like a
little hero, to the admiration of all who saw her."

When the inspector told them that they would be detained
at the police station, Constance pleaded that she might be held
as a hostage and William given a bed at the hotel. Although at
first reluctant he was so impressed by her personality that he
arranged the matter with the landlord as she wished, but
"William wept bitterly at being parted from her".

Locked into the common charge-room Constance seated
herself upon a bench and confronted, dry-eyed, the humiliating
end to their brave plan, which her shorn head would advertise
to the world until her hair was grown, and the retribution which
was bound to follow. Peering through the grill from time to time
the officer on duty noticed that she sat as though frozen into
immobility, never once altering her position on that hard
bench.[1]

2

Mr. Kent had been absent in Devon and, when he stepped
from the train next day, was "met with the hue and cry which
had been raised". But by the time he reached his carriage he
learned that a message had been received from the Bath police
and a trap sent to bring the children home.

The children's flight has often been attributed to Mr. Kent's
"tyranny" as "a grim Victorian father who ruled his household
by authority rather than by tenderness" instead of to his wife's
"harshness". But he spent more time absent from his home than
present within it, and, as some authorities have pointed out,
while he was away, Mrs. Kent was in supreme control. But for
the treatment which was now meted out to the children they
are both equally to blame. They had managed to live down the
domestic scandals of the past, so now, threatened with a new
one, their united fury knew no bounds and descended like an
avalanche upon the heads of the strained and exhausted
culprits.

[1] Their flight is supposed to have inspired Charles Dickens in *Edwin Drood*.
Helena and Neville Landless who were brought up by a cruel stepfather, ran
away as children, Helena cutting off her hair and dressing up as a boy. It was
written in 1870.

William broke down completely under the thrashing he received: Constance, her cheeks smarting and her ears ringing from blows, was thrust down into the cellars and the key turned upon her. Here, in the dank darkness, among the rats, black-beetles and festoons of cobwebs, she was kept for two days and nights—local legend says for even longer, and that it was by no means the first time that she had been subjected to this partic-ularly brutal form of punishment. Be this as it may, one thing is certain: from now on she developed a silent and unconquerable reserve towards her step-mother.

3

The story of the flight was soon public property, and it was generally agreed that children do not run away from home unless they are acutely unhappy. Dr. Stapleton records that people were asking: "What motive of apprehended punishment, of suffering or injustice was operating in their minds when they set forth as wanderers and in disguise from their father's house? . . . Nor, while it remains unexplained, can any fair or reasonable complaint be made of that criticism which on the part of the public and the authorities has supposed some defect in their education and moral discipline, and domestic treat-ment."

The "authorities" as represented by the Board of Factory Commissioners asked Mr. Kent for an explanation. His answer was to make Constance the scapegoat. The whole escapade had, according to him, been the result of her "intractable dispo-sition", of which evidence was to be found in the lack of "feminine delicacy" with which she had cut off her hair and assumed boy's clothing, and, still more, in the only reason she could be induced to give: that "she had wished to be inde-pendent"—a shocking sentiment on the lips of a Victorian young lady.

But if this explanation satisfied the Board, the sympathy of the public remained with the children. The wretched business did at least bring the culprits one advantage. Both were sent to suitable schools: William to one in the Midlands and Constance

to one in Hertfordshire. But while William was allowed to
return home for his holidays, Constance—presumably with the
intention of extending her punishment—was made to spend hers
at school.

Neither Mr. nor Mrs. Kent were blessed with forgiving
natures, especially where their *amour-propre* sustained an
injury. From now on the former bore these two children of his
a grudge, while his wife's disdain of William hardened, and her
dislike of Constance turned to hatred.

A few weeks after the flight Mrs. Kent gave birth to a son
who was christened Francis Savile.

4

Constance was away from home for nearly two years. On her
return she found the atmosphere unaltered. Mary Ann and
Elizabeth, sunk in apathy, were incapable of uttering a word of
protest on their own behalf, far less on that of anyone else.
William, much grown, but as awkward and timid as ever, was
continually disparaged by his father and contrasted unflatter-
ingly with his little half-brother Savile, the only one of his
children to claim Samuel Kent's affection. He spent his time
running errands for his step-mother and wheeling out in the
perambulator her latest baby, Eveline.

Constance's rebellion had been that of a child of ardent
temperament defying its own impotence in the face of adult
injustice. She had paid—and was still to pay—a bitter price for
it. Time and other influences had subdued her, and of these
perhaps the greatest had been Edward's death. This had occurred of yellow fever at Havannah in 1857, when he was on
the point of returning to England on leave and soon after
Constance had been sent away to school in disgrace. His death
was a crushing grief to her: it robbed her of the one person in
the world upon whose unfailing affection and understanding she
could count. His last act had been to bequeath her their
mother's Bible.[1] She knew full well the value he had attached to

---

[1] He left the rest of his property, which amounted to £150, to be equally
divided among his three sisters.

it, and as the salt of her tears mingled with the salt of the sea which had stained its pages when the *Kenilworth* foundered at Balaclava it seems as though the essence of those lessons which they had both learned from their mother returned to inform and sustain her spirit: so that when, in the spring of 1859, she took up once more the threads of her existence at Road-hill House, it was with a more mature philosophy and a greater self-discipline.

She undertook her share of the household tasks, submitted as dispassionately as possible to her step-mother's spitefulness, and made an immediate conquest of the spoilt and wilful Savile, for he, like all other children, was irresistibly drawn to her and she alone could coax him out of his moods of petulance and peevishness. She went for walks, exchanging greetings with the villagers and lingering to play with their children—to the disapproval of her family. She cultivated a corner of the grounds which became known as "Miss Constance's garden" and memories of which still linger in Road.

She now went, first as a day pupil and that autumn as a boarder, to a school at Beckington, a village half-way between Road and Frome, two miles from each. This establishment belonged to two ladies, the Misses Scott and Williamson, and consisted of about forty girls from kindergarten age upwards.

Constance had always been happy at her schools. This one proved no exception. Her studies provided activity for her brain and in the communal life she could express her personality and find an outlet for her affections. Her slender-fingered hands and delicate wrists could perform the finest tasks with dexterity and she shewed a talent for sketching and designing which her mistresses encouraged. Rather small for her age, her figure was compact and neat and though the fashions of the period were calculated to bestow an air of over-maturity, yet nothing could disguise her natural elegance, or the look of lively intelligence which accompanied it.

Term ended on the 17th June and Constance, having been awarded the second prize for good work and behaviour, took leave of her mistresses and friends in the confident belief that she would be amongst them again as soon as the holidays were over.

But four weeks had scarcely passed before she was arrested on a charge of wilful murder.

CHAPTER SIX

ROAD-HILL HOUSE: THE EVE OF THE CRIME

I

UNLIKE Walton Manor and Baynton House, Road-hill House stands four-square and conspicuous, confronting the village of Road across its green, as though challenging the world to believe that evil or cruelty could ever have taken place within its walls. Unaltered in any main essential it retains all the charm and distinction which the eighteenth century never failed to bestow. As in 1860 some twelve acres of garden and meadows surround it through which the River Frome meanders. But the curved carriage-way which formerly led to its pillared porch from the south-east corner of the grounds has today been replaced by a straight drive entered from the road through a pair of handsome wrought-iron gates of Italian workmanship.

The accompanying plan of the house is a copy of the one made at the time of the crime, and is neither entirely accurate nor properly to scale for the reason that Mr. Kent refused permission for one to be made. But it will serve the purpose well enough. The main discrepancy relates to the back staircase which should be shewn as extending from the ground to the top floors, while at its foot was a door by locking which—and that leading from the hall into the back passage, as was done every night—the back premises could be completely shut off from the rest of the house leaving the back door as the only means of exit.

The only approach to this was through the high-walled courtyard, the gates into which were locked before the family retired to bed and a savage Newfoundland dog let loose within it.

Dr. Stapleton describes the half-dozen or so cottages in the lane at the side of the house as constituting a rural slum—"a piece of St. Giles set down in rural surroundings"—and declares that their occupants were particularly ill-disposed towards Mr. Kent. As to the first charge, there is no evidence to support anything so improbable; while as to the second, it was disproved not only by police investigation soon after the crime, but also by the fact that three of the occupants were employed by Mr. Kent himself.

Within the house the first floor was occupied solely by Mr. and Mrs. Kent, their children and the nurse. This "segregation of the first family with the servants at the top of the house when there were vacant rooms below" provoked considerable comment. Only one of these rooms was furnished, the other two being used as "lumber-rooms", although there were box-rooms on the floor above.

2

In June 1860 the indoor staff at Road-hill House consisted of Sarah Kerslake, cook-general, who had created something of a record by retaining the situation for over a year; Sarah Cox, the housemaid, and Elizabeth Gough, the nurse.

Sarah Cox, who had succeeded only a few weeks before to a long line of predecessors, was to be one of the principal witnesses in the case, and almost the only one whose evidence never varied from beginning to end of the complicated proceedings. She was devoted to Constance, and until the day of her death cherished the basket—now the equally treasured possession of her daughter—in which she had carried Constance's lunch to her when she stood charged with the crime.

Elizabeth Gough had been eight months with the Kents. She came from Isleworth, was entirely urban in upbringing and outlook, and it is surprising to find her in such rural surroundings. With the *chic* and sophistication of one who had recently held a situation as a lady's-maid, it is equally surprising to find her returning to her original occupation of nursemaid, especially in so humdrum a household; and although she was an exceedingly attractive young woman of twenty-one, she sought neither admirers nor diversions in the neighbourhood. A baker's daughter, she sprang from precisely the same class as her mistress—a fact of which gossip was soon to inform her if it had not already done so—towards whom she behaved with a nice blending of deference and affability. Although her nose was too long and her jaw too heavy for beauty, and she suffered the additional blemish of a missing front tooth, Elizabeth Gough's attractions were considerable and she made a deep impression upon the people of Road where she is still spoken of as a "smart girl". Besides a good figure, she possessed the striking combination of fair hair and dark eyes.

She only had charge of Savile and Eveline. The care of Mary Amelia, the eldest child, who slept in her parents' room, together with all the heavy work of the nursery, devolved upon Emily Doel, a village girl who came in daily.

Another indoor employee was Mrs. Holcombe, mother of the groom-gardener, who came in every Saturday to do the scrubbing. She and her son lived in one of the cottages in the lane.

The outdoor staff consisted of Holcombe, John Alloway, the odd-job boy who lived at Beckington, and Daniel Oliver, an elderly labourer belonging to the village, who milked the cows and helped in the stables and garden. Mrs. Esther Holley, who also lived in the lane, took in the family's washing.

3

Mr. Kent's official salary was £800, and his private income between £300 and £400 a year, making a total which, even in those days and without taking into account his personal extravagances, was barely sufficient to provide for the upkeep of Road-hill House and for the requirements of a large family to which yet another addition was due in a few weeks' time. Rumour said that he was pressed for money, and that his account with his wine merchant was unduly large.

A vacancy had recently occurred on the Board of Factory Commissioners. Mr. Kent was now fifty-nine, and promotion was no longer a matter of ambition—it had become an urgent necessity. He knew that his past domestic scandals had created prejudice against him, and he had canvassed the support of all

the most influential men in his area for his application for the
vacant seat. That application had now gone in, backed by some
200 signatures, and though sanguine of success he knew that any
fresh scandal must irretrievably ruin his chances. It was perhaps
this need for caution which accounts for the period of halcyon
calm that seems now to have descended upon Road-hill House:
a calm, the surface of which was ruffled only by Alloway who,
on 23rd June, asked for a rise in wages, and on this being refused
gave a week's notice.

4

As a rule all the household with the exception of Mr. Kent
went up to bed before eleven o'clock. His own time for doing so
varied. He might remain in the library, which also served him
as an office, until nearly midnight, especially when he had
arrears of work to deal with. But however busy he might be he
never failed to feed and loose the dog and lock the gates at
about eleven o'clock; and, however late he might be, he never
omitted to make a tour of the ground-floor, lighting his way
with a dark-lantern kept for the purpose, to see that all doors
and windows were securely fastened, before locking the door
from the hall into the back passage, extinguishing the gas-lamp
in the hall and going up to bed.

That spring had been one of gales and heavy rain: the gales
blew themselves out, but the rain persisted well into June. Then,
towards the end of the month, a comet made its appearance, and
simultaneously the weather turned fine and warm. On Sunday,
24th, Mr. Kent attended morning service at Road-hill Church,
only a few yards from his door, taking Savile with him. He was
regular in his attendances and the vicar, the Reverend Edward
Peacock, although a considerably younger man, was a close
personal friend.

On Tuesday, 26th, he was to leave home for a couple of days,
and before doing so he handed his lantern to Kerslake, pointing
out that the glass had got broken the previous night and order-
ing her to have it repaired at once so as to be ready for him on
his return.

On Friday, 29th, the sweep came at 6 a.m. to sweep the chimneys of the kitchen and the nursery. As soon as he had finished Elizabeth Gough and Emily Doel set to work to give the nursery a thorough cleaning. Savile had awoken in one of his most petulant moods, and made such a nuisance of himself to the two girls that at last Elizabeth Gough snatched him up and carried him downstairs to his mother, asking her to take charge of him until she had finished her work.

"Very well," said Mrs. Kent, "but you must put him down. You know he is too heavy for me to carry."

He was an exceptionally large child for his age, strong and well-developed, with a lively, alert intelligence which knew well how to take full advantage of the indulgence which both his parents, but especially his mother, shewed him. His worst trait was the habit of tale-bearing—in which no doubt Mrs. Kent encouraged him. "He was always running to his mother with stories of all he heard and saw. . . . He told his mother everything that went on in the house."[1]

Always anxious about her children's health, Savile's in particular, Mrs. Kent decided that his fretfulness was probably due to the need of a purge, and immediately despatched a note to Dr. Parsons asking him to prescribe. The doctor made up a calomel pill which he sent back with instructions that it be given at bedtime.

Meanwhile Constance had taken charge of Savile and carried him off to play out-of-doors, and there most of the household saw them "romping together" happily in the sunshine. When Mr. Kent drove into the courtyard later that day Savile's peevishness had passed and he ran forward to greet his father, trotting along beside him as he made his way to the house and chattering animatedly of all that had happened in his absence. Mr. Kent, with the indulgence reserved only for Savile, allowed him to follow him into the library, where he seated himself at his desk: an hour later, when Elizabeth Gough came to fetch the child to his supper and bed, she found him perched on his father's knee making pot-hooks on the margin of an official report which Mr. Kent was drafting.

[1] Statements of Elizabeth Gough.

5

The Kents, like most middle-class families, used the dining-room as a general sitting-room. That evening, as was customary, Cox served tea there at nine o clock, and at 9.45 she, Kerslake and Elizabeth Gough came in to join the family prayers.

When these were over Cox carried the tray away to the kitchen, and after refilling the teapot she and Kerslake sat down at the table to have a cup themselves. Elizabeth Gough, who usually kept aloof from the kitchen, came in and asked for some tea for herself, which she drank standing and then left.

Cox was responsible for locking up the front of the house, Kerslake for locking up the back premises—which she was engaged in doing when at 10.30 Mr. Kent came in to get the dog's food. Cox was then in the drawing-room. It was very rarely used and its fitted carpet was covered with white drugget. Of the three sash windows reaching from floor to ceiling, which formed a bay at the far end of the room, only the middle one was ever opened. It was awkward and heavy, squeaked loudly when it was raised, while considerable strength was needed to lift it higher than six inches, at which point it stuck and for which reason it was seldom opened wider. That night, as Cox lowered and latched it, she thought the room smelled fusty and needed a thorough airing. She closed the shutters, fixed in place the iron bars which secured them, then, leaving the room, she locked and bolted the door. It was 10.45 when she and Kerslake went up to bed, locking the door at the foot of the back stairs behind them. A few minutes earlier, when she had put Mr. Kent's lantern ready for him, all the rest of the family had gone up and he and his wife were alone in the dining-room.

Mrs. Kent had given Savile his pill at eight o'clock when he had been put to bed. At ten she had looked into the nursery to see that all was well, and kissed the child as he lay fast asleep with his head resting on his arm. On her way downstairs she had paused on the half-landing and called to the nurse to come and look at the comet; and as they stood together at the window she remarked that she was very tired as she had not slept well the previous night. An hour later, on her way to bed, she again glanced into the nursery. All was peaceful. The nurse was not present, but as the door leading into her dressing-room was shut Mrs. Kent concluded that she was undressing. The nursery door, unless one was accustomed to shutting it, squeaked, and a loose ring around the handle jingled: Mrs. Kent shut it without a sound and went into her bedroom opposite.

William had gone up at 10.15 and Constance followed him almost immediately. At 10.30 the elder sisters went up, and Elizabeth quietly opened Constance's door to see that she was in bed and her candle out. She seemed to be already asleep and Elizabeth crossed the landing to William's room. She did not go in, but listened to make sure that all was silent, and stooped to see that no light was shewing under the door. She then lingered for a long while at the landing window gazing up at the comet and out over the shadowy garden, still and tranquil in the short midsummer night. When at last she made her way to her room Mary Ann was already in bed, but it was nearly midnight before she lay down beside her sleeping sister.

So far, and with a fair degree of accuracy, one can trace the movements of the various inmates of the house on the eve of the crime up to the time each went to bed; except in the case of Mr. Kent, who, according to his own statement, went up at 11.45, but this could not be corroborated by anyone but Mrs. Kent.

The day had passed smoothly and uneventfully, as in thousands of other English homes. Mr. Kent had been affectionate and good-humoured with Savile; Mrs. Kent, solicitous and tender. Constance and he had played together happily. William had been absent from midday until the evening. Mary Ann and Elizabeth had passed the long daylight hours as submissively and inconspicuously as ever. There had been a complete absence of friction. Nothing had occurred to arouse anyone's animosity. Yet during the brief summer darkness, before dawn came at a few minutes before four o'clock, one of the nine adults under that roof committed a crime of unsurpassed brutality, apparently without the slightest motive.

All were to declare that they had heard no sound—by which they meant no *unusual* sound: for had any of them caught the sound of movement at that hour when the crime was committed

—the opening or shutting of a door; a board creaking under a footfall—their drowsy, unsuspicious minds would automatically have attributed it to Mr. Kent, making his nightly round and then coming upstairs.

Outside the house, however, anything unusual in its appearance stood some chance of being observed. And so it was that at 12.45 P.C. Urch of the Somerset Constabulary, stationed at Road, was surprised to see, as he went by on his nightly patrol, that the gas-lamp was burning in the hall. He "had never known it to be alight so late unless Mr. Kent was entertaining friends".[1] He also noticed that the light behind the nursery curtains was unusually bright, and that all the other windows were in darkness. Suddenly the silence was shattered by a short spasm of barking from the dog, which ceased as abruptly as it had begun. Urch paused and listened, but no other sound broke the stillness until, a few minutes later, the church clock struck one. Reassured, he turned his footsteps homewards.

In the meadows below the house a night-prowler named Moon was loitering on the banks of the Frome in the hope of taking one of Mr. Kent's trout. At the sudden barking of the dog he froze into immobility. But his straining eyes and ears could discern no movement nor caught any further sound, and, as he heard the church clock strike, he moved cautiously on.

6

That night was to see the end of the second cycle in the life of Samuel Kent. It has already been said that each of these two cycles was set in motion by almost identical impulses, that each closed in a sudden death, and that each was marked by a startling chronological similarity. This last is as follows:

(A) 1. In 1844, when Mary Pratt was engaged as nurse, the first Mrs. Kent was 37 years of age and expecting a baby.

2. She—the first Mrs. Kent—had three children living: two girls and a boy.

[1] P.C. Urch in evidence.

3. She had been married 16 years.
4. Mary Pratt was 21.

(B) 1. In 1860, when Elizabeth Gough was engaged as nurse, the second Mrs. Kent was 37 years of age and expecting a baby.

2. She—the second Mrs. Kent—had three children living: two girls and a boy.

3. She had been intimate with Mr. Kent for 16 years.

4. Elizabeth Gough was 21.

CHAPTER SEVEN

THE CRIME: SATURDAY, 30TH JUNE —MORNING

I

AT 5 A.M. Holcombe left his cottage in the lane, crossed the front lawn and passed round the far side of the house before unlocking the wicket into the stable-yard. The grass was dry under his feet, and the morning fine and warm. At six o'clock Alloway joined him for his last day's work at Road-hill House and was sent to water the plants in the greenhouse, and then to collect the boots and knives for cleaning.

Kerslake aroused Cox:

"It's gone six, and time to get up."

They came out of their room in their print dresses, white caps and aprons, Cox turning left for the front stairs and Kerslake crossing the passage and going down the back stair-case, unlocking the door at its foot. She then unlocked the back door and, going into the kitchen, raked out and relighted the range, and put on the kettles for the children's bath. In the adjoining scullery or "back-kitchen" was a "boiler-stove" which provided hot water for the sink and to heat the airing cupboard beside it: in summer it was never refuelled at night and was therefore burned out by the morning, but Kerslake did not relight it until after breakfast at 8.30.

Cox, on her way downstairs, noticed that the drawing-room door, which she had locked and bolted the night before, now stood ajar. She hurried in, to find the shutters of the middle window pushed apart and the sash raised. Her first instinctive fear, of burglary, soon subsided, for nothing was missing or out of place, while neither the window, which was only open its usual six inches, nor the shutters bore any sign of being forced. She therefore concluded that one of the family had gone into the room after she had locked it up the night before, noticed its fustiness and opened the window to air it, forgetting to close it again. So, thinking no more of the matter, she went on with her work.

At 6.30 Mrs. Holcombe arrived for the weekly task of scrubbing the back premises, and then Emily Doel, who filled the hot-water cans from the kettles and took them upstairs to the nursery, getting the children's bath from the lumber-room on her way. As she entered Elizabeth Gough, who was making her bed, glanced sharply over her shoulder, but went on with what she was doing "without uttering a word". Emily noticed with surprise that Savile was not in the room, and, with even greater astonishment, that the little girl Eveline had already been dressed. It not being "her place" to ask questions, she got the bath ready just the same, during which she "went in and out of the room several times, but the nurse did not say a word".

2

Mrs. Kent awoke and saw that beyond the curtains the day was bright. She vaguely remembered having awoken earlier, when the light beyond them had been grey, to a sound like the opening squeak of the drawing-room window and, thinking drowsily that the servants were already up and about, had fallen asleep again.

Her husband was lying turned away from her with the bed-clothes pulled high over his shoulder. She glanced at his watch and told him that it was 7.15. He did not reply, but "she knew that he was awake".[1]

She got out of bed, thrust her feet into her slippers and was pulling on her dressing-gown when there came a knock on the door. She opened it to find Elizabeth Gough.

"Well, Nurse, what is it?" she asked. "Are the children awake?"

"Neither of them," the nurse said.[2]

[1] This and the conversation which follows is taken from Mrs. Kent's evidence.

[2] This reply was alleged to have been given after Emily Doel had seen that Savile was absent and Eveline already dressed.

"What? Neither of them?" exclaimed Mrs. Kent.

"Master Savile?" the nurse asked awkwardly. "Is he with you?"

"With me?" Mrs. Kent cried. "Certainly not!"

"He's not in his bed."

Brushing past her Mrs. Kent went straight to Savile's cot.

No bed in which a child had slept normally could have presented the appearance which his did: the pillow bore an unnaturally deep indentation made by his head, the mattress a similar impression made by his body; yet the upper sheet and the counterpane were carefully smoothed, folded together, turned down and neatly tucked in.

The sides of the cot were too high to allow the child to climb out of it unaided, and Mrs. Kent asked:

"Did you put the chair near the cot?"

"No, ma'am."

"When did you miss him?"

"At five o'clock."

"*At five o'clock!* Why didn't you come and tell me at once?"

"I thought perhaps you had heard him cry and had come and fetched him."

"You wicked girl, how dare you say so! You know perfectly well he is too heavy for me to carry—only yesterday when you brought him to me I told you to put him down because he was too heavy for me. I have always told you to come to me at once if there is anything wrong with the children. Go upstairs to his sister's room and see if he is there."

Mary Ann, half-dressed, opened her door to the nurse's knock.

"Is Master Savile with you? He is not in the nursery." The nurse "spoke in loud tones" and her voice brought Elizabeth Kent to her sister's side and Constance to her door.

Mary Ann said "No" and asked:

"Have you told Mrs. Kent?"

"Yes, I have—she hasn't seen him either."

According to Elizabeth Gough's statement when she returned to tell Mrs. Kent that Savile was not upstairs she found her still standing beside the cot. There is no evidence of what deductions Mrs. Kent may have drawn from its peculiar state, or from the nurse's strained face and distracted manner,[1] nor of any further conversation between herself and Elizabeth Gough —and none that she went to report the child's disappearance to her husband. All one knows is that she now went downstairs, looked into the various rooms, was told by Cox how she had found the drawing-room window, and could nowhere see any trace of the missing child.

Yet there were certain unmistakable conclusions to be drawn from all that she had seen and heard—conclusions which were to strike minds far less acute than her own.

The child was missing from a cot which he could not have got out of unaided; the upper bed-clothes of which had been smoothed and replaced in a manner which clearly shewed a practised hand, and, obviously, *after he had left it*.

No forced entry had been made through the drawing-room window: *therefore it must have been opened from inside*. But not by the child: he could neither have opened the shutters nor raised the sash himself. Nor was the opening wide enough for him to have squeezed out through it.

The front and back doors were both found locked and bolted: if he had gone out by either, *then someone must have fastened it again afterwards*.

Someone, then, must either have connived at his going, or carried him away. But so headstrong a child would never have submitted to being taken from his cot and carried out of the house in the small hours of the morning without a vigorous protest—certainly vigorous enough to awake the nurse whose bed was within a few feet of his own. *And why was he gone? And where was he now?*

It is impossible not to believe that Mrs. Kent, confronted with facts of such significance, did not then have at least a blind understanding of what had occurred, for she possessed feminine intuition to the full.

Her child was nowhere in the house: yet she gave no orders for the grounds to be searched or the police to be fetched. She was notoriously sharp-tempered: yet she made no scene. In silence she returned upstairs.

[1] See page 68.

It is impossible to believe that any man so violent in his reactions as Mr. Kent, and credited with a deep attachment to this particular child, should have remained lying in bed, as he admitted he did, awake and within earshot of what was occurring, without troubling to get up and make inquiries—*unless he dared not*.

What now took place between husband and wife no one was ever to know. In her deposition Mrs. Kent said that when she returned to her bedroom she found Mr. Kent lying in bed just as she had left him, that she said to him, "Savile is missing: he is nowhere in the house"; and that, replying, "Then we must see where he is," he got up and went into his dressing-room. This laconic interchange is contrary to all one knows of human nature in such an emergency, especially in the case of two such intemperate people as Mr. and Mrs. Kent.

What transpired later supports the view that within the next few moments Mrs. Kent was in possession of the whole terrible truth: that in spite of her bitter grief—in spite of the outrage and humiliation which the knowledge brought her—she perceived with hideous clarity as she looked upon the man cowering before her that the only hope of saving her two little girls, her unborn child and herself from the appalling calamity which had overtaken them lay in saving *him*—at all costs. Upon this she instantly concentrated every faculty.

A quarter of an hour later he was galvanized into activity— a wild, combative, distraught activity, but with a plan to put into effect. A quarter of an hour later the nurse had become the eyes and ears of her master and mistress.

The attitude Mr. Kent adopted towards the investigations which followed was defensive and obstructive: in the course of them he and the nurse frequently contradicted their own statements; fear induced them to make blunders which landed them in perilous situations: but out of all their predicaments they were extricated by a coolness and cunning which neither of themselves possessed. From then onwards to the bitter end, five years later, Mr. Kent was a haunted man fighting desperately, often painfully, always fearfully, and frequently on the verge of collapse, to save himself, aided by an attorney of exceptional resource everlastingly at his elbow, by a counsel of ability close at hand, and sustained in the background by an invincible will.

But that first plan—although other interpretations were to be put upon it—was hastily devised to get Mr. Kent out of the way, and to ensure, so far as it was humanly possible to do so, that the ordeal which it was beyond his powers to face —the discovery of his child's body—should occur during his absence.

While he was dressing he shouted for William. Dashing upstairs, the boy was instructed first to tell Holcombe to get the phaeton ready as Mr. Kent was going to Trowbridge to inform Superintendent Foley; secondly to impress on everyone that on no account was Mrs. Kent to be disturbed, *"not even if there should be bad news about Savile"*; and thirdly, to run to the village and fetch P.C. Urch. William sped to perform these errands.

Holcombe, having obeyed his order, had just joined Alloway and Oliver, who were standing by the wicket between the stable-yard and the garden at the rear of the house, when Mr. Kent, with his hat on his head and clad in an overcoat, although it was a warm morning, came "running fast" round the corner of the house by the drawing-room window. Seeing the men he stopped, "shouted" to Holcombe, "Master Savile is lost: he has been stolen and carried away", then, turning about abruptly, "ran back the way he had come".[1]

3

On receiving William's message P.C. Urch was concerned as to whether he had authority to comply with the request, since Road-hill House stood over the county boundary in Wiltshire: he therefore decided to consult James Morgan, whose powers, as parish constable, had different limitations. Morgan at once undertook to go with him, and as the two men neared the house they saw Mr. Kent's phaeton, with its hood up, drive out of the gates and turn towards Trowbridge. They hurried to intercept it, and asked Mr. Kent "what the trouble was".

[1] Holcombe in evidence.

"I've had my little boy stolen," he said. "I'm on my way to Trowbridge to fetch Superintendent Foley."

"You needn't go further than Southwick, sir," said Morgan. "The policeman there will forward the information to Trowbridge, and you can return back as soon as possible."

"I shall go on," retorted Mr. Kent; then, catching sight of Thomas Benger, a smallholder who was grazing his cows on the green, he shouted to him: "My little boy is lost. There'll be ten pounds to the man who finds him." And with that he drove off.

That Mr. Kent, leaving no responsible person at home, should insist upon himself driving the four miles to Trowbridge to inform the police of his child's disappearance, when there was already a policeman on his doorstep and another at Southwick half the distance away, and when Holcombe on horseback could have carried a message equally well and probably more quickly, is curious enough; but that he should have done so without even glancing into the nursery, without putting a single question to the nurse, and without so much as organizing a search for the child, is inexplicable except on the grounds that he was a man distraught.

4

As Mr. Kent drove off in a swirl of dust Thomas Benger —a character well known to everyone in the village of Road —raised his shrewd, wise eyes and beheld William Nutt, the cobbler, approaching from his cottage in the lane. Nutt, a solemn and portentous individual, announced that he had just heard that Mr. Kent's little boy was missing.

"Well, William," said Benger, "let's go and look for him."

The cobbler shook his head. Soon after Mr. Kent had taken Road-hill House—which had stood empty for a couple of years previously—and before he had actually moved in, Nutt had been caught helping himself, as was the common practice, to apples in the neglected garden, and Mr. Kent had immediately prosecuted him.

"Come on, William," urged Benger, "Mr. Kent's not going

to prosecute anyone for looking for his lost child. More likely there'll be five pounds for the man that finds him!"

Nutt was reluctant, but Benger was persuasive, and in 1860 five pounds could purchase a cow.

There is still living in Road an old gentleman whose mother, when he was a little boy, used to send him out in Benger's care, for Benger was not only beloved by children but trusted by their parents; and from Benger's own lips he heard the story of how he and William Nutt found the body of little Savile Kent.

They began their search in the shrubbery which, extending from the entrance gates and widening with the inward curve of the drive, formed a dense thicket between the latter and the wall that divided the grounds from the lane, and effectively concealed the privy. Presently Nutt observed oracularly:

"If the child is not in the house, Thomas, we may as well look for a dead one as a living one."

The door of the privy stood open. Nutt glanced in, then recoiled in horror, crying:

"Oh, Thomas! It is as I predicted!"

Benger hurried to his side. On the floor was "a pool of blood about the size of a man's hand". Benger pushed past Nutt, lifted the lid from the seat and peered down; in the darkness of the vault something white gleamed.

"Go, get a light, William," said Benger urgently.

Mrs. Holcombe, scrubbing the back steps, heard the running crunch of Nutt's boots and glanced up into his dazed face.

"Go, get a candle, Mary," he gasped.

"Why, what's the matter?"

"The child's been murdered in the privy!"

"God save us!" she cried aghast, and dropping her brush scurried into the house to return with Kerslake carrying a candle.

Benger held the light over the vault.

"Oh, William, here he is," he cried.

Reaching down, he drew up a small blanket, streaked with night-soil and stiff with congealed blood. Dropping this on the seat he said:

"Look, William!"

Nutt looked down. Wedged between the splashboard and the back of the vault lay Savile's body. It lay on its left side, the left hand and foot thrown up.

Putting down the candle Benger lifted the body out. As he did so the head fell horribly backwards—for the throat had been severed to the very vertebrae of the neck. He laid it on the blanket which Nutt spread out. A stream of blood had trickled along the left cheek to the temple where it had matted the fair curls: the little face was white as wax, except about the mouth where the flesh was dark as though it had been bruised. The child had died a most violent death—*yet the eyes were not wide and staring, but peacefully closed, and the expression was reposeful and serene.*

"He's been cruelly murdered," said Benger deeply, and, folding the blanket about it, he placed the body in the arms of Mrs. Holcombe, who stood transfixed in the doorway.

5

The arrival of Morgan and Urch did something to relieve the atmosphere of suspense and calamity which afflicted the household. Mechanically and with tense faces the "young ladies" had set about the first of the morning tasks, laying the breakfast table. Constance had Eveline on her arm. William, nervous and unhappy, fidgeted in the background. The two maids went about their work stolidly. Elizabeth Gough, her face pale and drawn, roamed upstairs and down, out-of-doors and in again, but always to return every few minutes to the kitchen to which, though she had seldom condescended to enter it before, she now seemed as irresistibly drawn as a needle to a magnet—or as someone to the place which holds an anxious secret.

The two constables questioned Cox, who shewed them how she had found the drawing-room window. They asked to see the nursery, and Elizabeth Gough took them upstairs. Glancing up from the cot Morgan asked the nurse incredulously:

"Do you mean to say this is how it was?"

"Yes."

"Is this how you found it?" he repeated.

"It is. I haven't touched it."

"Have you lost anything besides the child?"

The nurse, he recorded, "hesitated perceptibly" before replying:

"*There was a blanket taken from the cot.* Nothing else is missing."

"What time did you miss the child?"

"At five o'clock. I didn't make any inquiries as I thought he was with his mother."

Questioned about the previous night she said that she had gone to bed at eleven o'clock and had fallen asleep at once "as she was very tired and slept heavily on account of the extra work" occasioned by the sweep's visit in the morning.

One does not know if it struck the two men as odd that a strong and healthy young woman should be so exhausted after turning out, with the aid of another young woman—who did all the scrubbing and polishing—a room of moderate size such as the nursery, and Urch next asked her if she had heard the dog bark.

"No," she said, "I didn't."

The constables then examined the cellars, and had just emerged and were about to continue the investigation out-of-doors when the vicar came hurrying up and said that he had only just heard of the loss of the child and would like to see Mr. Kent.

"He's gone to Trowbridge, sir, to fetch Superintendent Foley," Morgan explained, and at that moment the little procession bearing the body came into sight.

Mrs. Holcombe parted the folds of the blanket, and Mr. Peacock gazed down upon the mangled corpse of the child whom he had last seen so vigorously alive. He was profoundly shocked. He stayed only to put a few brief questions before hastening home to order his horse that he might ride after Mr. Kent "to break the fearful news to him".

The procession, augmented now by Morgan and Urch, entered the house through the back door and tramped along the passage to the kitchen.

In the kitchen the whole household, except Mrs. Kent and William, was gathered. Constance was at the window, still with Eveline in her arms; Kerslake and Cox stood beside the range; Elizabeth Gough hovered in the background; Mary Ann and Elizabeth, standing by the table, had their backs to the door, towards which all turned apprehensively at the sound of so many footsteps.

Mrs. Holcombe, with the men close upon her heels, went straight to the table and as she laid the body upon it, Benger said again:

"He's been cruelly murdered."

With a cry Mary Ann and Elizabeth reeled "as though they would fall" and Nutt "stepped forward and supported each round the waist with an arm".

Constance and the maids stood as though paralysed. But Elizabeth Gough slipped through the door and went straight upstairs to Mrs. Kent's room.

6

Mrs. Kent's account of what took place upon Elizabeth Gough's entry into her room is as incredible as her account of what had taken place in that same room half an hour previously between her husband and herself.

"The nurse came to assist me in dressing . . . she spoke of the missing child; she was brushing my hair; she knew the child had been brought in dead, but was not allowed to tell me."

From this one is expected to believe first of all that the nurse, as soon as the body was brought in, ceased loitering in the kitchen and hurried upstairs for no other purpose than to assist her mistress in dressing: and, secondly, that within a minute or two of viewing the defiled and mutilated corpse of the child she had tended and for whom she professed a great fondness, she was so little affected by the sight that she could speak of him as though he were still only missing, and could conduct herself with such *sang-froid* as to be able to conceal her knowledge from the sensitive awareness of a mother, presumably awaiting in a state of acute anxiety for news of her child's fate.

Nor is it less remarkable that Mrs. Kent, apart from her initial outburst of indignation, should have displayed no sign of *animus* towards the nurse who was responsible for the safety of the child and in whose care he had been when he had so mysteriously vanished. No mother—even one far less absorbed than Mrs. Kent in her children; far less emphatic in the rules she laid down for them and far less subject to anger over their smallest breach—could have adopted the attitude which she did towards Elizabeth Gough unless the necessity to do so had been compelling. All through the long hours of that terrible day Mrs. Kent remained secluded in her room, all but her husband and the nurse being excluded from her presence. All through the days and weeks which followed, the more closely suspicion centred upon the nurse the more protective became Mrs. Kent's attitude towards her. Yet it is curious that, although Mr. Kent's own lack of animosity against Elizabeth Gough aroused the keenest criticism, her own, which was no less open to conjecture, was completely overlooked. The explanation lies, no doubt, partly in the fact that, whereas his complicity in the crime was immediately suspected, Mrs. Kent's innocence was obvious; and partly because the very motive to be alleged made her suffering the more bitter, while her advanced state of pregnancy added a poignancy to the whole tragedy which, where she was concerned, obliterated all other feelings than those of profound compassion. Nevertheless, it is extraordinary that no one has since detected in her the source from which originated those mysterious happenings which took place at Road-hill House so soon after the crime.

7

Mrs. Hall, the turnpike-keeper at Southwick, saw Mr. Kent's phaeton approaching and went out to take his fee and open the gate. He asked for a return ticket and, as she was giving it to him, said:

"I have had a child stolen *and carried away in a blanket*."

"When did you lose it, sir?" the woman asked.

"This morning, and if you see anyone suspicious coming, you are to stop them.[1] Do you know where the policeman lives?"

"Mr. Heritage? Yes, sir. It isn't far."

She directed him. As he drove off she noticed it was eight o'clock.

Mrs. Heritage was dusting her parlour when the phaeton stopped at her gate, and she saw Mr. Kent offer a halfpenny to a little boy to knock at her door. She hurried out at once.

"Is your husband at home?" Mr. Kent asked.

"He's in bed, sir."

"You must call him up. I have had a child stolen out of my house last night—or rather we missed him at five o'clock this morning. A little boy aged three years and ten months, supposed to have been taken out of the drawing-room window."

"Have they taken any clothes, sir?"

"No—*wrapped up in a blanket*. Tell your husband he must get up immediately and make every inquiry. I'm going to Trowbridge to give information to Foley."

"There's no need for you to go on, sir," she pointed out just as Morgan had done. "Heritage will inform the Superintendent at once."

"I shall go on," Mr. Kent replied, and as he gathered up the reins she asked:

"Your name and residence, sir?"

"Kent—Road-hill House."

At 8.30 Mrs. Hall beheld the Reverend Edward Peacock riding hard towards the gates. She hastened to open them. His face was white and shocked, and she exclaimed:

"This is a sad affair at Road, sir."

"The child is found," he said shortly.

"Where, sir?" she asked as he passed through the gate.

"In the garden," he answered as he galloped off.

About a quarter of an hour later she saw Mr. Kent returning at a smart pace. She greeted him gladly.

"Then, sir, the child is found?"

"Yes," he said, hurrying on, *"and murdered!"*

[1] It was the duty of turnpike-keepers to co-operate with the police and assist in apprehending criminals.

8

By nine o'clock Mr. Kent was back at Road-hill House, and a few minutes later Dr. Parsons arrived from Beckington with William, who had been sent to fetch him, seated beside him in his gig.

The doctor was shewn into the library, where he was joined by Mr. Kent, who, after a few words of explanation, led him along the passage to a disused room opposite the kitchen, which had formerly been the laundry and to which the body had been removed. He opened the door for Dr. Parsons but did not himself enter.

Of Dr. Parsons, John Rhode writes that he

"seems to have been an ordinary country surgeon, possessing the ordinary medical knowledge of the time. His chief idea was not to offend the gentry as opposed to the common folk, and his evidence of fact shews a deplorable tendency to vary according to the latest theory adduced".[1]

That this charge is fully justified the course of events will presently make clear.

Until the coroner's order authorizing a *post-mortem* had been obtained Dr. Parsons could only make a preliminary examination of the body. He had been told that the child had been missed by the nurse at five o'clock and was therefore "surprised to find so much rigidity". He noted "the blackened appearance round the mouth", the livid, protruding tongue-tip, observed that the wound in the throat "almost amounted to decapitation" and that no blood had issued from two small cuts on the first and second fingers of the left hand. He then went to examine the privy, and here he was presently joined by Superintendent Foley, who had arrived from Trowbridge with two of his men, P.C.s Heritage and Dallimore, and had just come from viewing the body.

Except for the small pool of coagulated blood on the floor,

[1] *The Case of Constance Kent!*—John Rhode.

E

which Dr. Parsons estimated at "not more than 2 or 3 ounces at most" and a drop or two on the front of the seat, there was no other blood visible anywhere. Calling attention to this Parsons remarked that if the throat had been cut while the heart was still beating its pulsation would have caused the blood to spurt out in such powerful jets through the severed arteries that, in so confined a space, the walls and seat would have been sprayed with it. "I should have expected to find no less than three pints from so large a child," he said. He suggested to Foley that the crime had been committed elsewhere and advised him to have a thorough search made.

Foley, however, had other ideas, and considering that Stephen Millet, the local butcher, was better qualified to give an opinion as to the quantity of blood present, sent for that worthy.

> "Of Superintendent Foley and his conduct of the first and vital investigations," writes John Rhode, "it is difficult to speak without impatience. He was a partially educated man who had risen to the rank of Superintendent through no particular merit of his own, and the occurrence of a crime in the house of a man whom he regarded as far above him in station upset his faith in human nature and in the essential fitness of things. . . . He was entirely incapable of carrying out such an investigation as was required in the present case."[1]

All this is true, and more besides—for all the muddle and misery which was to ensue was mainly due to his ineptitude and incompetence. He did not long survive the shame which his handling of the case brought him, and in that classic, *The Moonstone*, which Wilkie Collins published two years later, he is supposed to figure as the original of Superintendent Segrave.

P.C. Urch in the meanwhile had submitted a report to his own headquarters at Frome, in response to which Sergeant Watts had been despatched to Road—he was to play a memorable part in the investigations before the day was over—and Foley detailed him, with Urch and Heritage, to make that

[1] *The Case of Constance Kent*—John Rhode.

search which Dr. Parsons had recommended while he himself continued his examination of the privy.

This quickly yielded what appeared to be a clue. He observed an object floating on the surface of the night-soil, which, on being hooked up, proved to be what he described as "a female breast-flannel".[1] It had been expertly cut from a piece of expensive material, and its edges neatly bound with narrow tape, a length of which had been sewn to each side so that the two could be crossed at the back and tied in front. They were, in fact, still tied, but one had been torn away from its stitches. The breast-flannel was saturated with blood.

"It was," said Foley, "a new article and the blood on it was principally in the centre, as though it had dripped upon it . . . and had congealed drop by drop as it fell."

Wrapping it in a piece of paper he gave it to Dallimore to take to the police waggonette, which was standing in the stable-yard under the charge of a constable, and, hoping that the vault might yield further clues—perhaps the weapon itself— he arranged with Fricker, the village plumber, to drain it with the help of Thomas Benger; then, taking Dallimore with him, he turned his attention to questioning the servants.

Where this inquisition took place is not clear, for, "fearing to intrude upon the family privacy", Superintendent Foley had obsequiously refrained from entering the house.

"Such," said the *Bath Herald*, "was the delicacy and servile deference Mr. Foley exhibited when having to deal with a gentleman, though his house was the scene of a murder. If it had been a labourer's cottage he would have behaved differently. . . . Here were two and a half hours lost, and that much time given to the murderer, if an inmate of the house, to destroy traces of his guilt."

9

When news of the crime reached Dr. Stapleton at Trowbridge he passed it on to Mr. Rowland Rodway, who was Mr. Kent's

---

[1] A prototype of the modern brassière.

solicitor and his own. They immediately set out for Road-hill House, which they reached about 11.30.

Here they found Mr. Peacock and Mr. Sylvester, the district coroner, in the library with Mr. Kent. They also found that, as Dr. Stapleton expresses it, "no steps had been taken to put the police at their ease by formally delivering every place and person into their custody". But when they suggested that Superintendent Foley should be immediately released from this painful dilemma, Mr. Kent "expostulated against the necessity, vehemently and repeatedly, asserting that the murderer would be found outside his house and not within it".[1] At last, however, their efforts were successful, and—close upon noon—the police were permitted access to the scene of the crime.

Both these gentlemen—the one as Mr. Kent's personal friend and the other as his attorney—visited the nursery and interviewed Elizabeth Gough. The former records the peculiar condition of the cot but refrains from drawing any conclusions from it; but of his interview with the nurse he says, "Her statements seemed unnecessarily and even dangerously elaborate in detail." Mr. Rodway for his part thought that her "countenance exhibited signs of emotion and fatigue" and was haggard as though from want of sleep; but when he voiced these opinions to Foley the latter scouted them, declaring that the nurse was "wholly innocent of the crime and ignorant of its perpetrator"—a conclusion at which he had arrived, as the *Bath Herald* acidly remarked, "with singular nimbleness". Mr. Rodway's further suggestion that a Scotland Yard detective be called in caused the superintendent to bristle with indignation.

What is described as a "conference" now took place between Mr. Kent and his visitors, at which his obstructive attitude towards the investigations grew more pronounced and his general behaviour more extraordinary.

> "His mind," says Stapleton, "seemed to wander irregularly, discursively and unsteadily over a wide field. He suggested a succession of suppositions all equally vague and improbable and unsupported by any testimony or by the evidence of a single fact."

[1] J. W. Stapleton.

With wild eyes and haggard face he furiously declared that instead of wasting their time in the house the police should search the cottages in the lane and "expressed the conviction that the murderer would be found there".[1] Did not William Nutt bear him a grudge for prosecuting him? Had he not had a quarrel with Benger over a short-weight in coal which he had carted for him? And had not these two gone straight to the privy and found the body?

Then suddenly he would change his tune and assert as positively that the child had been murdered by gypsies, or by someone who had concealed themselves in the house for the purpose; or by the nursemaid who had preceded Elizabeth Gough —one Emma Sparks—because when she had been dismissed she had used threatening language and described his children as "horrid".

Between one such outburst and another he would fling himself out of the room to see what the police were doing, to pester them with questions, to demand to be told what theories they were forming, and generally to impede their activities; and to repeat to them the crazy denunciations he had been making in the library.

But however crazy his words and demented his behaviour, however overwrought his state of mind, there was none the less method in his apparent madness. Concealed indoors were articles which must lead inevitably to the identity of the criminal should the police discover them. When the officers could no longer be excluded from the house; when all attempts to divert the investigations elsewhere had failed, he could only resort to any device which would have the effect of imposing impediments. With this end in view he insisted on the police carrying out intensive searches in particular rooms, in their penetrating the spaces under the roof and routing about in the rambling cellars. Every moment lost by these delays and fools'-errands was for him a moment gained; for with nightfall he would be relieved of their vigilance and could make an opportunity for destroying those vital clues.

[1] J. W. Stapleton.

10

Elizabeth Gough, in the first statement she made to Foley, told him, as she had previously told Morgan and Urch, that she had gone to bed at eleven o'clock and immediately fallen soundly asleep, and had not awoken until 5 a.m. She had then noticed that Eveline had kicked off her bed-clothes, and, on kneeling up in her bed to replace them, had glanced across the room and seen that Savile's cot was empty. She thought he must have cried out and his mother, hearing him, had come in and taken him. She had then gone back to sleep and, waking an hour later, had got up and dressed, said her prayers and read a chapter of the Bible. At 6.30 she had knocked on Mrs. Kent's door, but had got no reply. She had then dressed Eveline, and at 7.15 gone and knocked again, when Mrs. Kent had opened the door.

At noon, when he had at last been permitted to "intrude", Foley, accompanied by Superintendent Wolfe of Devizes, who had been sent to assist him, went up to the nursery. Standing beside the cot he asked the nurse:

"Have you rearranged the bed-clothes?"

"I have not touched them. You see the cot now exactly as I found it."

"Is anything missing?"

"Yes, a blanket."

"When did you discover it was missing?"

"When the body was brought into the kitchen wrapped in it."

It will be remembered that she had told Urch and Morgan *before the body had been found* that she had missed the blanket. Her statement had no doubt been reported to Foley, for he pressed her on the point.

"You had not noticed it was missing before that?" he asked.

"No," she said, and went on to explain somewhat elaborately: "The cot was made up with the blanket between the sheet and the counterpane. It was smaller than either, so could not be seen when the cot was made up, and the sheet and counterpane turned down."

As the two Superintendents made their way downstairs, Mr. Kent came out of the library, and Foley asked him if he had known that a blanket was missing from the cot before he left for Trowbridge.

"I did not," he replied.

"You didn't know anything about it, sir?"

"Certainly not," he declared emphatically.

Yet he had distinctly told both Mrs. Hall and Mrs. Heritage at Southwick that the child had been *"carried away in a blanket"*.

II

Dr. Parsons performed the *post-mortem* early in the afternoon. When the clothing was removed he found another wound in the body: this was a stab which had entered just below the left nipple and had been delivered with such force as to pierce through the blanket, night-shirt and flannel vest, sever the cartilage of two ribs and extend three-quarters across the chest. It had passed below the pericardium and diaphragm, displacing, though not injuring, the heart. It had evidently been made by a "long, strong, sharp-pointed knife, like a carving knife" and the blade, in its passage or withdrawal, "had been violently twisted or wrenched round, as was evident from the torn appearance of the muscular fibres, and the scraped, irregular appearance of the exposed rib at the posterior angle of the cut".[1] No blood had flowed from this wound and "there was no retraction of the parts".

The total absence of blood either in the privy or anywhere else and the fact that no blood had issued from the stab seemed to indicate that neither it nor the wound in the throat were the primary cause of death. The blackened appearance around the mouth, the protruding livid tongue, suggested to Dr. Parsons that the child had actually been suffocated by the pressure of a hand "holding some soft substance"; that the child had been dead "or almost dead" when the throat was cut and that the body had been drained of blood before the stab in the side had been inflicted: while, to judge by the rigidity and by the fact

[1] Stated in evidence.

that the calomel pill had passed from the stomach into the bowels but had not yet acted, the time of death must have been about midnight.

Dr. Stapleton had been present at the *post-mortem*. He says that there were three knives in the house capable of inflicting both the wounds. He also suggests that the body was carried down the back stairs, under which, he says,

"was a cupboard where some damp and dirty socks were found after the murder in suspicious circumstances.[1] At the bottom of the staircase was a door, by locking which all communication with the bedrooms could be cut off, and next it the kitchen where the knives were kept and a fire smouldering where bloody relics could be destroyed, and a passage leading to the back door, which led direct through the stable-yard to the closet, only 25 feet away."

As soon as the *post-mortem* was concluded the undertaker's mother was admitted to lay out the body. She asked for assistance, and Dr. Parsons suggested the nurse and Mrs. Holcombe. But "Elizabeth Gough did not come forward" and Sarah Cox took her place. Since the nurse had previously related how she had performed this service for a little girl who had once been in her care, her defection now seemed odd: however, she afterwards "went in with the weeping family to see the dead child".

12

Dr. Parsons now accompanied Foley in a search of the bedrooms.[2] In Constance's chest-of-drawers they found a list of her clothing made out in her own handwriting, no doubt for school use. They checked it and found it correct. She had three night-dresses: a clean one was in the drawer; one lay folded

---

[1] These socks are mentioned nowhere else in any of the records of the crime: nor does Dr. Stapleton himself allude to them again. It will never be known, therefore, what made the circumstances of their discovery suspicious.

[2] Whether this search included the bedroom of Mr. and Mrs. Kent, and the former's dressing-room, is not clear.

upon her bed, which they examined and found free from any stain; the third had been taken down to the airing cupboard by Cox.

In the meantime Foley had sent for the wife of P.C. Dallimore, whom the police employed as a "female searcher". She reached Road-hill House about four o'clock and after searching the persons of the "young ladies" and the two maid-servants, she searched their rooms as well. In that occupied by the elder sisters she discovered a night-dress belonging to Mary Ann—which presumably Foley and Parsons had overlooked —with stains upon it. The stains appeared to be due to natural causes: nevertheless Mrs. Dallimore took possession of it and handed it over to Foley so that a medical opinion could be obtained. Dr. Parsons had by then gone, so Foley had the garment taken to the police waggonette, in which the breast-flannel already lay.

Mrs. Dallimore then went to the nursery. She noticed, as she entered it, that the door squeaked and the brass ring around the handle jingled, but after a few trials she discovered that, once the knack was known, it could be opened and shut quite silently.

As soon as Elizabeth Gough saw her she demanded:

"What do you want with me?"

"You must undress yourself," said Mrs. Dallimore.

"I cannot."

Mrs. Dallimore explained that she was acting under orders and that the young ladies and the maids had already submitted to the ordeal. Elizabeth Gough then complied, and, as she undressed, Mrs. Dallimore plied her with questions.

"Well, Nurse," she began, "this is a very shocking thing about the murder."

"It is."

"Can you give me an account of it, do you think?"

"I got up at five and missed the child from his bed; then I lay down again."

"Why did you lie down again after you had missed the little boy?"

"I thought he was with his Mamma, because he generally goes in there of a morning." Then she suddenly burst out: "This is done through jealousy! The little boy goes into his Mamma's room and tells her everything."

"But no one would murder a child for doing a thing like that!" protested Mrs. Dallimore. "Who do you think would do it?"

But Elizabeth Gough was on her guard again.

"I cannot tell," she said.

On going downstairs again Mrs. Dallimore lingered a few minutes in the kitchen before taking her departure, and here a small incident occurred which imprinted itself upon her retentive memory. Elizabeth Gough had also come downstairs and was standing with her back to the door when footsteps sounded along the passage and Fricker entered, hot and dirty. She turned round and asked sharply:

"What have you been doing, Fricker?"

"I've been opening the closet."

"Have you found anything?"

"No."

"Then you won't."

CHAPTER EIGHT

THE CRIME: SATURDAY, 30TH JUNE
—EVENING

I

WHILE the recently established "electric telegraph" was conveying the news of the crime to the Press, the columns of which were to be filled with it for months to come, Mr. George Groser, who reported the case for the *Daily News*, got a lead over his colleagues by being already on the spot, and during the afternoon he contrived to find his way into the hall of Road-hill House.

Low down on the wall near the library door he claims to have seen a smear of blood to which he drew the attention of Superintendent Summers, of Frome, who had then just arrived. Summers was on the eve of being transferred to another part of England, and his connection with the case was brief and superficial. When, some weeks later, this point was referred to him, he wrote denying all knowledge of it. Mr. Groser was equally positive that the incident had occurred, but the matter could not be put to the proof for the smear had vanished. There seems no particular reason to doubt Mr. Groser's assertion, while the record of the police in the case inspires little confidence in their denials. Mr. Groser, indeed, won something of a reputation as an authority on the case, and was to be the means of verifying an important incident later on.

Meanwhile the police had decided that the drawing-room window had been opened as a blind, and although Mr. Kent's assertions that someone had concealed themselves in the house for the purpose of killing the child could be disregarded, there remained the possibility that someone had been admitted from outside by a member of the household. This theory pointed to the nurse, and it was suggested that she might have admitted a lover through her dressing-room window, the sill of which was on a level with the flat roof of the dining-room; that the child, usually a sound sleeper but made restless by the pill, had awoken and been killed to prevent him giving the alarm. But there were no traces of anyone having been on the roof; no footprints on the ground beneath; the ivy growing up the dining-room walls would not have supported the weight of a boy, far less a man; the only available ladder, some distance away, shewed no signs of having been disturbed; and finally Elizabeth Gough was found to have no friends of either sex in the neighbourhood—she admitted to having an admirer in Isleworth with whom she corresponded, but it was quickly established that he had never been anywhere near Road in his life.

But nevertheless Foley had some highly suggestive lines to work upon. While the whole nature of the wounds on the body shewed that strength greater than that possessed by the average woman had inflicted them, there was also evidence to indicate that two persons had been concerned in the crime and that one of them must have been a woman. In the first place the criminal could not, while holding the child, have remade the cot in the neat way in which it had been found, for it would have needed the use of both hands, nor was it likely that he would have returned on purpose to do so; secondly, burdened with the child he could hardly have found his way through the shuttered darkness of the house, unlocking doors as he went, without making a noise unless someone had gone before to guide him; thirdly, the practised manner in which the cot had been remade, the child's eyes closed and his features composed, and the presence of the breast-flannel in the vault of the privy all pointed to the accomplice being female.

Dr. Parsons had impressed upon Foley that the arms, hands and garments of the criminal must have become heavily blood-stained: if two persons were involved the likelihood was that the garments of the second would also bear marks of the deed. But up to 5.30 p.m. that day the only stained garment found had been Mary Ann's night-dress.

No weapon had been discovered; the number of knives in the kitchen drawer was correct and Alloway had stated that he had noticed nothing unusual about those he had cleaned that morning. But one object was missing—Mr. Kent's dark-lantern which Cox had put ready for his use at about 10.45 the previous night. And this would have been ideal for lighting the criminal's way, for its beam could be instantly obscured with the shutter on the least alarm.

The question as to whether the lantern and the blood-stained garments still remained concealed in the house, or had already been made away with, must surely have been exercising Foley's mind.[1]

At 5 p.m. Dr. Stapleton drove into the stable-yard and, leaving his carriage there, joined Mr. Kent and some other friends in the library. Hearing of his arrival and anxious to obtain a medical opinion on the nature of the stains on Mary Ann's night-dress, Foley sent P.C. Dallimore to the waggonette to fetch it, and, knocking on the library door, asked Dr. Stapleton to spare him a few moments. They went into the dining-room, where the two officers held out the garment between them and where, as Dr. Stapleton relates, he

> "heard all the circumstances regarding it. . . . *It belonged to a member of the family—not Constance: the marks on it and the circumstances connected with them . . . furnished unequivocal evidence as to their nature and refuted the possibility of their being associated with the murder.*"[2]

At this same moment Sergeant Watts and P.C.s Urch and Heritage were concluding a search of the kitchen under the

[1] It was soon to be suggested that their destruction was the real object of Mr. Kent's hasty departure for Trowbridge that morning. This is hinted at by the *Somerset and Wilts Journal* in the following article:

> "Regarding Mr. Kent's hasty departure for Trowbridge we would ask one question: he left within a quarter of an hour of the loss being known, meeting the Road policeman as he came out. The order for the horse to be put into the trap must have been given, therefore, sometime previously. The dead body was not discovered for some time, say at least a quarter-of-an-hour, after his departure. The Rev. Mr. Peacock then rode after him and caught him before entering Trowbridge. The distance is less than five miles: how is it that Mr. Kent was so long on the road? Surely with even only ten minutes' start, driving as he should have driven, it would have been impossible so to gain on the trap as to overtake it in a four-mile ride? We should like to hear an explanation of this circumstance."

Much later Mr. Kent was to state in the witness-box that Mr. Peacock met him when he was *returning* from Trowbridge. If Mr. Peacock was ever questioned on the point his answer has not survived.

[2] The italics are Dr. Stapleton's.

eyes of an interested audience consisting of Kerslake, Cox, Mrs. Holcombe, Elizabeth Gough and Fricker—the last, no doubt, happy in the knowledge that every snippet of information he could glean would earn him later on that evening many a pint at the "Red Lion".

At 5.40 Watts and the two constables went through the communicating door into the scullery to pursue their search there. The scullery had a second door opening into the passage.[1] Sergeant Watts stooped to peer into the boiler-stove, which, owing to the prevailing disorganization in the house, Kerslake had omitted to relight that morning. He put his hand into the flue. It touched something: an object which had been pushed far enough up to escape notice, yet not too far to be consumed by the flames when the fire was rekindled. He noted these details before he drew the object out.

It was a brown-paper parcel, hastily made up: not tied with string, but with the ends of the paper twisted together. Parting the paper he just had time to notice that it contained a "very bloody female garment" before, glancing up, he beheld Fricker peering intently over his shoulder, and framed in the doorway Elizabeth Gough.

Hurriedly thrusting the parcel under his arm he signed to Urch and Heritage to follow him, and, leading the way to the coach-house, he entered it with the men and closed the door. Secure from observation the garment was then examined. Unlike the orthodox night-gown—a loose garment with long sleeves, buttoning up to the neck—this "night-shift", as Watts called it, though made "in a coarse material like a servant would wear", was shaped somewhat to the figure, had short sleeves, and two flaps back and front, which fastened at the waist. It was, in fact, a copy of the latest fashionable whim.

It was of a size to fit a grown woman, and, although not new, was still serviceable. It had worn thin under the arms and about the knees and been carefully darned. But beneath one arm was a newly-made rent, and it had been in use, Watts judged, for a week or longer since it had last been washed. From the waist

---

[1] The kitchen has since been converted into a billiard-room, and the scullery is the present kitchen.

downwards, to within a few inches of the hem, were large "splashes" of blood.

"It was very bloody. The blood was dry then, but I do not think the stains had been on it a long time. . . . Some of the blood was on the front and some was on the back: more was on the front."[1]

He looked for initials, or some distinguishing mark, but found none. Determined not to let it out of his hands until he had placed it in Foley's, he opened the coach-house door —and there, immediately outside it, stood Mr. Kent!

Instantly he demanded to be shewn what had been found.

"I must see it," he said, "and Dr. Parsons must see it."

But Watts replied that he must give it to Superintendent Foley and went in search of him, accompanied by Heritage, in whose presence he handed it over to Foley at about six o'clock.

Up to this point the history of this garment—which, to avoid confusion, will be referred to as the *night-shift*—is perfectly clear; but its subsequent adventures are enveloped in a deliberately contrived mystery, the solution of which has never been seriously attempted, and since the subsequent course of the case was to hinge on the *night-shift* it is essential to try and solve the riddle of its fate.

J. B. Atlay, though convinced that this garment "could only have been that worn by the murderer", believed it to have been a man's night-shirt;[2] but Watts' description of it—and every contemporary reference to it—leaves no doubt that it was the garment of a woman, and a woman, moreover, of the servant class.

It will be recalled that Dr. Stapleton, after examining Mary Ann's night-dress, somewhere about 5 p.m., had returned to the library, where he spent the next two hours. Some time during those two hours Mr. Kent had left the room, for at about six o'clock Watts had found him outside the coach-house door. Some time before then, presumably, he had learned of Watts' discovery, doubtless from Elizabeth Gough.

[1] Watts in evidence.
[2] *The Road Murder*—J. B. Atlay.

Dr. Stapleton, after expressing his conviction that the stains on Mary Ann's night-dress furnished "unequivocal evidence as to their nature and refuted the possibility of their being associated with the crime", had assured Foley that it would therefore be useless to exhibit the garment as evidence. But when, at seven o'clock, he went to the stable-yard to find his carriage and go home, and learned from the constable in charge of it that the police waggonette "contained some things which the Superintendent was taking away", he says that he "felt some anxiety about the night-dress which had been shewn him" (though on what grounds he does not state). He therefore "went to the police cart and there observed the same garment which he had seen two hours previously and made the remark that *under the circumstances it would be proper to mention it to the authorities*".

What caused Dr. Stapleton, after so emphatically rejecting the night-dress as evidence only two hours before, suddenly to change his mind? The reason can only be that now he was looking not at Mary Ann's *night-dress*, but at the *night-shift*, of the discovery of which he was entirely unaware. He failed to notice that he was looking at a different garment, but he did notice that the stains upon it were not from natural causes. This view seems to be confirmed by the sequel which took place at 10.30 a.m. on Monday, 2nd July. As he and Mr. Sylvester, the coroner, himself a surgeon, were leaving Road-hill House to attend the inquest, they saw the police waggonette again in the stable-yard and looked into it to see if it still contained Mary Ann's night-dress, which it did. A glance was sufficient, says Dr. Stapleton, to satisfy them, and "both concurred in dismissing it, being fully convinced that the marks upon it had no connection with the murder". This time there can be no doubt at which garment they were looking, for by then the night-shift had ceased to exist.[1]

Some time about six o'clock on Saturday, 30th June, Watts, in the presence of Dallimore and Heritage, had handed the

---

[1] "It was," writes J. B. Atlay (*The Road Murder*), "owing to the incompetence of the police allowed to be destroyed. . . . It opened up a new and extremely interesting aspect of the case . . . and is not the least astonishing of the bungling and reprehensible methods that revealed themselves in its handling."

parcel from the boiler-stove over to Foley, informing him of its contents, and the time and place of its discovery. They were in the grounds, and Foley, realizing that they might be under observation from the house, merely parted the paper and took a hasty look at the garment before giving the parcel to Dallimore with instructions to put it in the waggonette along with the other things he was taking to Trowbridge.

Foley had been on the case since nine o'clock that morning, and his mind, never very bright, was probably still further dulled by fatigue. He was later to declare with shrill self-pity that "not a bite or sup had passed his lips all day" though on closer inquiry he reluctantly admitted that "he had accepted refreshment from the cook—port wine and water". At eight o'clock that evening he had an interview with Mr. Kent, whose friends had now departed, and this, it has been suggested, was probably accompanied by further "refreshment". When Foley emerged from it at about 9 p.m. he informed Watts that he could go off duty, but that he would require Urch "to keep watch that night with Heritage upon the inmates of the house". Urch, therefore, and Heritage, "were to go home and have their suppers". From the instructions which Watts passed on with this order to Urch it seems clear that Foley gave him to understand that the watch was to be set secretly and was to centre upon the staircases, for Watts told Urch that "he was to see that his lamp was well-trimmed, and take up his position within the drawing-room doorway" and that, should he hear anyone coming down the staircase, he was to wait until they neared its foot and then "shine his light upon them and see who they were".

The instructions which Foley himself gave to Urch after Watts had gone were, however, widely different. He and Heritage, he told him, were to make their return at eleven o'clock "with caution" as the inmates of the house, except Mr. Kent, were not to know of their presence; they were to tap on the library window *when Mr. Kent would admit them and tell them what to do.*

That the Superintendent in charge of the investigations into such a crime as this should place his officers at the disposal of the man in whose house it had been committed and was himself,

D

therefore, numbered among the suspects, passes belief. Yet this was what Foley did. He was putting a plan into operation: the source from which this plan originated will not long remain in doubt.

All through the long hours of that ghastly day two desperate women and a desperate man had known that a vital clue had fortuitously escaped the destruction planned for it and might at any moment fall into the hands of the police and so inevitably bring about their downfall. When it was discovered their anxiety knew no bounds, and within a few minutes Mr. Kent was at the coach-house door trying by bluff and bluster to regain possession of it from Watts.

It is quite plain that Foley was fully alive to its importance as a clue, and, up till eight o'clock that night, when he had his interview with Mr. Kent, it had been his intention to take it, the breast-flannel and Mary Ann's night-dress back with him to Trowbridge. After the interview his intentions had changed and a plan had been formulated of which the following is the essence. After the household had gone to bed, and while Mr. Kent was secretly admitting Urch and Heritage at the front door, Foley and Dallimore were to replace the parcel containing the night-shift in the boiler-stove, then drive off out of the stable-yard with a great clatter. Hearing them go, and in ignorance of the fact that Mr. Kent had in the meantime introduced the two constables into the kitchen, its owner would then creep downstairs to retrieve it, and the two officers would merely have to step through the communicating door to take her in the act. That he was himself the intended victim of the trap he was baiting did not occur to Foley.

That Dallimore and Heritage were privy to the plan seems certain. It seems equally certain that Urch was not. When at eleven o'clock he and Heritage approached the house "with caution" and tapped on the library window they were admitted by Mr. Kent, and after a whispered word or two they tiptoed in his wake along the passage to the kitchen. There they found a supper of bread and cheese and beer awaiting them, of which Mr. Kent invited them to partake: he then withdrew, and while their attention was engaged with the food and drink *he quietly locked them into the kitchen.*

Not until 1.30 did Heritage discover this, and simultaneously that the parcel over which the watch was set had disappeared. He immediately began to thunder furiously upon the door, whereupon Urch, still ignorant of what it was all about, protested that "he was making enough noise to wake the whole house". But it was twenty minutes before Mr. Kent, still fully dressed, came and opened it, and "offering no explanation for his action said that he had been walking about". Heritage shot past him and out of the house, and set out, presumably on foot, for Trowbridge to report to Foley the sorry outcome of the night's proceedings. Mr. Kent thereupon relocked the door upon Urch, who remained once more incarcerated in the kitchen until 5 a.m., when Mr. Kent returned, unlocked the door and told him to go "as the servants would soon be about".

2

Foley, realizing how completely he had been befooled and outwitted, and the inevitable consequences to himself should his appalling blunder become known, entered into a conspiracy with Heritage and Dallimore to keep the whole episode of the discovery and loss of the night-shift a close secret, while the bewildered Urch was easily persuaded to keep silent on the subject of his own and Heritage's imprisonment in the kitchen. Fortunately for all of them Sergeant Watts was next day superseded by Inspector Pitney and took no further part in the case; and when a few days later he happened to come across Dallimore at a local fair and asked him what had transpired concerning the night-shift the latter had a story ready. It had turned out, he said, to be only an old and dirty garment belonging to one of the servants, stained with blood from natural causes: after the inquest on Monday he had been going to replace it in the boiler-stove so that the poor girl could retrieve it when the nurse called him away: he had put it down beside the stove and when he returned it was gone.

But in spite of all attempts to stifle the affair, a rumour reached the village—perhaps through Fricker—that the police had found a woman's blood-stained night-dress. Next day this rumour was followed by another: that the garment was "lost", and in the minds of the excited people Mary Ann's night-dress was identified with the night-shift, though the owner remained unknown.

That Saturday night Elizabeth Gough stayed with Mrs. Kent in her bedroom until 11.30, by which time Mr. Kent had the night-shift safely in his possession, and spent the remainder of the night with the two maids, ostensibly because she was nervous, but possibly in order to make sure that they did not interest themselves in what was taking place downstairs, where Mr. Kent, with the police safely locked in the kitchen, was busy destroying the clues, which he very likely did in the greenhouse furnace.

After the nurse had gone to the maids' room, Elizabeth Kent spent the rest of the night with her step-mother, Constance taking her place in Mary Ann's room—circumstances which completely refute Mr. Kent's subsequent statement that none but his wife "knew that he was to be up all night". William was the only person in the house that night to sleep alone, and he locked his door "for fear".

Fear, indeed, lay heavy upon all the inmates of Road-hill House: shock, grief, suspicion, suspense—all the aftermath of bloodshed and violence—afflicted their minds and played havoc with their senses. Guilty and innocent alike, none knew and all dreaded what the coming day might bring; and one and all felt the void created by the absence of that vital, demanding little personality who had gone to bed the previous evening confident that he was surrounded by love and secure against all harm, and who now lay a blood-drained and mutilated corpse under lock and key in the gaunt, disused laundry.

CHAPTER NINE

THE EVE OF THE INQUEST

I

ALL the circumstances of the crime, as it was first reported in the Press, were calculated to horrify the public and arouse the deepest sympathy for the family in which it had occurred.

The child of a gentleman of some consequence had been kidnapped from beside his sleeping nurse, and from the room next to that of his parents, so silently and craftily as to disturb no one and leave no trace, then brutally done to death, and his body, with wanton obscenity, cast into the vault of a privy. That such a deed was possible chilled the heart and sickened the mind of every parent in the kingdom: it was feared that a maniac was loose among them and that at any moment their own offspring might furnish his next victim. Sympathy, especially for the grief-stricken mother so soon expecting another baby, was universal, and the attention of a whole nation was riveted upon Road-hill House as it anxiously awaited the disclosures which the inquest was expected to yield.

But the reporters who were forthwith despatched to Road found a strange state of things existing there. The inquest had been timed to open at 11 a.m. on Monday, 2nd July, and on Sunday morning James Morgan, in his capacity as parish constable, performed the duty of empanelling the coroner's jury—twelve "good men and true" with Mr. Nutt, the village grocer—father of William who had discovered the body—as foreman. But in the course of the evening it became known that influence had been brought to bear upon Morgan to warn off Nutt and replace him with the vicar. There was no personal feeling against Mr. Peacock, but as a close friend of the family, and as one who had been constantly with Mr. Kent since the crime, it was felt with justification that he was ineligible for the office: and since two more members who had been previously chosen were also warned off and replaced by others, it was difficult to avoid the conclusion that the jury was being packed. To make matters worse, it was common knowledge that the coroner himself was also a friend of Mr. Kent and had been an equally frequent visitor to his house.

2

On Monday morning, 2nd July, people flocked to Road from all over the neighbourhood. Sensation seekers tried by guile or impudence to get past the police and gaze their fill upon the privy. Hour by hour the crowd waited, gaping at all who entered or left the house. It noted the arrival of Captain Meredith, the Chief Constable, making his first appearance on the scene, who after an examination of the premises reappeared among them "to make the official and authoritative statement that in his opinion two persons had been concerned in the murder".[1]

Mr. Rodway, Dr. Stapleton, the coroner, and "several gentlemen interested in the case" had already gathered in the house. Mr. Peacock's arrival was followed by that of the jury, whose faces were grave and anxious.

They were taken to view the privy; to view the wax-white body in the laundry; they were conducted along the passage into the pillared hall: they were countrymen, looking and feeling abashed and awkward in their best suits as, gripping their hats, they tried to walk quietly in their heavy boots through that house of tragedy—a house, to their eyes, so large and resplendent, the home of a man so far above them in station. But none the less they were fully conscious of their responsibility and determined to see that justice was done.

Up the stairs they trooped and stood around the cot in the nursery; they trooped into each of the unoccupied rooms, their attention being drawn to the cupboards in which an assassin might have concealed himself. They trooped downstairs again and into the drawing-room where they were shewn how the window and the shutters had been found that Saturday morning. And while they thus perambulated the house,

[1] J. W. Stapleton.

guided by the coroner and shepherded by the police, there, lurking unobtrusively in the hall, was Mr. Groser, who had once more contrived to slip indoors while his less enterprising colleagues kicked their heels outside.

3

The ladies of the house had sought refuge from this invasion in their bedrooms. But even in the darkest hours of grief and tragedy domestic necessities must still be fulfilled, and human needs ministered to, and out of these arose an incident, trifling in itself, yet destined to assume proportions upon which hung life and death.

Sarah Cox, summoned to give evidence at the inquest, had first of all to perform her Monday task of collecting and sorting the soiled linen. This was always done in the "lumber-room", and when the sorting was finished Cox informed Mary Ann, who then came and entered the items in the laundry book; then Cox packed the articles into two baskets for which Mrs. Holley, the washerwoman, called in the afternoon.

While this was being done on Monday, 2nd July, Constance was in her bedroom looking for her purse which she had mislaid.[1] The morning was warm and she felt thirsty, but so long as the police and jurymen were tramping up and down the stairs she refrained from going to fetch herself a glass of water. At last the house seemed quiet and she decided to venture forth. There was no one on the first-floor landing, and she was half-way down the next flight when she saw a stranger standing in the hall. It was Mr. Groser and he glanced up. Constance turned round and retraced her steps. Back on the first-floor landing she caught sight of Cox in the lumber-room packing the linen. Mary Ann had already returned to her room. It then occurred to Constance that she might have left her purse in the pocket of a petticoat which she had put out to go to the wash, so stepping just inside the doorway she asked Cox to look and see if it were there. Cox delved down into the basket which she had just finished packing, and found the petticoat,

---

[1] It had fallen behind the chest-of-drawers.

but its pocket was empty. As she was repacking the basket and covering it down with a dress of Mrs. Kent's, which she tucked in round the sides, Constance asked her if she would fetch the glass of water for her "as there were people in the hall". As she went, Constance automatically followed her to the top of the back stairs. Cox "was not gone near a minute", and when she returned she found Constance standing just where she had left her. Constance drank the water and went up to her room, and Cox completed the packing of the second basket which she covered down with a table-cloth. The first basket, as she afterwards stated in evidence, "looked just as she had left it", and there was nothing whatever in its appearance which gave her the impression that it had been disturbed since she had covered it down with Mrs. Kent's dress only a minute or two before.

4

Through Foley's incompetence the night-shift—the one and only piece of tangible evidence which would have led directly to the identity of the criminal—was gone for ever. The only hope of incriminating anyone now depended upon the ability of the police to build up a sufficiently strong case on circumstantial evidence alone. The criminal's gravest danger lay in the inquest, for it is only at an inquest that *all* the evidence relating to a case can be heard: once the inquest is closed the case can only be re-opened upon a specific charge, when only evidence relating to that charge is admissible. It is therefore the duty of the coroner to examine all persons in any way connected with the case, and to adjourn the inquest as often as is necessary until he is assured that he and the jury are in possession of all the ascertainable facts; it is then incumbent upon him to marshal the facts in such a way that they form a logical direction to the jury as to their verdict; and it is important that they should, if possible, fasten the guilt upon some person or persons, for their verdict, once given, influences all the investigations and proceedings that follow.

Throughout the week-end Mr. Kent had been engaged in endless consultations with a number of his friends, many of them persons of considerable local influence, and among them Mr. Sylvester, the coroner himself. The result was a scandalous collusion to keep Mr. Kent and his family from being examined at the inquest, and, in order to facilitate this end, the jury was deliberately packed. Among these friends were members of the Bench of Magistrates itself: men whose duty it was to see that justice was done, but who, in a period when class privileges were being jealously guarded against the growing threat from below, were far more concerned to protect one of their number from the consequences of a deed which threatened to overwhelm him and his whole family. "The magistrates were all hand-in-glove—and Mr. Kent was one of them."[1]

That Monday morning Mr. Kent informed Mr. Rowland Rodway, his solicitor, that, since neither he nor his family were to be present at the inquest, he wished him to attend it in order to "watch his interests". Mr. Rodway very properly objected on the grounds that "the public having already come to the conclusion that the murder was committed by an inmate of the house . . . the presence of an attorney on behalf of the family might probably be misconstrued into a desire on their part to conceal rather than discover the criminal". To this Mr. Kent obliquely retorted that "the magnitude of the crime and the detection of the murderer were considerations which led him to disregard any possible consequences". Like Dr. Parsons, Mr. Rodway "had no wish to offend the gentry", and he reluctantly agreed to comply with his client's request.

5

Mrs. Holley, agog at the rumours concerning the "loss" of a night-dress, could by noon on Monday no longer restrain her curiosity and determined to call for the Road-hill House laundry at once. She was familiar with every item of the Kent family's clothing, having taken in their washing ever since they

[1] From the letter of a resident of Frome.

D*

had come to Road. If a night-dress were missing she would spot it in a moment and know whose it was.

Accordingly she and her daughter, Martha, went over to the house; they were assisted downstairs with the baskets by Kerslake and the moment they got them into their cottage they dragged out their contents. In their first excitement they overlooked the fact that the laundry book had not been enclosed, for it took them barely a minute to discover that, of the young ladies' night-dresses, only two, instead of the usual three, had been included. These two had frills of lace at the wrists and down the front which identified them as the property of Mary Ann and Elizabeth. Constance's night-dresses were plain: the night-dress omitted, therefore, was Constance Kent's.

CHAPTER TEN

THE INQUEST: MONDAY, 2ND JULY

I

A ROOM at the "Red Lion" had been engaged for the inquest although it must have been obvious that it would be far too small to accommodate a tithe of the crowd which was bound to assemble. Perhaps it had been deliberately chosen for the very purpose of excluding as much of the public as possible, for the Temperance Hall, on the opposite side of the green from Road-hill House, was both larger and in every way more convenient.

The narrow village street, hemmed in between grey stone cottages of which the "Red Lion" itself was little more than one somewhat enlarged, was packed with a tightly wedged mass of humanity through which the representatives of the Press had to elbow their way only to find that no accommodation had been reserved for them and every particle of space was occupied. Already the heat in the little overcrowded room was growing unbearable, while the noise from the street outside made hearing almost impossible; which, combined with the indignant protests of the reporters and the representations of the jury, compelled Mr. Sylvester, as soon as the latter had been sworn, to order an adjournment to the Temperance Hall.

It was past noon when the proceedings were resumed. After Sarah Cox had given evidence as to how she had found the drawing-room window and shutters the previous Saturday morning, Elizabeth Gough was called.

"I am nursemaid at Mr. Kent's," she said in answer to questions. "I have been there rather more than eight months. The deceased was a very good-tempered child; it was no trouble to take care of him. He was in the habit of sleeping in a cot by himself, in the corner of my bedroom; another child, a girl two years of age, sleeps in a cot in the same room. I usually put the younger child to bed about half-past seven, the deceased about eight o'clock. I put him to bed at that time on Friday night; he was in excellent health and good spirits. Mrs. Kent always comes into the room after prayers to see the children; she did so that night at a quarter to eleven; the child was then lying, as he usually did, with his face to the wall and his arm under his head. After I had been in my room a little while Mrs. Kent came up to bed and shut my door as she passed. I usually left my door open for Mrs. Kent to shut when she came up, so that if the little girl who was sleeping in her room should cry I should hear her. I did not go to sleep until about twelve, and heard nothing during the night. I awoke about five o'clock; the nursery door was a little open and I missed the deceased from his bed. The impression of the child was there as if he had been softly taken out. The clothes were smoothly put back as if either his mother or myself had taken him out. When I saw deceased had gone I thought his mother had heard him crying and had come in and taken him out. He wore at night his night-dress and a little flannel shirt, but no piece of flannel.[1] The piece of flannel does not belong to the house; it was not worn by anyone in the house.

"I went to Mrs. Kent's room about a quarter or twenty minutes to seven to ask for the child, supposing she had him. I knocked twice at the door but obtained no answer, and as Mrs. Kent was unwell I went away and came again at a quarter past seven, when Mrs. Kent was in her dressing-gown and said she had not seen the child. I then went to the Misses Kents' bedroom upstairs, but they had not seen him either. Then I went downstairs and searched all over the house, and looked into the garden and kitchen garden, and all round the shrubbery. The housemaid told me how she had found the drawing-room window open. I looked for footmarks but did not see any, except on the drawing-room carpet where there were impressions of two hob-nailed boots, one distinct, the other very faint; they were of a large foot.[2] There is a little piece of

[1] I.e. the breast-flannel.
[2] They were, in fact, Morgan's footprints, so Elizabeth Gough could not have seen them until later in the morning.

gravel a person would have to cross in going where the child was found. I did not find him; I did not go there to look.

"I can state positively that no one was in my bedroom or the dressing-room which opens out of it, as we had a sweep that morning, and in the evening everything was put away. I pushed a stool and a box under my bed and went into the dressing-room. I put the things in order in my bedroom and lit the night-light. . . . I know of no one who could have had any dislike of the child. My room has a latch on it and a bolt, but I was never allowed to bolt it, in order that Mrs. Kent could come in if the children cried. The door opens very noiselessly; it is bound round with lint to make it do so, that I might not wake the children. . . . I noticed no footmarks in the nursery; the room is carpeted all over. . . . I heard nothing whatever that night. I was asleep the whole time. The deceased was a very heavy sleeper, and would sleep especially soundly that night as he had no sleep during the day, which he usually did, because the sweep was there."

Thomas Benger then described how he and William Nutt had found the body, the main points in his evidence being that there was no blood on the walls or seat of the privy, only the small clotted pool on the floor; that the blanket was lying on top of the body, not wrapped about it; that the expression on the child's face "was quite pleasant and his little eyes were shut". Benger then went on to relate how he had helped to empty the vault in which "there were five feet of water, but nothing of importance was found".

William Nutt corroborated the first part of Benger's evidence.

Superintendent Foley was next called, and produced the breast-flannel which, he said, had been lying directly below the body. He had searched the whole grounds, but had discovered no blood anywhere else.

Stephen Millet, the butcher, was then called: he displayed two portions of *The Times* of 9th July which he had picked up in the privy and upon which "something bloody had been wiped . . . the blood on them was moist and the pieces sticking together".

Captain Meredith then asked for Elizabeth Gough to be

recalled and in the course of a further examination she said: "The boy William is about fifteen; he had been home from school about a fortnight; he generally goes to bed before his father and mother. There was no dog in the house; in the evenings the dog outside is let loose in the stable-yard. I did not observe on Saturday night that the dog seemed as if he had been drugged.[1] I had bread and butter for supper on Friday night; I had had no beer or anything of that kind; I never take anything of that kind. I had had a hard day's work on Friday because of the sweep. I don't usually have tea at night, but I did take a cup at about eleven that Friday night from the general family tea-pot."

Stephen Millet, recalled, said that he estimated the total amount of blood on the floor, clothes, blanket and body, and in the night-soil, at not more than "three half-pints". He would have "expected more from a child that size".

Dr. Stapleton, taking advantage of the "remarkable informality" which distinguished the proceedings, then intervened, and, indicating Dr. Parsons, said: "We medical men think that is not enough. We should think that three pints of blood from a child like that should be accounted for, and that has not been done."

And now Dr. Parsons himself gave evidence.

"I am a surgeon and reside at Beckington," he said. "On Saturday morning last a little after eight,[2] Mr. Kent's son came to me and told me that his brother had been found in the privy with his throat cut, and begged me to come to the house immediately. I did so, driving him back with me. I found the body in the laundry; the blanket and the night-dress, stained with marks of blood and night-soil, were still on. There were two small cuts on the left hand, evidently made by a sharp instrument after the body had been drained; there was no appearance of blood on them. The throat was cut to the bone by some sharp instrument, from left to right; all the membranes, blood-vessels, nerves and air-tubes were completely divided. There is no doubt that the cut was made by a single sharp, clean

[1] There was a rumour that it had been.

[2] It must have been later than that: William Kent did not leave the house until after the body had been found, which was at about 8.15, and he had then to reach Beckington on foot—a mile and a half away at least.

incision. I found afterwards a stab on the body, evidently made by some broad, sharp, long and strong instrument, as it penetrated through the flannel-shirt and night-dress, passing below the pericardium and diaphragm, severing the cartilages of two ribs, and extending three-quarters across the chest. I judge it was done by a sharp-pointed instrument; *it could not have been done by a razor.* It must have been, I think, a sharp-pointed, long, wide and strong knife. The wound was not less than four inches deep, and when it was inflicted the body must have been previously drained of blood.

"I examined the interior of the stomach to ascertain if the child had been drugged, but he had not. I found the internal parts healthy. Deceased was a child of remarkably fine development. I am satisfied that no drug had been given him. I am of the opinion that he had been dead at least five hours before I first examined him about nine o'clock in the morning. He was quite cold and I was surprised at so much rigidity. My opinion is that there has not been produced today so large a quantity of blood as was likely to be caused by the wounds I have described. A child of that size would have sent out with a gush at one jet a quantity of blood not less than three pints, whereas I do not think we have seen anything like a pint. The arterial blood would at first come out with a rush, and the venous blood would drain out afterwards. I should have said that there was a blackened appearance around the child's mouth which we do not usually see in dead bodies; it was likely to be produced by the violent thrusting of a blanket into the mouth to prevent him crying out, or it could have been done with a hand. The tongue was not cut. I did not make a regular *post-mortem* examination until I received the coroner's orders to do so in the afternoon."

To the general surprise no further questions were put to Dr. Parsons as to the immediate cause of death, but as he sat down he said aloud that "it was his belief that the child had been smothered by the pressure of a soft substance over the mouth".

Foley then got to his feet and said that he had found a quantity of blood-soaked paper in the privy, and was of the opinion that the child had been taken to the privy and murdered there; to which Dr. Parsons replied that "in his belief there was a great deal more blood yet to be accounted for, and that in his opinion a proper and sufficient search had not been made".

All present had followed the proceedings in attentive silence; but when the coroner, without calling any further witnesses, now began to address the jury and to instruct them that the evidence required a verdict of murder against some person or persons unknown, voices in the hall "demanded to know why none of the family had been summoned to appear", while, "with the single exception of their foreman, the jury protested vigorously against the closing of the inquest without the taking of further evidence and further investigation". As their foreman made no move "they insisted that he should voice their demand that the family should appear for examination". Mr. Peacock complied, "but he did so very reluctantly, saying that he could not see any earthly good in any of the family being examined, and that he considered it their duty to spare the feelings of the family as far as possible".

The coroner said that "he concurred with the foreman's views and that the feelings of the family ought to be regarded". At this there were cries of dissent, and the jury repeated their insistence that it should be done; whereupon the spectators, who had signified their disagreement or concurrence with the recent exchanges by hisses or hand-clappings, broke into cheers and echoed the jury's demand. Above the noise the coroner was heard to say, "I can see no good that can come of it", which provoked a fresh storm of protest, in the midst of which Dr. Parsons rose to say that Mrs. Kent's state of health would not permit her to appear. When order had been restored the coroner said:

"If you insist and are determined to examine any part of the family I shall adjourn the inquest to the house."

This meant, of course, that the public would be excluded, and the coroner's announcement caused a new outburst which again held up the proceedings. When it had subsided the coroner asked:

"What part of the family would you like to be examined?"

Some of the jury cried, "The two youngest!" Others said: "Try them all! Shew no respect to one more than another."

The coroner then rose, gathered up his papers and left the hall. At first the jury refused to follow him, but it was explained to them that he could compel their obedience, and as Mr. Rodway, who had hurried over to Road-hill House a few minutes previously, now returned and assured them that Mr. Kent had authorized him to say that he was quite willing for any of his family to be examined, they left the hall and crossed the green to the house in the wake of the coroner.

They were conducted into the kitchen, where they stood about awkwardly, together with a handful of reporters, until Mr..Sylvester joined them; and then Constance and William—and those two only—were brought before them.

"To my thinking," wrote Mr. Timothy Penney, one of the reporters, "the examination of the younger children was of a cursory and superficial kind. The coroner did not take notes and he put several of his questions in a leading form."

Constance's evidence was as follows:

"I am sixteen years of age. I knew nothing of this affair until after my brother was found. About half-past ten on Friday night I went to bed, and I knew nothing until seven o'clock. I generally sleep soundly. I did not leave my bed during the night. I do not know of anyone having a spite against the boy. There was no disagreement in the house, and I am not aware of anyone having a grudge against the deceased. The nurse was always kind and attentive to him. On Saturday morning I heard he was missed; I was then getting up."

William said:

"I am brother to the deceased. I went to bed on Friday night at ten-thirty, and got up at seven o'clock on Saturday morning. I did not get out of bed during the night. I have nothing to add about his death—I wish I had. The deceased was a great favourite of us all, not of one in particular. I did not see deceased after dinner-time[1] on Friday; I was out. I always shut my door at night, but I do not lock it usually; I did last night for fear."

The jury had gone to Road-hill House fully expecting that

[1] Mid-day dinner.

all the family would be summoned for examination, but only these two children had been brought before them. Now the coroner ordered an adjournment back to the Temperance Hall, and the jury, too bewildered to protest, sullenly obeyed. As soon as they had taken their seats Mr. Sylvester resumed his address. He cautioned them to dismiss from their minds all preconceived opinions and suspicions, and to rely solely on the evidence before them. He expressed it as his opinion that the fatal injuries had been inflicted in the closet, as no blood had been found in the house, and he believed that it would have been possible to staunch the blood so as to prevent it from being splashed upon the walls. One of the chief difficulties in connection with the case was their ignorance of the motive. The only conjecture he felt himself at liberty to give was that some person had secreted himself in the house overnight, and committed the horrible deed out of spite to the parents.

"Gentlemen," he said, "this is a most mysterious and atrocious murder,[1] committed by some person or persons, but I fear it will not fall to your lot, under the present aspect of the case, to criminate any person or persons. It would have been a satisfaction to you and to me to have traced the crime to the perpetrator of it; but as you cannot do that you will return your verdict that this murder has been wilfully committed by some person or persons unknown."

A juryman here interposed to say, "There is a strong suspicion on my mind, for it is clear that no one could have got into the house from outside."

"Whatever suspicions you may have in your mind," the coroner answered, "must not influence you in giving your verdict. You may have suspicions in your minds tending to implicate some member"—he was about to say "member of the family" but quickly substituted the word "person"—"some *person*, but you must remember that suspicion is not proof. We have no direct evidence before us, circumstantial or otherwise, and you must therefore decide upon that which is before you and upon that alone. I think you cannot but agree with

[1] The coroner treated the case as though murder were a foregone conclusion, and never instructed the jury to consider the possibility of manslaughter.

'me, and record it in your verdict, that a murder has been committed by some person or persons unknown. . . . You must remember, gentlemen, that our duty is merely to inquire, and we are not responsible for our inability to discover the author. It is not your place to find out who murdered the child, but how the child met his death; your duty is to find expressly the cause of death. It is the duty of the magistrates to investigate and find out the perpetrator of the crime, and no doubt they will do so after the close of the inquest.

"And then, gentlemen, we must also recollect that although the action was concealed from the eyes of men, yet it was seen and recorded by One above; the eye of Providence saw the deed and can penetrate the mystery, and although it has not fallen to our lot today to point out the offender, yet our conviction is that sooner or later the murderer will be discovered."

Having thus shifted the inquiry and misled the jury as to the scope of their duties, Mr. Sylvester determined to force their verdict while their minds were still bemused. He allowed them no opportunity to "lay their heads together and decide upon their verdict . . . nor did the foreman, or any member of the jury, speak up and return a verdict as the verdict of the jury, but . . . the coroner filled up a printed form of inquisition and read it over and signed it, and requested the jury to sign it. . . . But some of them got up and spoke aloud, and objected to the closing of the inquest without further inquiry; and especially Mr. Edward West . . . rose up and, addressing the coroner, put his hand upon his breast, and, in an impressive and excited manner, said he felt that they had not done their duty. . . ."[1]

Another juror named Martin then got up and said that "Dr. Parsons, the vicar, and the coroner wished to hush the matter up and they held back certain evidence. Mr. Nutt senior had been warned off so that the vicar could be warned on."[2]

But in spite of their protests the printed form was passed

---

[1] Quoted from the affidavits made later in the case of *The Queen v. Sylvester*: see page 176 *et seq. infra.*
[2] *Ibid.*

to them for their signatures and one by one, reluctantly, they signed it, though "much dissatisfaction was shewn, and one of the jury, named Marks, said aloud as he signed his name that he had never signed anything so against his inclination before".[1]

Mr. Sylvester was booed as he left the Temperance Hall and voices called out that the jury had been packed; that Mr. Kent should have been forced to appear, and that all the family, not only the two youngest, should have been examined.

2

The Press was unanimous in condemning the way in which the inquest had been conducted.

The *Morning Post* demanded to know for

"what reason the personal friends of Mr. Kent and his family interested themselves with such a person as the parish constable to procure the withdrawal of one juror and the substitution of another", and stressed the need to explore "all the combinations and intrigues by which it was sought to pack the jury".

The *Daily News* said:

"We must seriously object to the course pursued in appointing one who was avowedly an intimate friend of the family as foreman of the jury. . . . A man who is beyond suspicion of partiality was the only proper person to occupy a position of such responsibility."

The *Bath Express*, after observing that the crime "now engages public attention almost to the exclusion of every other topic", repeated the objections against Mr. Peacock sitting as foreman of the jury and continued:

"It is always desirable to confront a guilty person in the first agony of consternation and confusion and before he has had time to recover his composure, to abolish all traces

---

[1] Quoted from the affidavits made later in the case of *The Queen v. Sylvester*: see page 176 *et seq. infra.*

of his crime, and to prepare his defence. If he has one or more accomplices . . . no time should be given them for framing a consistent and convincing story.

"All this advantage was lost by the imbecile conduct of the coroner, who was content with affirming a murder, but made no effort to discover the murderer. . . . After only five witnesses had been examined, one of whom was the surgeon . . . the coroner strangely deemed the taking of further evidence unnecessary 'wishing to spare the feelings of the family'. . . .

"The coroner himself admitted in his charge that 'it was impossible for anyone to have gained ingress from outside'. How was it that he did not see the irresistible conclusion, *viz.*: that the persons who composed the household must be held collectively responsible for this dreadful event? . . . Supposing the murderer to be one of the household, it seems impossible that the guilt of that person should not be suspected by the rest of the household, or at all events by one or more of its most sagacious members. . . . There may not be an accomplice, but there may be *accessories after the fact*—namely those who infer guilt, but would screen the murderer. This shews that the feelings of no one person ought to be considered."

3

The moment the inquest was over Mr. Rodway had an interview with his client "for the purpose", as he wrote later to the *Morning Post*, "of consulting on the measures to be further adopted". But he was unable to "collect . . . materials for forming any decided opinion. I suggested to him what I considered to be the probable solution of this mystery; but I found that our views of the crime, and of the mode and direction of its investigation, widely differed; and as I could not adopt Mr. Kent's views, nor he mine, I abstained from further interference."

This explanation provoked the following comment from the *Bath Herald*:

". . . Mr. Rodway says—'I could collect no materials for forming an opinion'—but Mr. Rodway *did* form a very decided opinion: to wit that Mr. Kent's ideas, both as to the nature of the crime and the mode and direction of investigations, were so wild and absurd that he could not, with any regard to conscience or self-respect, consent to act upon them; whereupon he threw up his brief and left Mr. Kent to find some more compliant counsellor. As Mr. Rodway will not tell us what those impracticable ideas were, we will ourselves inform the public. Mr. Kent seriously maintained that the murder was committed by some tramp, or possibly by a discarded servant; but, at all events, by no one connected with Road-hill House. The investigation might range far and wide, provided it kept clear of the only place where the criminal was likely to be found. Mr. Rodway refused to go on this wild-goose chase, and he speedily ceased to be Mr. Kent's solicitor."

Elsewhere the same paper had suggested that, whereas Mr. Rodway wanted a real and thoroughgoing effort to discover the murderer, Mr. Kent wanted only a sham and make-believe investigation. Nevertheless it criticized Mr. Rodway severely for his conduct at the inquest.

". . . When this gentleman saw what a farce the inquest was as conducted by Mr. Sylvester, how scandalously he was excluding evidence, and how bent he was on closing the inquest at one sitting, without even an attempt to execute the one and only end of it—the fixing of the accusation on someone—for a child of four years old could hardly be a suicide—how came it that Mr. Rodway did not admonish the coroner of his duty and insist on an adjournment of the inquest? He is bound to give some further explanation to the public; for whatever was his motive, his conduct on this occasion was that of one endeavouring to obstruct, not to promote, the discovery of the criminal; if not by active exertions, yet by silence and patent connivance at this foul prostitution of that valuable instrument for the discovery of crime—the Coroner's Inquest. . . ."

"The more compliant counsellor" with whom Mr. Kent replaced Mr. Rodway was Mr. Dunn of Frome, a lawyer of considerable astuteness. Mr. Rodway later caused much surprise by consenting to act on behalf of "Mrs. Kent and the second family".

4

As soon as the inquest was over permission was given for the funeral of the dead child to take place; but Mr. Kent dared not hold this at Road, for the public was shewing its disgust at the "combinations and intrigues" which had distinguished the coroner's proceedings by making hostile demonstrations outside Road-hill House. Accordingly very early in the morning the little coffin was placed in a closed carriage, and with Mr. Kent seated on one side of it and William on the other was swiftly conveyed, under police escort, to East Coulston, where, by an ironic twist of fate, the grave of the cruelly wronged wife was opened to receive the cruelly mutilated body of her supplanter's son. What were Samuel Kent's emotions as he stood beside it, knowing that in the minds of many the deaths of both those who were now to lie within it were attributed to him?

The following Sunday—8th July—when he and his wife attempted to go to church the police had to make a way for them through a crowd which shook its fists in his face and shouted, "Murderer!" "Who killed his own son?" so that Mrs. Kent "in a fainting condition had to be helped into the cover of the church porch".

CHAPTER ELEVEN

THE THIRD NIGHT-DRESS

I

ON THE morning of Tuesday, 3rd July, Mrs. Holley called at Road-hill House for some money which was owing to her, and although she took the opportunity to ask Cox for the washing-book she said nothing about the absence of Constance's night-dress from the wash—"That was where I was wrong," as she afterwards confessed.

When on returning home she found that three night-dresses had been listed she grew so flustered as to what she ought to do that she consequently did nothing; but that afternoon her agitation gave way to alarm when she saw no less than four policemen coming up her garden path, and, as she hastened to open the door to them, she gratuitously blurted out the falsehood that "the clothes were right with the book".

The next moment she bitterly regretted her imprudence, for all they had come for was to shew her the breast-flannel and ask her if she could identify it or had ever seen one like it in the wash: questions to which she was able to reply, truth-fully, in the negative.

But fearful as to what the consequences of her lie might be, as soon as the police had gone she sent Martha up to the house to tell Cox that "Miss Constance's night-gown was not among the clothes, and would she send one to make the washing right with the book, because the police had been to her house and might come back".

Cox informed Martha that her mother must have made a mistake, as she was certain that she had put three night-dresses into the basket and that one of them had been Constance's. She then went to fetch Mary Ann and returned with her and—surprisingly—with Mrs. Kent as well, who declared positively that "three bed-gowns had been put into the basket".

Next morning (Wednesday, 4th July) Mrs. Holley, in a great state of agitation, went up to the house herself and asked to speak to Mrs. Kent. But Mr. Kent appeared instead and without more ado roundly accused her of stealing the garment and threatened that if she "did not return it within forty-eight hours he would have her apprehended under a special warrant". That same evening the police searched not only Mrs. Holley's cottage, but all the other cottages in the lane and those of Mrs. Holley's married daughters in the village.

And so the seed of the second crime which had been sown at Road-hill House the previous Monday morning had begun to germinate, and the remaining history of the case is largely the history of its growth and the fruit it was to bear.

2

Although all three of Constance's night-dresses had been accounted for by Foley himself on Saturday, 30th June, the police now dropped all other lines of inquiry and pursued this quest with surprising energy—perhaps because it afforded so timely a rejoinder to the rumour that they had "lost" a blood-stained night-dress on the Saturday night.

They questioned Cox closely: she repeated that she was "quite positive that she had put three night-dresses into the basket, that Miss Constance's was one of them and that there were no stains upon it". They questioned Mary Ann, who said that she "had listed the washing with Cox and had seen her put Constance's night=dress into the basket". They questioned Constance herself and asked her for the list of her clothes, and then for the night-dresses entered upon it: she shewed them two, and said that on the previous Monday morning she had put the third on the landing outside her door for Cox to collect for the wash. They asked Mrs. Kent if articles had ever been missed from the wash before, to which she replied that they had—twice: taxed with which Mrs. Holley declared that the only things that had ever been lost all the years she had done the family's washing had been "a ragged old duster and an old bath-towel".

3

On 7th July the Trowbridge magistrates met in consultation and decided to hold an inquiry into the crime *in camera* at the Temperance Hall at Road. This inquiry, which began on 9th July and continued, with frequent adjournments, for nearly a fortnight, had the effect of maintaining public excitement at fever-pitch right up to its dramatic climax on the 20th July.

Dr. Stapleton says that "it was generally understood that the principal object of these inquiries was to be directed towards the nurse"; that Mr. Kent was summoned to give evidence, but that Dr. Parsons certified to the Chairman of the Bench that he found him "in such a state of agitation and mental incoherence that it was impossible for him to give reliable or coherent testimony"; and he comments that "to this may be fairly attributed the partial and fragmentary character of the proceedings in every successive inquiry".

On the day the inquiry opened Mrs. Dallimore appeared in the kitchen of Road-hill House. Elizabeth Gough, as soon as she saw her, asked sharply:

"Mrs. Dallimore, what have you come for?"

Foley and two constables had entered hard upon Mrs. Dallimore's heels and she replied:

"These gentlemen will tell me what I am to do before I leave."

Foley then produced the breast-flannel—which Mrs. Dallimore had washed clean of blood and night-soil—and handed it to her saying:

"You must try this piece of flannel on those girls"—indicating Kerslake and Cox—"and the nurse."

She took Kerslake and Cox upstairs. The brassière proved too small for their well-developed bosoms, and in reply to her questions both denied ever having seen it, or any article like it, in the possession of any of the young ladies.

Mrs. Dallimore then went to the nursery.

"You must take your things off," she told the nurse.

"It's no use," said Elizabeth Gough. "If the flannel fits me, that's no reason I done the murder."

Mrs. Dallimore tried it on her.

"You see, Nurse, it fits you exactly, which it did not do the other servants."

"If it fits me, that's no reason to think I done the murder."

When they returned downstairs Foley told Elizabeth Gough to get ready to accompany him to the Temperance Hall. As the attitude of the crowd towards her was distinctly hostile it had been arranged that she should await her summons in the parlour of a cottage next door to the hall. This cottage was occupied by a harness-maker named Stokes and his sister, Ann, and the parlour window commanded a view of the entrance to the Temperance Hall.

The nurse was under examination for three hours, after which the inquiry was adjourned to Road-hill House for the purpose, it was stated, of examining Mrs. Kent and Constance. Upon the magistrates' return a number of other witnesses were examined, including Dr. Parsons, Holcombe, Kerslake, Cox, Mrs. Holley and Martha. It is curious to find that, although the proceedings were supposed to be strictly *in camera*, Mr. Kent's new attorney, Mr. Dunn, was present both at those in the Hall and those in Road-hill House.

"The examination," says the *Journal*, "was rigidly private, but we are sufficiently in possession of what transpired to know that although trivial points were elucidated to some extent, nothing occurred to throw light upon the main points of the crime."

It was rumoured, however, that much of Elizabeth Gough's evidence had been contradictory and had impressed the magistrates unfavourably.

When she was brought to Ann Stokes' parlour the following day to await a further examination—which was to last even longer than the first—she paced up and down "in a great state of agitation". At the close of her interrogation, after the magistrates had consulted together in low tones, the Chairman informed her that she would be detained "as a measure of security", whereupon she "went into hysterics and fainted".

However, she "quickly revived", and it was further explained to her that she was neither being charged with the crime nor put under arrest, but "by the magistrates' express orders" was merely being "lodged" for a few days with Mrs. Dallimore at Trowbridge. It was subsequently made public that this action had been taken not because the magistrates suspected her of being guilty of the crime, but because they felt that "she knew more of the facts of the murder than she had admitted, and during detention might be induced to reveal what she knows, or suspects, to free herself from suspicion".

She occupied a bedroom with Mrs. Dallimore and the latter subsequently stated on oath that "she spoke several times to her about the child". On one such occasion she asked her:

"Who do you think could have taken the child?"

"I don't know. I think someone must have concealed themselves in the house."

"I don't think so, Nurse—how could they get in?"

"I don't know anything about that—I can't say."

"I also told her," stated Mrs. Dallimore, "that it was quite impossible for one person to have done the murder; I asked her if she thought Miss Constance Kent had done it: she answered, 'I don't think Miss Constance would do it.' I asked her what she thought of Mr. William doing it with Miss Constance; she answered, 'Oh, Master William is more fit for a girl than a boy.' I asked her if she thought Mr. Kent did the murder; she said, 'No; I do not think for a moment that he committed the murder; he is too fond of his children.' I said, 'You said you thought it was done by someone secreted in the house, and the door creaks—how could it have been opened by a stranger without making a noise?' She said, 'A person accustomed to opening it could do it without making a noise.'"

Another conversation took place within the hearing of P.C. Dallimore himself, who later gave an account of it, also on oath.

"A night-gown is missing," he heard Elizabeth Gough say to his wife. "It is lost, I think, in the wash. You can depend upon it that night-gown will lead to the discovery of the murderer."

"Did you see the night-gown put into the basket?" asked his wife.

"Yes, I did."

"Then, Nurse, *you* saw it put in as well as Cox?"

"Oh no, I didn't!" the nurse then exclaimed.

"But you've just said so," Mrs. Dallimore pointed out.

"I didn't! I didn't!"

P.C. Dallimore then intervened himself.

"So *you* saw the night-dress put into the basket?"

"No, sir, but I didn't!"

"But you've just said so."

"No, I shall have nothing to say about that. I have enough of my own to contend with."

4

Elizabeth Gough's father had arrived from Isleworth and saw her at Mrs. Dallimore's; on 13th July, when she was summoned to appear again at the inquiry, he accompanied her to Road but was not admitted to the proceedings.

Feeling against her was now running so high that it was considered prudent to announce that she was *not* to be called, and it was only after the inquiry had been in progress for some time that she was hurried, heavily veiled, from the closed carriage which had brought her from Trowbridge into Ann Stokes' parlour. Although she was in a state of considerable nervous tension she had herself under good control until Ann Stokes, seeing from the window a wave of excitement pass over the crowd as the magistrates, followed by some of the police, suddenly left the hall and hurried across the green to Road-hill House in response to a message which had been brought from there, exclaimed:

"Something must have been found out!"

Inspector Pitney, of Frome, who was in charge of Elizabeth Gough, took a quick glance and said he would go and find out; then, in Ann Stokes' own words:

"The nurse became very excited and walked to and fro in the room, pressing her hands to her sides and saying she felt as if the blood had gone from one side to another. She also said that she could not hold out much longer, and that she could not have held out so long but that Mrs. Kent had begged her to do so. Some time after she remarked that she had pulled out some grey hairs from her head; that no one knew how she suffered, and that if anything else occurred she thought she would die."

Immediately upon the magistrates' return to the Temperance Hall, Elizabeth Gough was called, and when she emerged from what she had dreaded as an ordeal she shewed obvious signs of relief. The magistrates had apparently modified their suspicions of her, and she told the reporters who thronged about her at the door that she was returning to Mrs. Dallimore's at her own wish, but before leaving for Trowbridge she was going to see Mrs. Kent. To one question which they put to her she replied that when Mrs. Kent had been told that Savile was dead she had cried out at once: "Is he murdered? Good God! It is someone in the house who has done it!" And that she herself had answered, "Oh, ma'am, it's revenge!"

Later on she gave Ann Stokes an account of her visit to Mrs. Kent. She had said to her: "How can I bear it? I must give in—I can't hold out any longer." And Mrs. Kent had replied: "Oh, don't say that! You have done so well so far, do keep it up—you must, for my sake."[1]

It was reported that the message which had summoned the magistrates to the house had been from Mrs. Kent to say that she wished to amend her statement, made on 9th July, in which she had declared that she had never taken the child from his cot to her bed in the course of the night. She now said:

"I may have taken the child from his cot to my bed, but I cannot be positive. I said to her, 'Nurse, do not be frightened if I come in and take the child away.' I have always told my nurses not to be surprised at seeing me in the room at any hour of the night. I have been in the nurse's room, and sometimes she has been awake and sometimes not."[2]

So strange, and flat, a contradiction of her original statement seriously weakened the possibility of establishing a case against the nurse: hence the altered attitude of the magistrates towards Elizabeth Gough when the sitting was resumed.

[1] The above statements were made at an inquiry by Mr. T. B. Saunders (Chapter Sixteen).

[2] But in the evidence she gave later—4th October—in the case against Elizabeth Gough she reverted to her statement of 9th July.

CHAPTER TWELVE

CHIEF INSPECTOR WHICHER

I

THE first specialized detective branch of Scotland Yard, consisting of three inspectors and nine sergeants, had been established in 1842. "As with the old Bow Street Runners, anyone in England—and sometimes out of it—who chose to pay the expenses might employ one of these men."[1]

On that same day—Friday, 13th July—confronted with the total failure of their inquiry and of all the investigations so far attempted by the local police, and urged thereto by an insistent public demand, the magistrates decided to call in this expert aid; and one of their number, Mr. W. Stancombe, set out at once for London to arrange the matter with Sir Richard Mayne, Chief Commissioner of the Metropolitan Police.

Two days later—Sunday, 15th July—Chief Inspector Jonathan Whicher arrived at Trowbridge and took over the conduct of the case from Superintendent Foley.

Whicher had gained an European reputation for his skill in handling cases of a "delicate nature"; his methods of detection were regarded as unique, and in the practice of deduction he was, perhaps, the real forerunner of Sherlock Holmes. He was known to Charles Dickens, who has recorded some of his exploits under the name of Whichum in *Household Words* while Wilkie Collins has handed him down to posterity as Sergeant Cuff in *The Moonstone*.

The news that Whicher had taken over the case was received with gratification and the confident assurance that within a few days he would discover the criminal. Perhaps he shared this confidence himself, and, if so, therein lay the seeds of his failure. He began in the belief that a crime involving so few suspects and of such a wholly domestic nature must be easy of solution, whereas he should have been warned by the turn

[1] *The Story of Scotland Yard*—George Dilnot.

which the inquest had taken that there were hidden influences being brought to bear. As it was, either his self-assurance or his desire for a quick and sensational *coup* blunted his perceptions and caused him to be led astray even as Foley had been. But full allowance must, however, be made for the fact that Foley and his men deliberately kept the discovery and subsequent loss of the night-shift a secret from him, so that the only clues upon which he had to work were the breast-flannel and Constance's missing night-dress.

On Monday, 16th July, the magistrates resumed their inquiry at the Temperance Hall and Whicher attended the proceedings, which, as the *Journal* informed its readers, were "so profoundly secret that even magistrates who had not been in attendance throughout . . . were requested to withdraw". Mr. Dunn, however, contrived to be present. Mr. Kent had again been summoned to appear but "did not do so", and when an adjournment was made to his house "for the purpose of examining himself and his family, Mr. Dunn objected to many of the questions put to them and these went unanswered".[1] Dr. Parsons, the Reverend Edward Peacock, Mrs. Holley, Sarah Cox and Elizabeth Gough were among those examined, and the last-named emerged to inform the reporters that she was now at liberty to go where she pleased, but was returning to Road-hill House "at Mrs. Kent's special request".

At the end of the day's proceedings the Press were admitted to the hall when the Reverend R. Crawley,[2] the presiding magistrate, informed them that Chief Inspector Whicher "had been charged by the Home Secretary[3] with the pursuance of the investigations; that a reward of £200 had been offered for the detection of the murderer, and that any accomplice, except the actual murderer, would receive a free pardon on giving information". He added that half this sum would be paid by Mr. Kent, and that Elizabeth Gough had been released with full liberty to go where she pleased, but had "stated her intention of returning to the house".

---

[1] The *Advertiser*.
[2] He happened to be connected by marriage with the vicar of Isleworth to whom Elizabeth Gough was known, and the two clergymen had been in correspondence about the case.
[3] Sir George Lewis.

2

Whicher went carefully through the police reports which he received from Foley. At the same time there came to his ears a number of stories about Constance: stories so insidious and suggestive that though they were to be refuted first by his own investigations, and later by the evidence taken in court, their foetid breath clung about her like a miasma to the end of her days.

He learned that even as a child she had possessed an extra-ordinarily wilful and cunning disposition, as was evinced by her flight to Bath; that she had always displayed a vindictive spite towards her step-mother and had been insanely jealous of the dead child. He learned that only the previous year a very curious incident had occurred. Savile had had a cold and Mrs. Kent had instructed the nurse—Emma Sparks—to put bed-socks on his feet and keep him well covered up in bed. Looking into the nursery later on she had found him lying uncovered and without the bed-socks. Summoning the nurse, who had gone downstairs, she accused her of deliberately disobeying her orders, and an angry altercation followed, as a result of which Emma Sparks, having failed to produce the bed-socks, left next morning roundly abusing Mrs. Kent and describing the children as "horrid". After she had gone one sock was found under the nursery table, and the other on Mrs. Kent's own bed. Beyond the fact that Constance happened to be in the house at the time there was nothing whatever to connect her with this episode, but it was now suggested that she had done it with the deliberate intention of harming the child, or, it was even hinted, as a rehearsal for the crime itself. Whicher also learned that her mother had been mad, one of her uncles had been in an asylum and that her grandmother had been decidedly odd.

Although one would have thought that the very extrava-gance of these stories would have inspired him with caution Whicher made them the mainspring of his actions—and he moved with speed. Sergeant Williamson, who had been sent to

E

his assistance from Scotland Yard in response to his urgent telegram, was put in charge of the investigations at Road; Superintendent Wolfe was sent to East Coulston to make inquiries into Constance's behaviour as a child at Baynton House; he himself, armed with the breast-flannel, interviewed her school-mistresses and school-fellows at Beckington, the police at Bath and the landlord of the Greyhound Hotel.

Except that Sergeant Williamson unearthed the rumour "that some of the police had been locked up in Road-hill House on the Saturday of the crime"—a trail that was dropped when Foley "gave an explanation of it"—all these endeavours proved abortive. Wolfe returned to say that so far as he could ascertain Constance's behaviour at Baynton House had been that of a normal child; the Misses Scott and Williamson failed to identify the breast-flannel, and told Whicher that Constance had a pleasing personality, worked diligently, and that her general deportment had just earned her the second prize for good conduct; her school-fellows said that she was "very obliging" and that "they were fond of her". Nor had he any better luck at Bath: the landlord of the "Greyhound" had nothing to tell him beyond the details of her and William's arrival at his hotel, while at the police station where she had been detained they spoke of her with admiration.

He still had, however, the addresses of two girls who had been described to him as the closest friends she had had at school. The first of these, Louisa Hatherall, aged fifteen, the daughter of a yeoman farmer living near Road, declared that she had never seen an article like the breast-flannel in her life. She had nothing to say against the character of her friend, but admitted that they had exchanged confidences, which caused Whicher to think that if she were placed in the witness-box she might reveal something.

The second girl was Helen Moody, aged sixteen, who lived with her mother, the widow of a solicitor, in Warminster. Acting on the advice of Superintendent Abbott of that division, who had heard certain rumours, Whicher called, not directly upon the Moodys but upon their next-door neighbour, Mrs. Bailey. Although Mrs. Moody "did not visit with Mrs. Bailey" Helen had gossiped freely with her on the subject of the crime, and of her own intimacy with Constance, and stimulated by the visit of the famous detective she now enlarged loquaciously on all that had passed between them. Helen was observed "walking in the garden" and summoned to come over, whereupon, as excited as her hostess, she led Whicher to believe that she possessed an intimate knowledge of Constance and her affairs. He had not the breast-flannel with him, but, returning with it next day, he called, this time, at Helen's own home and shewed it to her, when she frankly admitted that she had never seen it, or any garment like it, among Constance's things.

<h2 style="text-align:center">3</h2>

Whicher had questioned and re-questioned Mrs. Holley, Martha and Cox; he had gone over Road-hill House and its grounds, and had searched Constance's bedroom. Now, on Wednesday, 18th July, he searched it again, and summoned her to it.

She entered to find him with the list of her clothes in his hand. It did not include any such article as the breast-flannel.

"Is this the list of your clothes?" he asked.

"Yes."

"In whose hand-writing is it?"

"It is in my own hand-writing."

"Here are three night-dresses—where are they?"

"I have two: the other was lost in the wash the week after the murder."

He asked to see the two: she took them from a drawer: both had been worn and were unwashed, for no laundry had gone to Mrs. Holley since Monday, 2nd July. Taking them from her Whicher tucked them under his arm, and, pointing to a night-dress and night-cap lying folded on her bed, asked:

"Whose are those?"

"They are my sister's."

He then left the room.

He had never entertained the slightest doubt that the crime had been committed by an inmate of the house. The presence of the breast-flannel in the vault of the privy implied that a woman had been connected with it. Her clothing, therefore, would have been stained with blood. No blood-stained garment—to his knowledge—had ever been found, but a nightdress, proved to have been Constance's, had mysteriously disappeared. With these factors in his mind he builded up his theory.

Constance, he argued, had possessed three night-dresses: A, B and C. A and B had been in her drawer and C in wearing. After committing the crime she had destroyed the bloodstained C and worn B for the remainder of the night. B it was, therefore, which Foley and Parsons had found on her bed next day and examined, and it was B which she had put out on Monday to go to the wash, placing A on her bed. After B had been listed and packed in the laundry basket she had employed the subterfuge of wanting a glass of water to get rid of Cox and retrieve it. A was then returned to her drawer and B taken back into use. Meanwhile responsibility for its loss would devolve on Mrs. Holley.

It was an ingenious theory, and Whicher fell as much in love with it as a reflection of his brilliance as did Narcissus with that of his beauty in the pool. He knew he had not a shred of evidence to support it, but Constance was young and impressionable and he felt convinced, as he afterwards acknowledged, that the psychological effect of a swift and sudden arrest, followed by that of imprisonment, would induce a confession of guilt, or, at least, some incriminating admission.

On Thursday, 19th July, he decided to ask for a warrant for her arrest.

Next morning, Friday 20th, "a rumour which had gone abroad that Mr. Kent and the nurse were to be taken" drew an even greater crowd than usual to Road. The shrubs which had once screened the house had been despoiled and the front lay open to view. The usually trim lawn was ragged and unkempt, and as white as the green itself from the dust churned up by innumerable vehicles. All entrances to the grounds were guarded by police. The expectant crowd noticed that "much excitement was apparent among the magistrates and all concerned", and that after the doors of the Temperance Hall had closed behind them at 11 a.m. they remained closed for three hours "during which time no witnesses were called".

Whicher's demand for Constance's arrest upon evidence of so frail and negative a character had created consternation among the authorities. Captain Meredith strongly opposed it, while the magistrates pointed out the damage it would do to her future even if—as seemed inevitable—the charge were to fail. As a compromise they suggested that she should be "lodged" as Elizabeth Gough had been, while he endeavoured to obtain further evidence. But Whicher was insistent.

At two o'clock he and Sergeant Williamson, accompanied by Captain Meredith and some of the magistrates, left the Temperance Hall for Road-hill House. As they passed along the lane opened for them through the crowd by the police, the reporters were invited into the Hall. For half an hour they waited, note-books and pencils in hand, for some pronouncement, but the remaining magistrates sat mute upon the platform as though in a state of suspended animation; and when at last an inspector of police strode in and handed them a message the reporters were requested to withdraw. A few minutes later the police inspector emerged, jumped into a waiting trap and drove off: it later transpired that he had been sent to Devizes to inform the governor of the gaol that an arrest was being made and he was to expect a prisoner.

The main body of the crowd, however, had its attention fixed upon Road-hill House, and surged forward eagerly as a posse of police formed outside the front door. A moment later this was opened to reveal Chief Inspector Whicher, with beside him—not Mr. Kent or the nurse—but Constance Kent. A deep gasp went up from the crowd, followed by a deathly silence, and then "a murmur of ' 'Tis Miss Constance!' was speedily heard in various quarters in mingled tones of commiseration and pity".[1]

They saw Whicher make some remark to her and offer his arm; they saw her recoil, then lay her finger-tips reluctantly upon it. Slowly they came forward, followed by Captain Meredith, Foley and some of the police, while the remainder went on ahead to clear a way. But there was no need for this,

[1] The *Advertiser*.

for the people fell back of their own accord and "stood silent and stared at her as though stunned".[1] The door of Constance's home had closed behind her, and not a single member of her family went with her, to stand at her side and support her through her ordeal. Her face was tense with shock, and her eyelashes moist with tears which she struggled to restrain. And so the second crime at Road-hill House bore fruit.

The proceedings in the Temperance Hall were brief and formal. Whicher, standing beside a table on which lay Constance's two night-dresses, stated that he had found a list of her clothing in her chest-of-drawers and had questioned her upon the number of her night-dresses. She had only been able to account for two of the three which figured on her list. He then continued: "This afternoon I again sent for the prisoner into the sitting-room. I said to her, 'I am a police officer and I hold a warrant for your apprehension, charging you with the murder of your brother, Francis Savile Kent, which I will read to you.' I then read the warrant to her and she commenced crying and said, 'I am innocent,' which she repeated several times. I accompanied her to her bedroom, where she put on her bonnet and mantle, after which I brought her to this place. I now pray the Bench for a remand of the prisoner, to enable me to collect evidence to shew the *animus* which the prisoner entertained towards the deceased, and to search for the missing night-dress, which, if still in existence, may possibly be found."

The two night-dresses produced were, he said, "only soiled by being worn". He then asked that "the remand should be for seven days, and pressed for it—against the wishes of the magistrates that it should be for longer—until it was granted".[2]

Constance sat still as death staring at the floor, her black-gloved hands folded in her lap, while the charge was being read. And so she sat throughout the long drive to Devizes Gaol.

---

[1] The *Advertiser*.
[2] *Ibid.*

4

Public reaction to Constance Kent's arrest was one of shocked incredulity. Locally, disbelief in her guilt was mingled with angry indignation. The *Advertiser* pointed out

> "that any other inmate of the house having committed the murder could easily have taken the garment from the bundle for the purpose of throwing suspicion by pointing it at Miss Constance. . . . This latter opinion is the view very largely shared by residents in the neighbourhood, who will not listen to the charge against her, but sympathize with her as one who has been put forward as a scapegoat."

It was a view shared by others besides residents in the neighbourhood, and found vigorous expression in an anonymous pamphlet entitled *Who Committed the Road Murder?*

> "What became of it"—(Constance's night-dress)—the author wrote, "is not the important question: but—WHO ABSTRACTED IT. Find me the thief, and the murderer (*if a murderer*) will be found. Find me the thief and I will find you the assassin; not that they exist in one person! . . . Hitherto all the brilliant detectives' effort has been to associate the loss of the night-dress with Miss Constance Kent, to prove that her guilt is wrapped up in it. . . . I perceive her purity in its loss, and, in its loss, another's guilt.
>
> "The thief purloined the night-dress to shield *herself*, by casting suspicion *on one of her own sex*. Had she purloined a *male* garment, the effect would have been beneficial only to her male accomplice (whoever he might be), in directing suspicion from him to the male whose garment she purloined. The night-dress is missing; seek no more for it, but bring every force to bear upon the probable circumstances of *the theft*."

The pamphleteer was not singular in his belief that the thief was Elizabeth Gough. It is possible that she was: yet there are reasons for thinking the theft was the work of another hand.

But first one must consider if Constance could have taken it herself.

That she originally intended to get the drink of water herself is supported by Mr. Groser, in a later statement,[1] who saw her coming downstairs that morning, and also saw her turn back on catching sight of him—exactly as she herself said. Cox, for her part, was positive that, when she went to fetch the water, she was "not gone near a minute" and that on returning she found Constance standing where she had left her, at the top of the stairs; she was equally positive that the basket which contained the night-dress, and which she had covered down with a dress of Mrs. Kent's after looking for Constance's purse and before running downstairs, shewed no signs of having been disturbed. Could Constance, therefore, have returned to the lumber-room from the top of the stairs, sought for and found the night-dress, extracted and concealed it, rearranged the basket with sufficient neatness not to attract attention, and been back at the top of the stairs in the very short space of time—"not near a minute"—that Cox was away getting the water? It seems improbable.[2]

Both Elizabeth Gough and Cox were due to give evidence at the inquest that morning at eleven o'clock. It was about 10.30 when Mr. Groser had seen Constance, so it was probably about ten minutes later that Cox left the lumber-room to go upstairs and get ready. Could the nurse, agitatedly preparing to face the ordeal before her and chancing to overhear Constance's request to Cox for the water, have had the mental agility to evolve on the spur of the moment so subtle and sinister a plot and put it into effect within the next five minutes before she, too, set out for the "Red Lion"? That also seems improbable.

Indeed the entire plot against Constance—like that to regain possession of the night-shift from Foley—exhibits the same resourcefulness and cunning which had distinguished the career of the erstwhile Mary Pratt: and on that morning Mrs. Kent had motive, opportunity and time both for fabricating the plot and putting it into effect. Suspicion had already fallen

[1] See page 169.
[2] Cox got the water from the pantry at the foot of the stairs.

upon her husband and the nurse. The night-shift had been destroyed, but no less than three of the police had reason for suspecting the truth about its disappearance. It was to their interest to keep their thoughts to themselves; but four other people—the two maids, Fricker and Watts—knew of its *discovery*, and rumours of its discovery and disappearance had already spread abroad. Awkward questions might be asked when no such garment was tendered in evidence. The disappearance of a night-dress now would furnish an answer to those questions and at the same time divert suspicion away from her husband and Elizabeth Gough towards the owner of that night-dress: towards Constance Kent, whom she hated.

From her bedroom nearby she could overhear Constance's request to Cox, and before Mrs. Holley should call for the baskets she had ample time to conceive and execute her deadly scheme.

5

In Devizes Gaol Constance Kent accepted the privileges which had been accorded her, and the kindnesses she received, with a simple gratitude which won the respect and affection of all who came in contact with her. They were, indeed, great privileges at a time when prisons were still places of horror: a cell to herself instead of one shared with numerous other persons awaiting trial; a camp-bed made up with sheets and blankets instead of a pallet of straw spread with sacking, and "extra and better food than the other prisoners".

On the evening of Sunday, 22nd July, Mr. Kent and Mr. Dunn drove together to Devizes.

"When they arrived at the gaol," recorded the *Advertiser*, "Mr. Kent was so deeply overcome by his feelings that he could not bear the ordeal of an interview with his daughter, and therefore remained in an adjoining room while the solicitor conferred with Miss Kent. We understand that she was perfectly calm. . . . Indeed she has continued to be so since her incarceration, although the painfulness of her

E*

awfully critical position naturally wrought somewhat of a change in her features; still her general demeanour has made such an impression on the officials of the gaol that they do not hesitate to state that her appearance, at all events, bespeaks her innocence of this horrid suspicion."

The *Journal* meanwhile recorded that "It is a very peculiar fact that Mr. Rodway of Trowbridge has been engaged by Mrs. Kent's friends on behalf of the second family."

Whicher in the meantime had been moving heaven and earth to obtain some evidence, however slender, of *animus* on the part of Constance against the dead child; but instead had only succeeded in bringing to light a report that she had brought home from school a little picture as a present for him, while he had been stringing beads to make her a necklace on the day before his death. Whicher even had the grave at East Coulston opened and the child's coffin searched for the night-dress; he had the river dragged for it, while a poster offering a reward of £5 for it was pasted on the door of the Temperance Hall. None of these endeavours yielded any result.

CHAPTER THIRTEEN

THE CASE AGAINST CONSTANCE KENT: FRIDAY, 27TH JULY

I

DR. STAPLETON writes:

"When Constance Kent was produced publicly before the magistrates, with a view to her commitment . . . those who undertook her defence did not think it necessary, or were not suffered, to extend their vigilance or inquiries beyond its limits. . . . Her liberation seemed already so secure, and was so easy of attainment that it could not tax that forensic talent which was employed on her behalf."

No witnesses were called for the defence: Constance Kent's "liberation" was attained solely upon the evidence of those called by the prosecution.

The proceedings opened at the Temperance Hall on Friday, 27th July. The Clerk of the Court conducted the case for the prosecution, Mr. Edlin[1] of Bristol that for the defence, and Mr. H. G. (afterwards Lord) Ludlow presided over the Bench of magistrates.

The case was due to begin at 11 a.m., but long before that hour a cordon of police had surrounded the Temperance Hall to keep back the crowd. Inside, chairs had been placed behind the Bench for a gathering of "distinguished visitors and fashionably dressed ladies", while the first three rows of seats in the body of the hall were filled by the Press. Immediately below the platform were two tables, one of which was reserved for the prisoner and her escort while at the other sat Mr. Dunn with Mr. Edlin on one side and Mr. Kent on the other. It was Mr. Kent's first public appearance since the crime, and

---

[1] Afterwards Sir Peter Edlin, Q.C.

throughout the proceedings he sat leaning forward in his chair, his elbow on the table and his hand shielding his face.

At 11.30 Constance entered by a side door accompanied by Mr. Alexander, the governor of the gaol. She paused an instant and glanced about her as though seeking some member of her family; but only her father was present and "on seeing him she went forward and dutifully kissed him". After a week's imprisonment she looked pinched and pale in her crêpe-trimmed mourning clothes and pathetically young and vulnerable; but her air was quiet and composed as she took her seat under the inquisitive eyes of that assembly. Nor did her composure desert her when the doors of the hall were thrown open and "the crowd came in with a rush occupying every available inch of space": nor when Whicher stood up and "roared for her missing night-dress as Othello for his handkerchief":[1] nor even when her two school-mates were summoned to give evidence against her. She sat grave and still throughout it all, her black-gloved hands folded in her lap.[2]

Elizabeth Gough, "looking considerably emaciated", was the first witness. After describing her movements on the morning of the crime from the time when she alleged that she had found Savile's cot empty until she went upstairs to see if he was with his sisters, she continued:

"While I was talking to them I saw the prisoner; she was standing at the door of her room nearly dressed; I spoke in a loud voice and she was near enough to hear all that passed; she made no remark to my recollection; I observed nothing unusual in her manner at the time; I have never heard her say anything unkind to deceased; I have never seen her conduct herself otherwise than kindly towards him."

After evidence as to the finding of the body had been taken Helen Moody was called. She described her meeting with Whicher at Mrs. Bailey's house and said:

"I was not surprised at seeing him there because Mrs. Bailey had taken an interest in the matter; I was much surprised to see Mr. Whicher at our house when he first called; Mr. Whicher

---

[1] *Murder and Murder Trials*—H. M. Walbrook.
[2] Not until the passing of the Criminal Evidence Act in 1898 could a prisoner be called to give evidence himself.

asked me questions in the presence of Mrs. Bailey; when Mr. Whicher called upon me first it was to shew me a piece of flannel; the second time to serve me with a summons."

At this point Whicher requested the Chairman to put a question to the witness, to which she replied:

"Mr. Whicher cautioned me to speak the truth and told me who he was."

She went on to tell the Court that she had been at the Misses Scott and Williamson's school for eighteen months, during the last six of which the prisoner had been there as a boarder. The Clerk of the Court then asked her:

"Have you ever heard the prisoner give expression to any feelings towards the deceased?"

Helen Moody: "I believe there was a dislike through jealousy."

The Clerk pointed out that this did not constitute a reply and repeated the question.

Helen Moody: "I have heard her say that she disliked the child and pinched it; but it was done in fun. She liked to tease them—not this one more than the others: the two younger ones —she was laughing when she said it. We were speaking about the holidays one day when we were out walking in Road, near the house, and I said, 'Won't it be nice to go home shortly?' She said, 'It may be to your home, but mine's different.'"

Asked if these were the prisoner's exact words, she replied:

"I do not remember her exact words, but she also led me to infer that she did not like the children."

Asked if the prisoner had given any reason for this, witness answered that she had not, except to say that the second family were better treated than the first. She had said, "My mamma would not let me have what I liked; if I wanted a brown dress, she would make me have a black, just for contrary." But no other conversation had the witness heard referring, except very slightly, to the child.

At this point Mr. Edlin rose and pointed out that the Clerk was cross-examining the witness instead of conducting an examination-in-chief. He then proceeded to cross-examine himself, but was content to elicit the information that Constance had carried off the second prize for good conduct at the end of her last school term and that Helen Moody's mother did not "visit at Mr. and Mrs. Baileys'."

Dr. Parsons was the next witness, and gave medical evidence which had not been brought out at the inquest. He believed that the blackened appearance about the child's mouth had been produced by forcible pressure during life; the tongue had been livid and was protruding between the teeth; there had been no abrasions within the mouth; the organs of the body had been completely drained of blood; the stab in the chest had not penetrated the heart, but had pushed it out of place, penetrated the diaphragm and wounded the right side of the outer coat of the stomach; the rigidity of the body had been complete when he had first seen it; the stab must have been made with a long, pointed knife and was about an inch and a half wide with a transverse notch on one side as though the knife had been drawn out in a contrary direction.

He had examined Constance Kent's bed-clothes, night-gown and night-cap; all were perfectly free from any stains; he could not say whether the night-gown "had on it the dirt resulting from a week's wear or not"; there was nothing on it that particularly attracted his attention; he could not say if it were cleaner than the others he had seen—"In my judgement," he said, "it might have been worn a week, or nearly so, by a young lady sleeping alone."

The deceased was a very heavy child for his age. The wound in the chest was made with a dagger-pointed knife, like a carving knife; it would require very great strength to inflict such a blow through the night-dress and vest, and to the depth to which it had penetrated. He had examined the linen in the drawers of the prisoner's room and "believed that he had seen a clean night-gown among them".

Louisa Hatherall had little to say: the prisoner had spoken of the partiality shewn to the younger children by the parents; William was made to wheel them out in the perambulator, which he disliked doing; the parents compared him unfavourably with Savile, saying what a much finer boy the younger one was; the prisoner had been an intimate friend of the witness, but had "never said anything particular about the deceased".

Mr. Edlin did not trouble to cross-examine.

Sarah Cox, who throughout her evidence studiously refrained from referring to Constance as "the prisoner", was first of all examined as to her movements on the morning of the crime and her answers in no way differed from those she had given at the inquest. She was then questioned on the events of the morning of Monday, 2nd July. She had, she said, as usual, found some of Miss Constance's soiled clothes on Sunday and some on Monday, some on the landing and some in her room; the night-gown was among those on the landing on Monday morning; after she had sorted the linen in the lumber-room she had called Miss Kent to put the numbers in the book. "I perfectly recollect," she said, "putting Miss Constance's night-dress in the basket on the Monday after the murder; I am certain of it; it was between 10 and 11 in the morning; I put the kitchen table-cloth over one basket and Mrs. Kent's dress over the other; I put the three night-dresses into one basket, and one of them was Miss Constance's; Miss Constance came to the door of the lumber-room after the things were in the basket, but before I had quite finished packing them; she asked me to look in her slip pocket to see if she had left her purse there; I did so and told her she had not; she then asked me to go down and get her a glass of water, as there were people in the hall; I did so, and she followed me to the top of the back-stairs, close behind me; I found her there when I returned with the water, and I was not gone near a minute, for I went very quickly; she drank the water and then went up the back-stairs to her own room. Between my room and Miss Constance's there is only a paper wall; I can hear very plain; on the night of the murder I did not wake at all."

Cross-examined by Mr. Edlin she said:

"On Saturday, 30th June, I took down a clean night-gown of Miss Constance's to be aired, and another the following Saturday; I can easily distinguish Miss Constance's night-dresses from those of the other Misses Kent because they have plain frills, while the others have lace and work; the dirty one I put in the basket on the Monday would, with the two I aired, make three; I am clear that these were Miss Constance's night-dresses; I observed no mark or stain on the one I put in the basket; it appeared to me to be as dirty as one would expect in a night-dress worn nearly a week; I am perfectly clear as to the airing of the two night-gowns; I am clear that these and the one I put into the basket were all Miss Constance's night-gowns.

"During the time I have been in Mr. Kent's service I have never heard or seen from Miss Constance anything unkind or unsisterly in her conduct towards deceased; she was romping with him the day before the murder; she went to see him with the other members of the family when they did; she appeared as upset as they were, and cried as they did; she kissed him.

"The book in which the linen is listed is sent with the clothes to the washerwoman; the clothes were entered on the Monday after the murder by Miss Kent; the next Monday, 9th July, the clothes were not sent to the washerwoman as usual because there was some dispute about the night-dress. I first heard the night-dress was missing on the Tuesday evening after the murder; a message was sent by Mrs. Holley's daughter, which I received from her; she said there were three night-gowns put down and only two sent; Miss Constance's was missing, and her mother said that I must send another to make the washing right with the book, as the police had been that day and she was afraid they were coming back; if one was not sent she would have to tell them about it. I told her I was sure that her mother must have made a mistake, because I was certain that I had put three night-dresses into the basket and that one of them was Miss Constance's; I also said that, if she would wait a few minutes, I would call Miss Kent. I went and told Miss Kent what she said, and Miss Kent said she was quite sure I had put Miss Constance's night-dress into the basket, as she had seen me do it. Miss Kent told her in the presence of Mrs. Kent that she was quite sure the night-dress had been put in the basket, and the girl then said she would go and tell her mother. In consequence of this the clothes did not go to Mrs. Holley as usual on Monday, 9th July; on the following Saturday I believe Miss Constance borrowed a night-dress from her sister, there being then two dirty ones belonging to her in the house—the one worn between 30th June and 7th July, and the other between 7th and 14th July.

"I observed nothing in Miss Constance's manner or behaviour after the murder except ordinary grief."

Mrs. Holley was the next witness; she said:

"I have washed for Mr. Kent's family ever since they have been here until the last three weeks. On the Monday after the murder I went to Mr. Kent's for the washing myself; it was in the usual room; Cook took one basket and I the other; the washing was in the usual state; Mrs. Kent's dress was over one basket and something else over the other; we went straight home and opened the baskets directly, as we had heard a rumour of Saturday that a night-dress was lost; we found one was missing; it was Miss Constance's. I did not have the book until Tuesday; it was not enclosed in the basket as usual. I sent my daughter up to the house on Tuesday evening, and afterwards went myself and saw Mr. Kent, who said that if I did not send the night-dress back within twenty-four hours he would have a search warrant taken out against me; my house has been searched by the police."

Cross-examined by Mr. Edlin, witness said:

"On Tuesday I went up to the house to get the book and receive my money; I did not say anything to the housemaid then about the night-dress being missing—that was where I was wrong. No one but my daughter assists me in the washing. The police first came to my house on Tuesday evening, and I was alarmed; it was then that I went to Mr. Kent's about the night-dress; the police came about a piece of flannel, not about the night-dress, but I told them that the clothes were right with the book; they came to me about the night-dress next day. Two things have been missing before: one an old duster, the other an old towel."

No other witnesses were called. Hardly a sound had been heard in the tightly packed court while the evidence was being given: now, as people relaxed for a moment, they became aware that it was five o'clock of a beautiful summer evening and that the sunshine was slanting in at the windows; they grew aware of the murmurous rise and fall of sound and movement among the crowd outside, of the whisper of a light wind among the trees, of the voices of children playing. But immediately Mr. Edlin arose to address the Court attention was once more riveted upon the proceedings.

Applause broke out when he began by adjuring the Bench

to release the accused at once and restore her to her friends. "I apprehend," he said, "that it will not only be your duty but your pleasure to say 'Aye' to that. There is not a tittle of evidence against this young lady—not one word upon which a finger can be laid to shew that she is guilty, nor can the finger of infamy in respect to this matter be pointed against her. I ask you to consider the effect of dragging this young lady from her home at such a time, if she is really innocent, as I believe she is. I know that an atrocious murder has been committed, but I am afraid that it has been followed by a judicial murder of a scarcely less atrocious character. I ask you, if this young lady is truly innocent, what will be the consequences of this procedure against her? If this murder be never discovered—and we know how dark are the paths of crime—it will never, never be forgotten that this young lady was dragged from her home and sent like a common felon, a common vagrant, to Devizes Gaol. I say, therefore, that this step ought to have been taken only after the most mature consideration, and after something like tangible evidence had been obtained, and not upon the fact that a paltry bed-gown was missing. . . . The steps you have taken will be such as to ruin her life—her prospects are already blighted—every hope is gone with regard to this young girl. If she is innocent, as I believe, it is really terrible to contemplate the result to her. . . .

"And where is the evidence? The sole fact . . . is the suspicion of Mr. Whicher, a man eager in the pursuit of the murderer, and anxious for the reward which has been offered: and it is upon his suspicion, unsupported by the slightest evidence whatever, that this step has been taken. The simple fact set up as the groundwork of that suspicion has been cleared up in a manner that must carry conviction, even to demonstration, home to every man in this room. . . .

"The prosecution's own witnesses have cleared up the point about the bed-gown. . . . There can be no doubt in the mind of any person that the right number of bed-gowns has been fully accounted for, and that this little peg upon which you seek to hang this fearful crime has fallen to the ground. It rested on the *ipse dixit* of the washerwoman only, and against that you have the testimony of several other witnesses. . . .

"I do not mean to find fault with Mr. Whicher unnecessarily; but I think in the present instance his professional eagerness in pursuit of the criminal has led him to take a most unprecedented course to prove a motive, and I cannot help alluding to the meanness . . . with which he has hunted up two school-fellows and brought them here to give the evidence we have heard. . . .

"But what does this evidence amount to? Nothing whatever; there is not a single word pointing to any *animus* on the part of this young lady towards her little brother. Was there anything strange that, in the unlimited confidences of school-children, she should speak of her step-mother, and say the younger children were preferred by her? . . . Where is the step-mother who will not prefer her own children to those of a former wife? But because the conduct of the step-mother formed a subject of conversation between these two school-fellows, you are asked, therefore, to find in it a motive which would induce this young lady to imbrue her hands in the blood of this dear little boy. Every fact of the case, on the contrary, not only rebuts the presumption of guilt on her part, but is consistent with the purest innocence. . . . A more unjust, a more improper, a more improbable case . . . was never brought before any court of justice in any place, as far as I know, upon a charge of this serious nature. . . .

"If, upon reading the evidence, you think that guilt is brought home, if not conclusively, at all events in a *prima facie* manner, to Miss Constance, your duty will be to let the matter come before you for further investigation. But if you regard all the consequences, and consider that for nearly a whole fortnight Mr. Whicher has been engaged in investigation, and has not succeeded in finding any one fact authorizing you to say that this young lady is guilty . . . I am sure you will order her discharge. . . .

"What Dr. Parsons said is well worthy of your attention. . . . The boy, he says, was unusually heavy for his age, and he expressly states that it must have required a blow of great force to have pierced through the night-dress and flannel vest, and penetrated to the depth of the wound found on the body of the deceased child. Is it likely that the weak hand of this young girl . . . can have inflicted that dreadful blow? Is it likely that hers was the arm which nearly severed the head from the body? It is perfectly incredible!

"And then with regard to her manner the following morning, which, we have seen, exhibited nothing which distinguished her from her sisters and other members of the family sharing a common grief. And we have the important testimony of Dr. Parsons as to the state in which he found her night-dress, free from any mark or stain indicating a participation in the hideous deed; and as to the fact, too, that according to his belief there was a clean night-dress in the drawer, which, together with the one returned from the wash that week and afterwards brought up, would complete the number, according to her own list, in her own handwriting, preserved in her own chest-of-drawers.

"It is true that Dr. Parsons expresses only his belief that he saw the clean night-dress in the drawer, but he says that Superintendent Foley also examined her linen on that morning —he is here in court, and although he has not been called on this inquiry, it is known to you that such also is his belief. And really this is tantamount to satisfactory proof that it was there, because, had it not been, the circumstance must inevitably have attracted their attention at the time; and then the two clean night-dresses are shewn to have been subsequently aired."

After discrediting Mrs. Holley's statement that she had not received the night-dress and describing it as "utterly inconsistent and irreconcilable with the other undisputed facts of the case", he concluded:

"There are no facts to justify this charge, there is no proof of motive. The first step taken in this case, in the absence of any legal adviser of the accused, it would be difficult to justify. Let me ask you to pause before you follow it up by another which would be equally unjustifiable. It would astonish any judge to be told, on reading the examination taken last Friday and today, that this young lady had been, thereupon, sent to gaol charged with having murdered her brother. Terrible and even fatal to her may even now be the consequences of what has been so hastily and imprudently done in this momentous affair. I pray you not to aggravate it. I call upon you in the interests not of humanity only, but of clear and simple justice, to detain her not one moment longer in custody, but to liberate her and to restore her to that home from which she ought never to have been taken.''

In the silence which followed Mr. Edlin's closing words the magistrates retired to consider their judgment. So tense was the atmosphere that when they returned and announced their decision, only the first part of it had any meaning for the public —that the prisoner was released. This was greeted with "loud and vociferous enthusiasm". It was not until later that the second part of the decision impressed itself upon the public mind in all its significance: that she was released upon her father entering into a bond of £200 for her to appear if called upon.

This meant, in effect, that she had not been acquitted of the charge. It had merely failed through lack of evidence, and Constance could at any moment be re-arrested upon it; while, so long as the crime was never brought home to anyone else, she would continue under a cloud of suspicion, perhaps for as long as she lived. As her Counsel had said, the consequences were indeed to be "terrible and even fatal to her".

But at the moment none of this had sunk home to the crowd: only the fact of her release from custody. And as she left the hall they gave her a "tremendous ovation".

Whicher for his part was greeted with imprecations and even some stones whizzed past his head; while a distinguished lawyer who had been present was overheard to say that Whicher himself "should have been in the dock for bringing such a charge against one who was as innocent of the crime as any of the Bench".[1]

Three days later—exactly one month to the day after Savile had been killed—Mrs. Kent gave birth to another son.

[1] This was Mr. T. W. Saunders, Q.C., of the Western Circuit.

CHAPTER FOURTEEN

REPERCUSSIONS

I

WHILE Whicher became an object of general execration, abuse being shouted after him in the streets and letters demanding his dismissal appearing daily in the newspapers, Constance was "considered a martyr", and even thought by some to be "the victim if the vilest plot that ever imagination conceived". The Press reported that she had received innumerable letters, some of them from "persons of consequence", expressing sympathy and belief in her innocence, one being from "a titled lady who offered her hospitality". Captain Meredith was also inundated with letters, and he let it be known that Constance's arrest "had been contrary to his advice and wishes".

A curious item also appeared in the *Advertiser* about Mr. Kent:

"It is stated on good authority that soon after the apprehension of Miss Constance, he applied, under the idea that she might be convicted, to her trustees to ascertain if the property to which she was entitled through her late mother, might be secured so as not to be confiscated to the Crown."

Since the case had now developed into a contest between the public and the authorities and was assuming the proportions of a Cause, it is more satisfactory to quote two reviews of it which were not published until the end of that year, rather than those which found expression in the heat of the moment. The *Annual Register* said:

"The grounds on which this accusation were made were so frivolous and the evidence by which it was attempted to be supported so childish, that the proceedings can only be described as absurd and cruel. The ground of the arrest was that one of the young lady's night-dresses was missing. . . . The only other evidence to support the charge was singularly empty and vexatious. Whicher produced two of the poor girl's school-fellows, who deposed to some silly expressions of jealousy by the young lady while resident at the boarding school, respecting the greater attention received by the children of the second family. . . .

"Notwithstanding the utter emptiness of the evidence the magistrates only discharged the accused on her father entering into recognisance of £200 for her appearance if called upon.

"By these indiscretions, the exertions of the detectives, so far from having tended to the discovery of the criminals, had rather diminished the chances of success; for in forming the theory that Miss Constance was the guilty party they had . . . directed investigations from the real track; while the clearance of the unfortunate young lady . . . checked further exertions by the fear lest suspicion directed against any other person should prove equally groundless. . . ."

An anonymous author, writing under the pseudonym "Barrister-at-Law", in a monograph on the case entitled *The Road Murder* thus summed up the character of the proceedings:

"The detectives were rash and cruel in arresting Constance Kent before they had even a skeleton of a case made out against her. A night-gown is missing, and upon the strength of that one circumstance she is charged with the most dreadful of all felonies. Literally there is not a particle more, even of circumstantial evidence. We are not assuming her innocence any more than we are begging the question of her guilt. We deal with the matter as one of proof, and would any barrister in England have taken upon himself, at the instigation of Mr. Whicher, to arraign that young girl as a murderer?"

2

"The general opinion," said the *Annual Register*, "was now with much more show of probability directed against Mr. Kent and the nursemaid." The public, indeed, was clamorous to know how it was that Mr. Kent had been permitted to avoid appearing at the inquiries; how it was that the discrepancies in the nurse's statements had gone unchallenged; and how it was that no official remonstrance had been provoked by Mr. Sylvester's conduct of the inquest. As the result of what appeared to be Mr. Kent's astonishing immunity from the ordinary demands of justice a rumour arose that he was receiving protection from persons in high places, and, aided by his name, developed into the legend that he was a natural son of Royalty. Gossip even went the length of fancying it could detect a resemblance between Constance and the Queen herself as she had been at the same age.[1]

On 1st August, however, the police made a move which at least had the nursemaid as its object. Captain Meredith and Superintendent Wolfe visited Road-hill House and, in the presence of the ubiquitous Mr. Dunn, put several questions to Elizabeth Gough and carried out an experiment. A dark cloth was placed in Savile's cot to represent the child, and Wolfe, "who was a very tall man", knelt up in the nurse's bed, in the position in which she alleged that she had first noticed the cot was empty. But neither over, nor through, the high sides of woven cane could he discern the cloth, which, if it proved nothing else, at least shewed that her story was founded upon a statement which was demonstrably false; and this, combined with the other evidence against her, was productive of a considerable weight of suspicion. She had no adequate explanation for the fact that she had allowed over two hours to elapse before giving the alarm, for her excuse that she thought the child's mother—in another room, across a passage and through two closed doors—had heard him utter a cry which had failed

[1] At one time an effigy of Constance Kent was exhibited at Madame Tussaud's, but was removed "as the result of a request from high quarters".

to arouse herself only a few feet away, was singularly unconvincing; she had made directly contrary statements within a
very short time of one another to Morgan and Urch in the first
place and to Foley in the second as to the time she had first
seen that the blanket was missing; the breast-flannel had fitted
her "exactly" and had fitted no one else in the house, while
she had in her possession a petticoat of a material so similar as
to appear identical; the rearrangement of the bed-clothes on
the cot was plainly the work of a practised hand; and finally,
as Mr. Rowland Rodway had pointed out, her manner and
appearance that morning bore all the signs of sleeplessness and
strain.

However, the authorities decided that none of this amounted
to evidence of sufficient strength to justify a charge, so on
27th August she was allowed to go home to Isleworth after
furnishing the police with her address and an undertaking to
return to Road if called upon. At the same time she informed
the reporters that it was only because Mrs. Kent had desired
her to be in attendance upon her during her recent confinement
that she had stayed so long.

3

The next step was taken by the magistrates of Bath, who
presented a petition to the Home Secretary—Sir George Lewis
—praying him to grant a Special Commission for the investigation of the crime on the ground that the ordinary means of
doing so had failed.

This was rejected on the argument that to supersede the
ordinary Courts of Justice and to establish in their place, by
Royal Authority, a Commission exercising new and arbitrary
powers hitherto unknown to English law would be unconstitutional.

"The rules which govern our ordinary courts," it was
stated, "are intended, not only for the detection of the
guilty, but also for the protection of the innocent from
unjust accusations; and when a crime is of so grievous a

nature as to excite a strong feeling of horror and indignation in the public mind, a strict adherence to these rules is absolutely necessary for the fair and impartial administration of justice."

This decision caused much dissatisfaction. The *Journal*, after alluding to the fact that the judge of a neighbouring county court had offered to act gratuitously as Special Commissioner, continued:

"Even this Sir George Lewis has felt it his duty to negative on the grounds that a Queen's Commission in such cases is unusual and impractical! . . . Here is red-tapeism and incapacity with a vengeance! . . . Is not the crime an unusual one, and is not its detection by ordinary means proved to be impractical?"

The *Bath Express* now organized the presentation of a memorial to the Home Secretary "largely signed by many of the most influential inhabitants of Bath," the main point of which was that

"a miscarriage of justice had occurred through the defective manner in which the coroner's inquest was conducted; that although all the circumstances of the crime pointed to it having been committed by one or more persons in the household, Mr. Kent and the members of his family had never been publicly examined or cross-examined; and that, although a Special Commission might be an unusual proceeding, the crime itself was extraordinary and unparalleled in character and circumstance."

But the tone of this petition, where it referred to Mr. Kent, was of so provocative a nature that, at the instigation of the *Journal*, a second memorial was drawn up couched in more politic terms, which purported to be from "the inhabitants of Road, and towns in its vicinity" and prayed that "however unusual such a course may be, a *Special Commission* may at once be appointed to discover the criminal and afford opportunities for statements on *oath* to be made by all concerned".

Sir George Lewis—whom Greville said "was as cold-blooded as a fish" and who used to refer to his ministerial duties as "the damnabilities of office"—was notorious for his inability to come to a decision. A student of the classics, it was his playful habit to fend off the importunate with renderings of *Hey-Diddle-Diddle* into Latin or *Humpty-Dumpty* into Greek. He now sought a compromise which was typical of his irresolution and in the words of the *Spectator* "utterly subversive to every principle of justice". He intimated to the Wiltshire magistrates his desire that "investigations into the crime should be diligently pursued by the police" and that, meanwhile, a responsible local solicitor, "experienced in criminal law", should be instructed to conduct a private inquiry into the case in his own office. But his powers were to be severely limited: he was not to make public the source of his authority, nor was he permitted to take evidence upon *oath*, which meant that neither could witnesses be compelled to obey his summons nor could he insist upon answers to his questions.

A Bath solicitor of the name of Slack was instructed accordingly; and the first hint of these "Star Chamber proceedings conveniently arranged by Government to hush the cry for justice which had reached it" became known on 4th September when Foley presented himself at Road-hill House and notified Mr. Kent that his servants would be required to appear the following day at Mr. Slack's office.

Mr. Kent immediately consulted Mr. Dunn, who wrote at once to Mr. Slack asking by whose authority he made this demand. Mr. Slack replied that he was "regularly instructed by a proper authority", adding that Mr. and Mrs. Kent would themselves be required to submit to an examination in his office on 9th September. Mr. Dunn retorted that, although his client was willing to submit himself and his wife to such an examination, he must first be assured that Mr. Slack's proceedings were by Government instruction and not "merely at the instigation of private individuals for some hidden purpose".

Mr. Kent in the meantime had written to a Mr. Waddington, Permanent Under-Secretary at the Home Office, to whom he had official access by virtue of his appointment, and on the same day that he received a reply an announcement appeared in *The Times* stating that Mr. Slack was acting upon the instructions of the Home Secretary himself. Accordingly Mr. Dunn wrote again to Mr. Slack, saying:

". . . I have Mr. Kent's instructions to say that if you should desire to put any questions to him, to Mrs. Kent, or to any member of his family or household, he would be prepared to receive you at Road, and I shall be happy to meet you there, and to afford you every facility for such purpose. . . ."

Commenting on these exchanges the *Bath Express* said:

"It is obvious that his" (Mr. Kent's) "position has been throughout a defensive one. . . . We should naturally have expected that the father of the murdered innocent would be clamorous for justice; that he would have besought the coroner not to close the inquiry, but to adjourn it. . . . He would, we presume, be advised by his lawyer that the abortive results of the coroner's inquest would render more difficult the proof of guilt in any subsequent stage. He indeed signed, or professed his willingness to sign, a local memorial for a Special Commission. But that movement was originated by others; he only adopted it when applied to for the purpose. How then can we avoid the inference that other persons, and those strangers, shewed more eagerness and exhibited more activity in endeavouring to discover the murderer than the father of the child himself? . . . Acting as a lawyer Mr. Dunn was justified in advising his client not to answer Mr. Slack's summons. But Mr. Kent was the parent, and in his parental instinct he ought to have spurned any legal punctilio and expressed his willingness to appear anywhere, he and all his household, to answer the most rigorous inquiries which either human sagacity or suspicion could frame. Instead of which he has had a Counsel and an attorney at his elbow to assist him in evading inquiries and restricting examinations, not in promoting them. . . ."

Elsewhere in the same article the *Bath Express* severely criticized the Home Secretary himself, pointing out that when Authority resorted to an "unusual procedure" it was indispensable to its proper effect

"that the step should be bold, unmistakable and determined. . . . The reverse of all this is the course taken by Sir George Lewis. Every possible fault has been committed by him in the miserably small, undignified and almost secret proceedings which he has now resorted to. . . ."

The article concluded with the following observations:

". . . The public have a right to expect that all that has transpired either in the offices at Bath or at Road-hill House should be made known. . . . It is the instinct of a timid and nervous person like Sir George Lewis in his dread of criticism to conceal all he can; he wanted to conceal the hand he had in the Slack investigations, and, knowing this, we doubt not that he would like to stifle all report of the evidence which has been taken under the present anomalous proceedings.[1] . . . Englishmen are not yet converted to the doctrine of secret tribunals."

Indeed the Press in general, which had urged the necessity for a Special Commission, was equally critical of Mr. Slack's "anomalous proceedings" both on account of their unconstitutional character and because they were singularly ill-calculated "to satisfy the public, whose experience of secret examinations and underhand proceedings in this case has been sufficiently lengthy and unsatisfactory". The *Spectator* said:

". . . The refusal . . . to issue a Special Commission has been followed by a most extraordinary innovation in the administration of the law. Sir George Lewis gets rid of the difficulty by a side wind, for it appears now that, although he refuses to initiate any proceedings, he yet

[1] This was never made public.

sanctions another course taken by the local magistrates
utterly subverse of every principle of justice. . . .

"The Road murder has been from first to last productive
of blunders; but the last is the most fatal, for even the
detection and punishment of the murderers would not
compensate us for the loss we sustain by the unconstitutional means employed."

The *Law Times*, however, pointed out that Mr. Slack's
investigations could never have been intended to fill the
place of a Commission of Inquiry and amounted to no more
than

". . . that which a solicitor makes when getting up his
brief: it is merely the preparation of the case for a public
examination before the magistrates, and therefore the
attendance of any witness is wholly voluntary. . . . Mr.
Slack's office is not to judge or report, but simply as a
solicitor to collect evidence for the hearing of the case by
the magistrates. But it would be desirable in such a difficult
matter . . . if, on the occasion of the hearing, they were to
be assisted by a Counsel experienced in the criminal courts.
The justices would be much aided by a practised criminal
lawyer advising them in the character of assessor. . . ."

4

In the course of his inquiry Mr. Slack questioned a great
number of persons—including some thirty former servants at
Road-hill House, among them Emma Sparks, and, as was
inevitable, scraps of information filtered through to the public:
that it was established that the murder had been committed
by an inmate of the house and that two persons had been
concerned in it; that Mr. Slack was satisfied as to Constance's
innocence; that Mr. Kent had recently made a habit of going
into the nursery last thing at night, after his wife had gone to
bed, and that he had done so on the night of the crime.

As for the practical results of the inquiry these became

apparent when, on 27th September, a warrant was issued for the arrest of Elizabeth Gough.

Superintendent Wolfe brought her from Isleworth to Devizes where she was charged and detained at the divisional police station as it was "thought inadvisible in the present state of public feeling to bring the prisoner to Trowbridge".

"The circumstances which have led to her arrest," stated *The Times*, "are as follows: Mr. Slack . . . forwarded the depositions of the various witnesses to the Attorney-General.[1] That learned functionary . . . appointed Wednesday last for a consultation, which was attended by Mr. T. W. Saunders[2] and Mr. Slack. The result was that an opinion was signed jointly by the Attorney-General and Mr. Saunders that there were sufficient *prima facie* grounds for issuing a warrant for the apprehension of Elizabeth Gough."

"Barrister-at-Law", however, considered that, in spite of the Attorney-General's decision that "not merely was there sufficient evidence to warrant her arrest, but they considered it their bounden duty to have her apprehended", the arrest of Elizabeth Gough was "too precipitate—more caution and delay might have resulted in further elucidation".

[1] Sir Richard Bethell: became Lord Chancellor in 1861.
[2] Mr. T. W. Saunders, Q.C., of the Western Circuit.

CHAPTER FIFTEEN

THE CASE AGAINST ELIZABETH GOUGH: 4TH OCTOBER

I

WITH the arrest of Elizabeth Gough it seemed at first as though the much criticized efforts of Mr. Slack had borne fruit, and that this might be but the first step in an important new development; for, as Dr. Stapleton says, "No man who was present at that trial can doubt the fact that the nurse's commitment on the charge of murder would not only have implicated Mr. Kent, but must, to have been consistent, have been followed by his immediate apprehension for a criminal purpose."

But actually there was never any great likelihood of such a contingency. As "Barrister-at-Law" declared:

> "the charge against Constance Kent was an imprudence, that against Elizabeth Gough was a burlesque. It was never intended or expected that anything would come of it. The transaction was got up in deference to the public outcry for a more ample inquisition"

—while the grounds on which the charge rested fully justified his comment that "attorneys, justices and policemen . . . are too eager to force artificial testimony where no genuine evidence exists".

Mr. T. W. Saunders, Q.C., of the Western Circuit, appeared for the Crown; Mr. Ribton, who was in practice at the Old Bailey, for the defence. The advice of the *Law Times* that a practised criminal lawyer should be present to advise the magistrates in the character of an assessor was not adopted, and Sir John Awdry, Chairman of the Wiltshire Quarter Sessions, presided unassisted. Though "impartial in his capacity as president of the Bench . . . even he allowed discussions and personalities which were totally out of place";[1] while he acquiesced unprotestingly in the curious reply he received to his request for the folio containing the findings of Mr. Slack's inquiry—that "it was not necessary to trouble the magistrates with it".

2

The hearing, in the overcrowded little police court at Trowbridge, began on 4th October and lasted four days—"a stipendiary magistrate from London would have disposed of the affair in twelve hours".[2]

Clad in black and wearing a thick black veil, the prisoner, whose father and uncle were in court, "looked as though she had been weeping", but remained remarkably alert. She appeared

"to watch with feverish anxiety the various questions of the learned Counsel and the answers of the various witnesses thereto. She made frequent notes, which she handed to her solicitor, who was sitting near her, and which were almost invariably passed on to Counsel for the defence."[3]

After the depositions had been read, Mr. Saunders, in opening for the Crown, gave a narrative of the case, recounting the suspicions which had led to Elizabeth Gough's previous detention at Mrs. Dallimore's, then said:

"I should like to mention to you that between the discharge of the prisoner and the inquiry instituted by Mr. Slack, another party was apprehended at the instigation of a detective from London—Miss Constance Kent. . . . The charge was preferred against her, and the result was she was liberated. I may here say, and I am glad to have an opportunity of saying so, that I believe from first to last there was not the slightest ground for justifying that proceeding against her.

---

[1] *The Road Murder*—"Barrister-at-Law".
[2] *Ibid.*
[3] The *Advertiser*.

I believe at this moment that the young lady ought to go forth to the world as clear from suspicion as any gentleman I have now the honour of addressing. I feel bound to say so. After having investigated very carefully and very clearly the particulars of this case, I have come to the conclusion, which I am sure every person would come to, who carefully examined into the case, that there was not the slightest shadow of a suspicion against that young lady."

This pronouncement was greeted with applause, which was quickly silenced, and Counsel continued:

"Mrs. Kent would confirm that her husband went to bed at 11.30 on the night of the crime. Strange to say, although they were sleeping in a room only separated by a passage from the nursery she did not hear anything during the whole night. Nevertheless the boy was murdered close to her own door, carried downstairs, bolts were undone, locks were undone, shutters were undone, a window lifted. . . . It is one of the mysteries of the case that all this took place without alarming anyone in the house. . . .

"The surgeon's evidence was that there were signs of suffocation and that the gash in the throat was inflicted after death, for there were no spurts of blood, only trickles. The gash in the throat was presumably inflicted for the purpose of misleading those who might be disposed to think someone in the house had done it.

"My own conclusion is that the child's throat was cut as a blind, for the purpose of drawing suspicion and evidence away from the proper quarter. . . . I suggest that the window was lifted up . . . as a blind, and that the child was taken out the ordinary way through the back-door. . . . It is utterly impossible to believe that one person committed the murder; . . . there must have been a second person in the room assisting in taking out the child, withdrawing the blanket and rearranging the sheet and counterpane so smoothly as to present the appearance of never having been interfered with. Was it likely that two strange persons went into the room to do that? If there were two persons does not the conclusion irresistibly force itself upon your mind that one must have been the nurse? Was it within the bounds of possibility that any person could have gone into the room and opened that door, which made a creaking noise, without the nurse hearing it? . . . It may be suggested that it was done by one person only —that it was done by the prisoner. Whether it was so, it is clear almost to demonstration that the prisoner was one of the parties concerned."

Here a model of the cot was produced and after describing its position in the nursery and the manner in which the bed-clothes were found, Counsel said:

"It is impossible that one could have done what was done. There must have been two. The prisoner had the knowledge that the blanket was gone. . . . She could only know of it by being conscious that the blanket was taken away and of having seen it done. She felt the pressure of that knowledge, and had remarked that it was gone to Urch and Morgan . . . and when the child was afterwards discovered covered with it she declared that it was the first time she had known it was gone with the child. It might be that hers was not the hand that committed the murder, but that the child was murdered and taken out of the room with the connivance and tacit consent of the girl there can be no doubt.

"A breast-flannel has been discovered beneath where the child lay in the privy. A female searcher has tried it on the other servants, the Misses Kent and Miss Constance Kent. It did not fit any of them, but it fitted the prisoner exactly. In confirmation of that episode the prisoner's flannel petticoat was of the same quality and texture. . . ."

After describing the experiment carried out by Superintendent Wolfe, he said:

"It was found by actual experiment that it was impossible for her to see whether the boy was in the cot. It is a small fact, but it shows that she was telling palpable untruths—that she was telling something to establish a case of innocence, which, when examined, showed itself to be a tissue of falsehoods."

Mr. Kent was the first witness to be called. Even at this stage an attempt had been made to keep him out of court, and Dr. Parsons had certified to Sir John Awdry that he was suffering from "mental incoherence and was so shaken by what he had undergone that no reliance could be placed on any testimony he might give".[1] This time, however, the attempt had not succeeded, and Samuel Kent gave evidence which was sometimes widely at variance with the known facts—as, for instance, when he said, "I had said to the members of my family that no one could have got into the house from outside; I am not aware that I mentioned that fact to the police—I may have done so; it was certainly my opinion from the first that no one could have entered from outside."

Questioned about the locking up of the police his answers were evasive and contradictory. "On Saturday night I had two policemen in the house; Mr. Foley sent them; they arrived at about eleven at night; I did not admit them into the house until I had heard the inmates go upstairs."

Mr. Saunders: "What was the object of their coming?"

Mr. Ribton objected to the question: Mr. Kent, he said, could have no notion of the object of the police except what they told him.

The Chairman pointed out that if the police had come at Mr. Kent's request he would know what reason he assigned for their doing so.

Continuing his evidence Mr. Kent said, "I took the two policemen into the kitchen; one of them was to leave at half-past two;[2] the other I let out at about five o'clock in the morning; I provided them with refreshment; I was in the library during a portion of the night, but left the house once or twice."

Mr. Saunders: "For what reason?"

Mr. Ribton objected to the question. He could not see how anything done or said by Mr. Kent could be evidence against the prisoner, though, no doubt, if the trial were to exculpate Mr. Kent himself—which he could not suppose to be its object—it would be relevant.

The Chairman ruled that anything *said* by Mr. Kent would not be evidence, but things *done* by him might be admissible. After some further argument the question was allowed to be put.

Mr. Kent: "I went out to see if the lights were out; I went

---

[1] Dr. Stapleton says that Mr. Kent was suffering from "intellectual palsy" which had "overtaken and frustrated his faculties" and "could neither be simulated nor concealed".

[2] Foley afterwards stated that he had given no such instructions: both constables were to remain until relieved.

out several times with the same object; the officers were at that time in the kitchen; they could have left the house if they had unbolted the doors."

The Chairman: "They could have let themselves out, but they could not go into the house?"

Mr. Kent: "Yes, they could have done so if the passage door was not locked, and I am not quite clear whether I locked the door or not; I locked the officers into the kitchen."

Mr. Saunders: "What reason had you for locking the door?"

Mr. Ribton objected to Mr. Kent giving his reason. He did not object to him deposing to any fact which had occurred to induce him to take this action, but objected to his stating his motive.

The Chairman (to Mr. Kent): "Had anything occurred to induce you to bolt the kitchen door?"

Mr. Kent: "I bolted the door that the house might appear as usual, that no one might know there was a policeman in the house."

Cross-examined by Mr. Ribton, Mr. Kent said:

"Before going to Trowbridge I looked round the garden and into the drawing-room for the child, and ordered my men to continue the search."

Mr. Ribton: "If you believed the child was stolen, why did you tell the men to search for it?"

Mr. Kent: "There was no fact known then beyond that the child was missing; I thought the child was stolen, and that was why I went to Trowbridge; the drawing-room window being open I concluded the child was stolen; Trowbridge is the nearest police station; . . . I had not been in the nursery before I went to Trowbridge; I got off as soon as possible; . . . I thought I could give the alarm quicker myself than if I sent; . . . there was a policeman at Southwick, and I called at his house and gave my message to his wife on my way; a policeman passes near my premises on duty every night; he lives at Road, but I did not try to find him; I saw Constable Morgan as I went out of the gate and asked him to give the alarm, and he said, I think, that he would tell the policeman; . . . the privy is twenty-two feet from the back-door, the drawing-room window a couple of hundred yards away; . . . the police came on

Saturday night by arrangement with Mr. Foley; I did not require it; it was not arranged with me that they were to come;[1] the policemen first went into the library, where they stood a few minutes, and then into the kitchen."

Mr. Ribton: "A plan of the premises would be of great assistance. We might be favoured with a plan, I think."

One of the magistrates tendered a copy of the *Bath Chronicle* which contained a plan. Mr. Kent observed that it was inaccurate. A whispered consultation followed between Mr. Saunders and Mr. Ribton, and the latter then asked Mr. Kent, "Have you refused to allow a person to go over the premises to get a more correct plan?"

Mr. Kent: "They have been over the premises and taken the measurements several times. There was a request sent to me, through Mr. Dunn, to have a plan of the house."

Mr. Ribton: "Did you refuse?"

Mr. Kent: "I did, through Mr. Dunn, my solicitor."

Mr. Ribton: "Through him, then, you refused to have a correct plan taken?"

Mr. Dunn: "That is not correct. I have had no application made to me."

Mr. Ribton: "If Mr. Dunn is going to contradict the evidence, he must do so on oath." (To Mr. Kent:) "You refused to allow a correct plan to be taken?"

Mr. Kent: "Yes."

The cross-examination then reverted to the subject of the two policemen, and Mr. Kent said, "I went into the kitchen with the police and remained there a short time; I bolted them into the kitchen; they did not ask me to do so; I had not told them that I meant to bolt them into the kitchen; they must have heard me do so for it is a noisy bolt; I gave them bread and cheese and beer; the door was not unbolted from a little after eleven until half-past two, when I let one of them out; . . . they told me they had knocked; . . . one of the policemen went away at half-past two, the other stayed in the kitchen until between five and six o'clock; . . . I bolted the door on the other policeman; I did not tell him I had bolted it; whether he knew I had bolted it or not I cannot say."

[1] Compare Foley's evidence, page 157.

Mr. Ribton: "Had you made any arrangement at any time with the police that you should bolt them into the kitchen?"

Mr. Kent: "None; my reason for bolting the door was that everything should appear as on other nights, that no one should suspect the police were in the house. . . . On Saturday I inquired of the matter" (the loss of the child) "of the other servants, not of the nurse; Mrs. Kent inquired of her, but not in my presence; I did not interrogate her because Mrs. Kent did so on the morning of the murder, and told me; I think in the course of the day the nurse told me how the bed was left; I don't recollect questioning her; she remained a month with me.after this matter; I might have asked her a few questions; I believe I did."

Mr. Ribton: "Then why did you tell me you did not?"

Mr. Kent: "Mrs. Kent gave me the account she received from the nurse and I asked her questions; I cannot positively say whether I questioned the girl or not."

Answering questions as to his movements on the morning of the crime and the previous night, Mr. Kent said, "I visited the drawing-room between eleven and twelve, and locked and bolted the door; I then went up to bed; it was twelve o'clock before I went to sleep; I awoke about 7.15; I was awoken by the nurse knocking; I did not get up; . . . I don't think I went into the nursery on the morning in question—everything was in confusion; . . . it was Mrs. Kent who first communicated to me the loss of the child, saying, 'Savile is missing'; I replied, 'We had better see where he is'; I was in bed; when she told me he could not be found I dressed and went down, but did not go into the nursery at all. . . ."

On the subject of the blanket he made the following statements:

"Before I started for Trowbridge I knew there was a blanket missing; when I went to wish Mrs. Kent good-bye, previous to starting, she told me so and seemed pleased with the idea as.it would keep the child warm; I told the turnpike woman of the circumstance; I never have, that I am aware of, denied knowing anything about the blanket."[1]

Asked why he had desired Mr. Rodway to watch the

[1] See Foley's evidence, page 157.

evidence at the inquest Mr. Kent replied that he had done so
"for his satisfaction"—"I did not know what might transpire
there, as it was reported that my son William had committed
the murder; I asked him to attend the inquest as my attorney
in consequence of that report."

The next witness was Mrs. Kent. She was dressed in deep
mourning, her face completely hidden by a heavy crêpe veil,
which she raised with evident reluctance when required to do
so. She gave her evidence in a clear and collected manner
"free from any bias against the prisoner, who seemed to take
particular interest in her statement and frequently looked
intently at her".[1] She said:

"I went into the nursery before nine" (on Friday night)
"while the nurse was at her supper; I went again at eleven
o'clock; I called the nurse to come and look at the comet, then
visible; after the first visit I went to the dining-room and stayed
there until eleven o'clock; Mr. Kent went out to feed the dog;
the others had all gone up to bed; about eleven o'clock I went
upstairs to bed; the nursery door was ajar; I went into the
room; the nurse was in the dressing-room, and the door was
shut; I shut the nursery door; if it is not shut carefully it
makes a creaking noise; Mr. Kent came to bed at about a
quarter-past eleven; I was then out of the room, but returned
to it directly and did not leave it again until half-past seven
the next morning; after going to bed I do not know how long
it was before I fell asleep.

"I awoke frequently during the night—several times;
because of my condition my nights were very restless; something attracted my attention early in the morning; it was just
light, like the light of a dull morning when I heard a noise; it
sounded as if the drawing-room shutters were being opened;
I did not call my husband's attention to it; I was not alarmed
at it because I thought it was the servants;[2] I did not hear the
dog bark that night;[3] at a quarter-past seven I looked at my

---

[1] *The Road Murder*—"Barrister-at-Law."

[2] This confirms the view that Mrs. Kent's ideas of time that night were
vague. The shutters must have been opened soon after the murder, when dawn
was just breaking; while the servants' usual time for coming downstairs was
about 6.15, when it would be already bright daylight.

[3] Urch, the policeman, and Moon, the poacher, heard it barking at 1 a.m.

husband's watch and commenced getting up; previous to that I had heard no knock on my door; I think I should have heard an ordinary knock at the door."

Mrs. Kent then told the Court how she had opened the door to the nurse's knock and learned that Savile was missing. The substance of this portion of her evidence, and of that which followed, has already been related. Questioned about the missing blanket, she was positive that she knew of its disappearance before Mr. Kent had left for Trowbridge, so confirming the nurse's original statement to Urch and Morgan, and contradicting her later one to Foley to which she had since adhered. "Before my husband left for Trowbridge I was aware the blanket had been taken with the child—the nurse told me so," said Mrs. Kent, and continued in answer to further questions, "After my husband had left she came to help me to dress, and did my hair; she spoke about the missing child and said, 'It's revenge! Oh, it's revenge!'; she told me she was a light sleeper."

Under cross-examination she said:

"I have never taken the child from the nurse's room to my bed while she was asleep; I may have taken the child from his crib early in the morning, but not without the nurse knowing it;[1] when the nurse knocked at the door, my husband was in bed; I had remarked the hour to him; he made no reply; he was between sleeping and waking; he was, I suppose, awake before the knock came; the knock did not wake him.

"The nurse was aware that I had had bad nights for some time past; she told me next day that she had knocked before, at a quarter to seven; I do not remember saying to her that I did not wonder at my not hearing that knock because after a restless night I slept soundly in the morning; I cannot tell if I slept so long as an hour during the night without being disturbed; it was before Mr. Kent left in the morning that the nurse told me the blanket was gone; I told him just before he went to Trowbridge, when he came to my door to say he was going.

"To the best of my belief the nurse was always particularly

[1] See page 110.

F*

kind to the child, and the child was very fond of her; I was too much agitated to notice if the prisoner was much distressed; I cannot tell how long Mr. Kent had been gone before I heard the child was found; Mr. Kent first told me that it had been murdered; they would not tell me of it before; it was after the prisoner knew that the child had been brought in dead that she said, 'Oh, Madam, it's revenge!'; I do not remember that I asked her more about it then; she had been directed not to tell me of its death; . . . she told me she had awoken at five o'clock and gone to sleep again; I did not see her kiss the child, but she told me she had done so; she appeared very sorry and cried because he was dead."

After completing her evidence Mrs. Kent asked to be allowed to make a statement. This was refused, but she was permitted to write down what she wished to say on a piece of paper, which was handed to her Counsel and then to the magistrates. It was reported that this was to the effect that Mr. Kent had not left her side for more than a quarter of an hour during the night.

Sarah Cox, Sarah Kerslake and James Holcombe gave evidence on the events of the morning, and then Emily Doel, the nurserymaid, was called. She said:

"I went into the nursery before any alarm was given for the missing child; . . . it was before eight o'clock; the nurse was making her bed; I went in and out several times; I did not say anything to her, nor she to me; I know she saw me because she looked round; it was before the nurse went to call Mrs. Kent that I was in the nursery."

The evidence of Mary Ann and Elizabeth Kent dealt mainly with the time at which they went to bed; then Constance was called and said:

"On June 29th I had been home from school about a fortnight; my deceased brother was a merry, good-tempered lad fond of romping; I was accustomed to play with him; he appeared fond of me, and I was fond of him; I slept in a room between that of my two sisters and that of the servants; I went to bed at half-past ten and went to sleep at once; my sister came to my room to see if my candle was out; I was nearly asleep then, and was completely asleep soon after;

I awoke about half-past six, and heard soon afterwards that my brother was missing.

"On Friday night I slept in a night-dress; I had put it on clean the previous Sunday or Monday; I was accustomed to wear the same night-dress for a week and usually changed it on Sunday or Monday; when I got up on Saturday morning I took it off and put it on my bed; the cook and housemaid usually make my bed.

"On the Saturday night I slept with my sister Mary Ann; my sister Elizabeth slept with Mamma; my Papa stayed up, and I slept with my sister for the sake of company; on the Saturday night I slept in the same night-dress I had worn the night before, and when I got up in the morning I put it back in my own room; on Sunday night I slept in my own room again; I am not certain whether I put on a clean night-dress that night or the Monday night; one night-dress went to the wash every week; I put a clean night-dress out to be aired on Saturday as I always do; on Monday morning the linen was collected for the wash; it was the housemaid's duty to collect it; it has been stated that one of my night-dresses has been missing; I know nothing of it; I did have three night-dresses."

Cross-examined, she said:

"Prisoner was examined as a witness when I was charged with this crime; she told me about the missing blanket, but I am not sure whether it was before or after the body was found; I heard her go to my sisters' door and inquire for my brother."

Morgan and Urch described how they had visited the nursery. In the course of his examination Urch said:

"The nursemaid shewed us the cot and the bed-clothes; they were quite smooth, as though the bed had only just been made; she turned back the bed-clothes and I saw where the child had been lying; the impression of the head was quite plain; I asked her at what time she had missed the child and she said at five o'clock, but that she had not made any inquiries about it before a quarter to seven; I asked her how that was, and she said she thought Mrs. Kent had heard the child crying and come and taken it away; I asked her if Mrs. Kent had ever done that before; she said, not in her time, but she had heard that she had done so when the previous nurse was there; I asked if there was anything else missing, and she said, 'Nothing except a small blanket which was between the sheet and the quilt'; she said it might have been drawn out without disturbing the bed-clothes, as it was narrower than they were. . . ."

Cross-examined, he said:

"Another constable, named Heritage, went with me to the house on Saturday night; we were told to place ourselves under the direction of Mr. Kent; we were placed in the kitchen at the back of the house; we stayed until twenty minutes past two, when Heritage, having to go then, began knocking on the door; I was sitting in the chair and I said to him, 'You are making noise enough to wake the whole house'; he said, 'I'm locked in and must get out'; after about twenty minutes Mr. Kent came and let us out, and Heritage said, 'I don't know how we came to be locked in like this'; Mr. Kent said nothing, but 'I've been walking about'; we don't know what time the door was locked; we found it locked at two o'clock; I stayed until six o'clock, when Mr. Kent came and said it was time for me to go as the servants would be getting up."

Heritage confirmed Urch's evidence; then Nutt and Benger gave evidence as to the finding of the body, after which Foley was called.

"At about half-past nine on Saturday morning," he said, "the prisoner shewed me the cot, and how it had been left when the child was removed; she told me the child had been covered with a sheet, a blanket and a quilt; she told me that she herself had covered the child the night before, tucking in the sheet and quilt on both sides of the bed, and that in the morning she found the sheet and quilt turned back but had never missed the blanket until the child was brought in wrapped in it; I cannot say whether she could have seen or not if the blanket had gone; I believe she could not."

The next question referred to the finding of the breast-flannel, whereupon Mr. Ribton interposed an objection. There was no evidence, he contended, that the breast-flannel was connected with the crime, and "the prosecution might as well produce the whole contents of the privy". This objection was upheld by the Bench, Sir John Awdry ruling that even if the breast-flannel was proved to belong to the prisoner, that would only serve to shew that the crime was connected with her room, which the loss of the child had already rendered sufficiently obvious.

Under cross-examination Foley said:

"The prisoner told me, I am sure, that she did not know the blanket had been taken until she saw it brought in with the child; Mr. Kent told me twice, in the presence of Mr. Wolfe, that he did not know the blanket had been taken away until he came back from Trowbridge; I have heard that Mr. Kent said here yesterday that he knew the blanket had been taken before he left for Trowbridge, but this does not shake my evidence on the point at all. . . .

"I knew that the two policemen had been locked up, and was very surprised when I heard of it; I did not understand they were to be locked up; it was arranged with Mr. Kent that the men should be at the house and he would sit up in the library; they had only the range of the kitchen; while the men were locked up anything might have been done in other parts of the house; I have never been able to find out Mr. Kent's reasons for locking them up; I must be excused from saying whether I have suspicions as to the reason for locking them up; when I saw Mr. Kent that Saturday he seemed very agitated; my arrangement with him, as I understood it, was that the police were to have the range of the premises."

The next witness was Superintendent Wolfe; he said:

"On Monday, 2nd July, I went over Road-hill House to see if any person could have been secreted in it; I went first to the spare-room, and Mr. Kent, who accompanied me, said, 'Here is a room which is not often occupied'; I saw that it was furnished ordinarily and said, 'Surely no one would secrete themselves here, for they would never know when someone might not come in'; the next room was a lumber-room, filled with children's toys and so on, and I said, 'No one could know but what someone might not enter this room also'; the only place I could find in which it was likely that anyone could have secreted themselves was under the roof, but I found nothing to indicate that anyone had done so.

"The prisoner, in shewing me how the bed-clothes were left,

said, 'It must have been done by a female hand, it was done so neatly'; on 7th August she said, 'Mr. Kent never alluded to the murder to me since it occurred from first to last: the young ladies have, and Miss Constance, and so has Master William who has repeatedly cried over it."

Witness confirmed Foley's statement that Mr. Kent had twice denied knowing the blanket had been missing before he left for Trowbridge, and continued:

"On 1st August I was with Captain Meredith and had a conversation with the prisoner; she said, 'The first time I missed the blanket was when the child was brought in dead. I went and looked in the crib when I went up to dress Mrs. Kent's hair'; she repeated this several times.

"Prisoner told me that when she first awoke, about five in the morning, she saw the child in the little cradle by her side was partly uncovered; she raised herself up on her knees to cover her up, and then saw that deceased was gone; I tried the experiment to see whether this could be done; I tried it in the presence of Mr. Dunn, who took a garment and put it in the cot, and I could not see it when kneeling on the nurse's bed; looking over the little child's cradle I could not see into deceased's cot; its sides were of cane and, looking at it in that position, sideways, the cane appeared solid and I could not see through it."

Cross-examined, Superintendent Wolfe said:

"The prisoner at all times manifested an inclination to answer all my questions; she said to me once, 'If I knew about the murder, do you suppose I could have kept it secret for five weeks?' On 7th July she said: 'I know nothing about it. Who came into my room and went out I cannot say. I did believe, and do now, that someone was secreted in the house that night. How is it that we so often hear of people secreting themselves in houses, sometimes for robbery?' . . ."

The next witness, Mrs. Dallimore, said that she had been summoned to Road-hill House on Saturday, 30th June, to search the servants. As she repeated conversations which she alleged had taken place between the nurse and herself, both then and subsequently,[1] the prisoner "closely regarded the

[1] These have been included in the text above.

witness" and communicated with her solicitor several times. The breast-flannel being handed to witness, she said, "The flannel is worn on the chest and reaches up towards the arms from under the stays." She went on to say that it fitted the prisoner exactly, and fitted no one else in the house.

Questioned about the night-dresses of the household she said that she had examined them carefully. "I examined that of Miss Constance and found nothing upon it; like that of the other young ladies it appeared to have been worn some nights, perhaps a week."

Dr. Parsons now gave evidence. He said that he had not examined the bowels, only the stomach, and found there no traces of the pill which would have passed into the bowels; it would not operate under six hours, and might take eight; no motion had taken place. As to the immediate cause of death he said, "My opinion is that the cut in the throat was made after pulsation had ceased," and he considered that "considerable violence must have been used in suffocating the child; . . . the tongue protruded between the teeth so as to be visible between the lips; the lips were of a very dark colour and livid; . . . the dark appearance on the mouth indicated strong pressure for a considerable time with a soft substance; the time might have been five to ten minutes; I should have expected to find marks of jets of blood on the child if the throat had been cut whilst it was alive, but I did not find any such appearances; it has since occurred to me that the circulation of the blood had been stopped by pressure upon the mouth before the throat had been cut; I think the stab occurred after death, because there was no retraction of the parts and no blood was flowing; the cuts on the hand were done soon after death; suffocation could not have been caused by the bed-clothes falling over the mouth; it was caused by considerable violence. . . .

"I went up to the nursery between nine and ten o'clock; the pillow had marks of the depression of the head, and also the bed of the body, but the sheet and counterpane were perfectly smooth; they could not have been folded down as they were without considerable trouble by a practised hand; if the blanket had been taken out, that must have been done before they were folded down.

"My opinion is that death was caused by suffocation, then the wound in the throat inflicted, and then the wound in the chest."

Cross-examined, he said:

"My opinion is that the child was first suffocated by pressure on the mouth, and after that the throat was cut; I cannot say positively that the wound had nothing to do with the death of the child; I cannot say positively that the child was quite dead when the wound in the throat was inflicted; I cannot say positively that the pressure on the mouth was the actual cause of death; I can only say positively that there *was* pressure."

The closing speeches of Counsel then followed: the main points of Mr. Ribton's speech for the defence were as follows:

It was not impossible that some person had been concealed in the house and, having committed the murder through malice towards Mr. Kent, had got away undiscovered. Meanwhile the suspicion pointed with equal force against Mr. Kent himself, and against Constance Kent, as it did against the prisoner. As to the three things urged against the prisoner, the alleged inconsistencies as to the time at which she discovered the blanket was missing shewed, even if they were proved, that in her agitation she was mistaken: regarding the flannel, even if it did fit and belong to the prisoner, of which there was no proof, this merely shewed that the murderer had been in her bedroom, which was already obvious from the removal of the child; while as to the possibility of seeing into the cot from the bed, it would be ridiculous to interpret the phrase "kneeling up" too literally.

The magistrates then retired, and, on the Court resuming, "the prisoner appeared greatly agitated". Sir John Awdry announced that the magistrates had determined not to commit the prisoner for trial although there was a case of grave suspicion against her, and material had been adduced which, with additions, might hereafter be brought to bear against her. They would accordingly bind her to appear when called upon in two sureties of £50 each.

And so the curtain rang down upon this grim farce—and now two young women, the one aged sixteen and the other twenty-two, lay under the ban of what amounted in reality to a verdict of *not proven* for the same crime. As Mr. and Mrs. Kent left the court they were hooted by the crowd. That evening Elizabeth Gough, accompanied by her relatives, went home to Isleworth.

A very curious sequel, however, soon followed. A sketch had been made of Elizabeth Gough in court and published in some of the papers; and somebody presently wrote to Sir John Awdry saying that a young woman of the same name as the accused and closely resembling her in appearance had been employed the previous year as nursemaid to the children of a gentleman, Mr. Hawtry of Eton; that she was "an artful girl" and "had been dismissed under suspicion of fraud".

Sir John passed the letter on to the Trowbridge magistrates, and Mr. Hawtry was requested to go to Isleworth for the purpose of identifying Elizabeth Gough. On his arrival he was conducted by a local police officer to her father's bakery: she was fetched from upstairs and on being confronted with her Mr. Hawtry "found that they were utterly unknown to each other".

But the strange part of the incident lies in the fact that not only were the two girls possessed of the same names—not a particularly common combination—and followed the same occupation, but the physical resemblance which Sir John Awdry's correspondent had noticed extended even to the loss of an identical front tooth. Yet in spite of this highly suspicious circumstance the matter was pursued no further, and the authorities rested content with the negative outcome of Mr. Hawtry's process of identification.

CHAPTER SIXTEEN

MR. T. B. SAUNDERS' INQUIRY: 5TH–12TH NOVEMBER

I

THE charge against Elizabeth Gough had at least succeeded in authenticating the persistent local rumour that two policemen had been locked up in Road-hill House by Mr. Kent the night after the crime, and Mr. Kent's attempts in the witness-box to vindicate himself had been singularly unconvincing. It was argued that he must have been fully alive to the seriousness of his action and therefore his motive for performing it must have been correspondingly compelling.

Soon after the case had ended a correspondent of *The Times* who signed himself "Commonsense" submitted the whole crime to a critical review and enumerated some of the questions which the public was asking.

"Sir," he wrote,

"It seems to be the general opinion that the murder was committed by, or with the connivance of, some inmates of the house. Now most of the inmates of the house were relatives of the murdered boy.

"In examining the evidence against various possible culprits it is therefore necessary to discard the arguments which have been pretty extensively pressed—that the boy's father, mother or his sister could not have been his murderer because they *were* his father, mother or sister.

"We know that parents have murdered their children, and sisters their brothers since the world began, and will do so again before the world ends, and it remains to see whether a crime of that atrocity has now been committed. Great stress has been laid on the fact that Mrs. Kent is supposed to have been a light sleeper, and that she was in a peculiar state of health that rendered her morbidly watchful; but, as there is no doubt that some person removed the boy from the room next to hers without being heard by her, it is clear that she slept sound enough on the night of the murder not to hear what was done; therefore her alleged wakeful disposition proves nothing. Moreover all sick nurses know how apt invalids are to protest that they have not closed their eyes, when they have unconsciously slept soundly for hours.

"It did not appear clearly in the evidence whether Mrs. Kent were asleep or awake when Mr. Kent first retired to bed, nor did it appear whether she had any means of knowing at what precise time he came to bed. She stated that he had not left her side *for more than a quarter of an hour* during the night. How did she know that? Did he leave her side at all? At what time, and for what purpose?

"No traces of the murder have been discovered on the premises—no bloody clothes or knife have been found.[1] Yet there was a pool of blood on the floor of the privy, and it seems scarcely possible that such an act could be committed without leaving some stains on the clothes of the murderer. Ought we not, therefore, to think which of the inmates of the house had the best opportunity of disposing of such evidence of the crime before the police arrived— before any search took place—before there was any suspicion of murder at all?

"Mr. Kent is stated to have left the house in his carriage to seek a policeman who lived at a distance. What sort of carriage did he travel in—who ordered it—who prepared it—who saw Mr. Kent enter it—did he leave the premises alone or accompanied by a servant—whom did he meet on the journey—is the precise road he took known—has it been searched thoroughly—what sort of horse did he drive —was it a spirited animal that would not stand alone while his master absented himself for a short while, or a quiet, dull beast?

"The nurse's conduct, to say the least, appears suspicious; it was undoubtedly grossly negligent, yet Mr. Kent has shewn no *animus* against her. He did not even dismiss her from his service after the event, while he had no scruple

[1] Sergeant Watts' discovery of the night-shift was still unknown.

in casting suspicion against a discharged nurse[1] who has been shewn to have had nothing to do with the matter.

"On the other hand the nurse describes the murdered child as a nasty little tell-tale, and openly avowing her suspicions of Constance Kent, has spoken highly of Mr. Kent's character of kindness to his children. Between Mr. Kent and the nurse there is clearly no ill-will.

"Everything tends to indicate that the murder was committed early in the night. Had it been committed before Mr. Kent went to bed, and had he a share in it, any noises in the house would have excited no suspicions in the inmates, and would have been easily explained by him had they disturbed any of the family. In that case the dog would not have barked, there would have been plenty of time to arrange the bed-clothes, and to prepare any bloody clothes for removal in the carriage in the morning.

"Why did Mr. Kent lock up the policemen? The men are said to have been sent to protect the family: against whom or what; and how could they do so if they were locked up?

"It is very possible that some or all of these questions may have been already answered satisfactorily by Mr. Kent, but it does not appear from the published evidence that they have been; they are in everybody's mind and in everybody's mouth, and it is for the interest of Mr. Kent if he is innocent, and for the interest of justice if he is guilty, that they shall be publicly met and dealt with."

The Times itself concluded a leading article on the case with the following observations:

"It has been pretty clearly established that the murder could not have been committed without at least the complicity of some inmate of the house. It has been reasonably concluded that more than one person was engaged upon the deed, and that the hand of a man is traceable in the proceedings. . . . Let there be no oblivion or surrender. Let it to be understood that this murder is to be discovered . . . and that justice, though it may halt for a time, is to overtake the criminal at last."

[1] Emma Sparks.

The *Morning Star* reviewed the steps so far taken to trace the criminal and voiced the rising demand for the quashing of the coroner's inquest and the institution of a new inquiry:

". . . A coroner's inquest, three magisterial inquiries, and a private inquisition of a character so unusual that there exists no name for it in our legal technology have been brought to a close leaving us very little wiser than we were before. It cannot indeed be alleged that these proceedings have been wholly fruitless. Evidence has been received, and admissions have been elicited from some witnesses, which seem to shed a strange light upon the history of this atrocious crime, and may serve as highly suggestive hints to those who may undertake the prosecution of further research. But the criminal still continues to elude the grasp of justice. Of the two individuals who have been accused, one comes forth from the ordeal pure and stainless, and against the other there exist no proofs sufficiently conclusive to serve as the safe basis for the verdict of a jury. . . .

"There is but one tribunal before which such a case as this can be thoroughly sifted, and that is a coroner's jury. . . . The coroner's inquisition in this case was conducted in a shamefully bungling fashion. . . . The Chief Justice of the Queen's Bench is, by virtue of his office, the supreme coroner of all England; it is for him to take cognisance of the mistakes of local officers and to quash the proceedings. . . . This is the only course which appears to offer any reasonable hope of discovering the perpetrator of the Road murder. . . . Let an immediate appeal be made to the proper authorities to take this step without delay; they can scarcely refuse to grant so reasonable a prayer. . . ."

2

The reaction of the local magistrates to the confirmation of the story that the two policemen had been locked up in the kitchen of Road-hill House was to announce that an inquiry would be held into the incident. This, as usual, was conducted *in camera*, and only meagre reports of it were made known. Captain Meredith declared that the incident had never been reported to him and observed somewhat lamely that the officers "could have got out through the back-door into the courtyard where the dog was". Since by so doing they would merely have exchanged confinement in the kitchen for confinement within a high-walled courtyard in the company of a savage dog, no one was surprised that they rejected the alternative. But the point was, not how they might have escaped from their predicament but what was the motive which had landed them in it, and why it had been followed by a conspiracy to keep the incident a secret. All attempts to elucidate this, however, proved unavailing.

Foley made the cryptic admission that he had sent the men to Road-hill House "to see that nothing was destroyed". He asserted that Mr. Kent had had nothing to do with their presence there; that he had been exceedingly angry when he had learned what had been done to them, and that the incident "had nearly cost them their positions". How this last could be true when he had never reported it, and why he should have swallowed his anger, remained unexplained.

At the conclusion he received an "official reprimand" and the magistrates went on to consider what further steps should be taken "in pursuance of the investigations".

On this subject one of those present held decided views. This was Mr. T. B. Saunders—not to be confused with Mr. T. W. Saunders who had appeared for the Crown in the case against Elizabeth Gough—a retired barrister who had gained a not inconsiderable reputation at the Court of Chancery, had now settled in Wiltshire and was a magistrate for the Bradford-on-Avon division. He had taken a vital interest in the case from the first and had formed his own theories concerning it. Now he rose and said that he had been informed that a great deal of evidence could be advanced which had not been publicly given; that it was the general opinion that the only hope of reaching the root of the matter lay in holding an *open* inquisition at which all persons who had information to impart should be **given** the opportunity of doing so; that he would pointedly refrain from using the word *murder* in connection with the crime, as it was possible it might be one of manslaughter only; that the locking up of the police was a most unaccountable proceeding, and he believed that if it were systematically investigated the motive for the action would be revealed and would throw new light upon the crime. He therefore moved the appointment of a special committee of magistrates to inquire *publicly* into the circumstances of the death.

Mr. Saunders' motion was opposed by Mr. Sotheron-Estcourt on the ground that it "would be inadvisible to keep up a continual agitation in the minds of those from whom they might hope eventually to obtain positive evidence, but rather trust to some incautious word or deed on their part hereafter": an argument to which Mr. Saunders retorted by saying that "he thought it unlikely that the criminals, who had so cleverly evaded detection when the hue and cry after them was at its height, would be so unguarded as to give themselves away once that hue and cry had abated".

But although Mr. Sotheron-Estcourt's view was upheld by the other magistrates, Mr. Saunders was determined that such an inquiry as he had suggested should be held, and that he himself, if need be, would conduct it. With the promised support of his brother magistrates of the Bradford Bench, and that of Captain Meredith, he submitted his proposal to the Home Secretary and asked for the necessary authority.

Sir George Lewis' reaction was characteristic: he sanctioned the proceedings, but refused all responsibility for them; and he withheld authority to take evidence upon oath.

To the criminals, who had good reason to hope that with the failure of the charge against Elizabeth Gough the case would perish of attrition, Mr. Saunders' inquiry spelled a new and potent danger: nor was it welcomed by the authorities themselves, for it threatened to expose both the "deliberate machinations" by which the coroner's jury had been packed and their own lack of vigour in prosecuting the case.

It could not be prevented, but it could at least be obstructed —by putting pressure on witnesses to keep them away, by encouraging a noisy *claque* to heckle and cause confusion, and by the copious use of ridicule.

Any man, however exceptional his qualities, would have had difficulty in achieving results against such determined opposition. And Mr. Saunders' qualities were not exceptional. He made his initial error by rushing the opening date of his inquiry and in not advertising it sufficiently, with the result that many who might have given evidence on the first day were prevented from doing so by previous engagements, while others did not even know that it had begun. After the first day the increasing disorder which hampered the proceedings discouraged potential witnesses from attending.

Having taken the Temperance Hall at Road for a week Mr. Saunders opened his inquiry on 5th November, with a number of magistrates and Captain Meredith beside him on the platform, and Superintendent Foley and members of the police, together with several reporters, in the body of the hall. He made an excellent opening speech, giving his reasons for refraining from using the word *murder* in connection with the crime, expressing the public desire for an open inquisition, and inviting all those who had information to impart to come forward. On the next and succeeding days, however, the support given by the magistrates and police gradually dwindled and the disorder increased, so that from then onward until the inquiry finally petered out on 12th November the course of evidence was frequently interrupted. Unfortunately Mr. Saunders had not the force of character to quell the disturbance, and under its influence his morale gave way and he lapsed into flippancies and absurdities which played directly into the hands of those who wished to smother his endeavours with ridicule.

But in spite of all this it was solely through the agency of this inquiry that Sergeant Watts' discovery of the night-shift in the boiler-stove was at last brought to light, while a number of minor incidents, which, although they may have been disclosed at various *in camera* inquiries, had never been made public, were for the first time revealed. Urch, for instance, related the conflicting orders given him by Watts and Foley on the night after the crime, and Heritage alleged that Foley had said to him: "Mr. Kent wants you to go to the house and stay there tonight. Go at eleven o'clock. Mr. Kent will tell you what to do. Move quietly because he does not want the servants to know you are there."

This did not accord either with Mr. Kent's evidence in court or with Foley's own statement to the Trowbridge magistrates that Mr. Kent had nothing to do with the presence of the police in the house. But now Foley admitted that he had sent the men there "to act under Mr. Kent's orders, as he required them. They were to knock on the library window where Mr. Kent was to be at eleven o'clock to let them in and confer with them." Asked why he had put them under Mr. Kent's orders he replied cautiously, "At that time the suspicion was not in the quarter it is now."

Alloway and Fricker reported the disappearance of the dark-lantern after the crime, while Inspector Pitney made an interesting deposition concerning the real feelings in the village towards Mr. Kent. "On the day after Miss Constance was discharged," he stated, "I said to Mr. Kent that I had come to make an investigation of the house. He said we had been long enough in the house, and it was time that we made some investigations outside. He spoke of the neighbours hating him. He said that Nutt bore him ill-will because he had prosecuted him; that others did because he had stopped their fishing in the stream. He referred to certain parties and expressed a wish that they should be looked to. I made an investigation and found the public feeling the opposite of what Mr. Kent stated it to be: that he was considered reserved, but little known; Mrs. Kent and the Misses Kent were much liked and respected."

Mr. Groser came forward and stated that he had been present in the hall of Road-hill House on the morning of Monday, 2nd July, and had seen Constance coming downstairs, and then turn back on catching sight of him—exactly as she had said she had done when she had been going to fetch herself the glass of water. Her statement was thus amply confirmed.

But the principal sensation was provided by Urch and Watts.

"I was present," said Urch, "when Sergeant Watts found a woman's night-shift in the boiler-hole; it was pushed far up; it was dry, but very dirty; it had been worn a long time; there were several places with blood splashes, some as large as my

hand; it was a coarse article like a servant would wear; it was
not a large article."

Sergeant Watts said, "Opening the door of the boiler-
furnace I saw something there wrapped up in a piece of brown
paper; I pulled it out; on opening the bundle in the stable I
found it contained a shift, which was dirty and very bloody;
it did not appear to have been partially washed; I wrapped it
up again; I was coming out of the stable when I saw Mr. Kent
just outside the door; he asked me what I had found and said
he must see it, and that Dr. Parsons must see it; I did not let
Mr. Kent see it, but handed it over to Superintendent Foley;
I have never seen anything more of it; I asked Dallimore some
days later what had become of it; he told me he was just going
to put it back in the place from which it had been taken, when
one of the servant girls came into the scullery and he put it
down at the side of the boiler-hole. I found the shift between
five and six in the evening; Fricker was close by."

Partly owing to the disturbance in the hall which accompanied the evidence of Urch and Watts the significance of their
disclosure was lost. The only night-dress of which anyone had
heard hitherto had been Constance Kent's, and the conclusion
arrived at was that the story of her night-dress being lost in
the wash had been a fabrication and now at last was being
revealed the real truth of what had become of it. Few, if any,
seem to have realized that the story to which they had been
listening concerned an entirely different garment.

While certain of the newspapers hurried the story into print,
others applied first to the authorities for confirmation, only to
learn that these were as much in the dark as themselves and
could do no more than promise an inquiry.

No sooner did the news reach Chief Inspector Whicher than
he wrote as follows to the Trowbridge magistrates:

". . . In reference to the recent disclosure relative to
the local police having found on the day of the murder a
blood-stained garment secreted in the boiler-hole at Mr.
Kent's house, which circumstance, it appears, was not made
known by them to the magistrates, I beg to state that it
was never mentioned to me by any member of the police

force during the fortnight I was engaged with them at Road assisting in the inquiry, and in daily communication with Superintendent Foley and his assistants, who, it now appears, were present when the garment was found. I beg to state that I was no party to it, for, as before stated, the fact was never known to me."

In the course of a private letter written about the same time to the Chief of the Bath Police, who was a friend of his, he makes a shrewd guess as to what actually happened, though he remains convinced, of course, that the garment must have been Constance's.

". . . I want to draw your particular attention to the most important fact which oozed out the other day at Mr. Saunders' inquiry which was stifled in its birth by the police concerned. . . I have no doubt that by some carelessness they lost possession of it" (the garment), "either by putting it out of their hands and Constance getting possession of it again, or they put it back in the boiler-hole to try to catch the owner coming to take it away, or it having been got away without their knowledge, a compact of secrecy was entered into with reference to it which was well kept. . . . I have little doubt that it was let slip in the way I have described, and that would account for what I never could get an explanation—*viz.*, why the men were secreted in the kitchen the same night. Foley never would explain that to me. . . ."[1]

[1] Neither of these letters was made public until 1865.

CHAPTER SEVENTEEN

JUSTICE'S LAST ENDEAVOURS

I

To Mr. W. Stancombe was entrusted the task of conducting the inquiry into this new mystery, and as soon as he had completed his preliminary investigations the Press was invited to attend a meeting at the Trowbridge police court over which Sir John Awdry presided.

The proceedings began with a statement by Mr. Stancombe, in the course of which he said:

> "An erroneous idea had got about that the garment in question was the missing night-dress. The magistrates were anxious that the public should be put right with regard to that matter; therefore they thought it right to have a more open meeting, and had called this meeting, with the police and others present, in order to give an opportunity for making public a description of the garment.
>
> "He had first sent for Foley, who had admitted that such a garment had been found; that it was very dirty, and there were marks of blood upon it; *that Dr. Stapleton had seen it,* and, satisfied as to the nature of the stains, had dismissed it with the words, 'Oh, put it away—it has nothing to do with the murder.' He had thereupon seen Dr. Stapleton who had said that he had no recollection of seeing more than one night-dress.[1]
>
> "After taking a statement from Sergeant Watts he had seen Dr. Parsons, who assured him that *he had seen no garment with a stain upon it.* He next interrogated P.C. Urch and had gone to Road-hill House and questioned the cook and housemaid; both denied any knowledge of the garment he described. He had examined the boiler-stove where it

[1] Mary Ann Kent's—see pages 77–80 *supra.*

was found; he could put his arm nearly full length up it. Sergeant Watts would now relate his part in the matter to them."

Sergeant Watts then repeated the statement he had made at Mr. Saunders' inquiry, adding the following details, "If a fire had been lit the garment must have been burnt; there was a great deal of blood upon it, nearly covering it in front and behind, extending from about sixteen inches above the hem upwards; the garment would have been fit to wear again if it had been washed and mended." In reply to a question he said that he had not noticed if the blood were dark red or light red; and that the stains had not been on it long.[1] More blood was in the front than on the back."[2]

Superintendent Foley was then questioned: his desperate attempts to vindicate himself were not only unconvincing but verged upon the grotesque.

"I was shewn," he said, "by the last witness, on 30th June, a dirty, stained garment. I did not keep it in my possession a minute; I did not like to touch it. I was the chief officer present; I said, 'You see it's a nasty, dirty chemise, so put it away—don't expose the girl.' After a good bit of talk I gave it to Dallimore, and I don't know that I saw it again until Monday; I cannot charge my memory that I saw it then. I could not actually swear that any medical man saw it, though I shewed Dr. Stapleton a stained garment. He did not see the night-gown until Monday,[3] and, if he saw the one in the cart in the yard, it must have been the one in question."

Mr. Stancombe: "I understood from you that Dr. Stapleton had seen it."

Supt. Foley: "I understood that he had seen it, but I cannot state positively whether he did or not. I shewed him one of the Misses Kents' night-gowns. I am sorry I did not keep the shift to shew it to him. Mrs. Dallimore had found the night-gown of Mary Ann Kent on Saturday. The missing night-gown was

[1] It had been established that Mary Ann Kent was the only woman in the household menstruating at the time of the crime.
[2] Sergeant Watts' further description of the garment is given on pages 78 and 79.
[3] Incorrect: he saw it first on Saturday.

not missed until the Monday.[1] It was on the Monday that I
shewed the night-dress to Dr. Stapleton.[2] This one that I
saw was an old stained chemise—not the missing nightdress."

Sir John Awdry: "By 'don't expose the girl' did you refer
to a matter of decency, or had you any other motive?"

Supt. Foley: "Solely and wholly out of respect for decency.
It appeared as though the person to whom it belonged had
worn it for a week or a fortnight. I told Dallimore to put it
back where it had been found. I don't know how it was that
I did not mention it to the magistrates, but I was satisfied that
it in no way related to the murder."

Dr. Stapleton was then asked to state his recollections of
the incident, and said:

"I saw a garment with stains on it on three occasions, and
I pronounced on them. It was on Saturday afternoon. The
stains were only on the back part. The garment now described
contrasts strongly with the one I saw on Monday. The one I
saw on Saturday afternoon was not like the one described by
Sergeant Watts."

After reviewing the evidence the magistrates stigmatized
Foley's conduct as "culpable", but there the matter was
allowed to rest. Mr. Stancombe's investigations had at least
established beyond doubt the fact that the night-shift found
in the boiler-stove was *not* Constance's lost night-dress; but
the extraordinary lenience shewn towards Foley, and the superficial character of the examination of himself and the constables concerned, suggest an overwhelming reluctance on the
part of the magistrates to probe too deeply into the matter, no
doubt for fear lest more damaging disclosures might be
produced.

The public, however, was not so easily lulled into silence.
Scathing comments filled the Press, while the demand that the
inquest should be quashed and a new one held grew so insistent
that it could no longer be ignored. On 24th November, therefore,
the Attorney-General, Sir Richard Bethell, applied to the
Queen's Bench for the issue of a writ *ad melius inquirendum.*

---

[1] I.e. Constance's.

[2] Incorrect: it was on Saturday that Foley shewed Mary Ann's night-dress
to Stapleton; on Monday Stapleton, in the company of Sylvester, saw it for
himself lying in the police waggonette.

"He urged the matter long and ably, and obtained a rule, calling upon the Coroner to show cause why the inquisition should not be quashed and a writ issued *ad melius inquirendum*".[1] His plea rested mainly on the fact that Mr. Sylvester had been guilty of committing technical breaches of the rules governing inquests—for instance: that the examination of Constance and William Kent had not been taken down in writing, and that the presentment had been written on paper and not on parchment, as the law directs in all cases of murder and manslaughter. This drew the following comment from *The Times*:

"It is a curious illustration of the occasional obliquity in the operation of our law that the Attorney-General was driven to a purely technical reason for reopening the inquisition into the Road murder. For some months past it has been a pretty general opinion that a precious opportunity was wasted during the three days immediately following the event, and the interests of justice were sacrificed at the inquest to considerations for the feelings of the family. Every subsequent investigation . . . has necessarily been conducted on the hypothesis of guilt on the part of some individual, and nothing has been gained but a provisional acquittal of two persons.

"An inquiry in the nature of a fresh coroner's inquest, even at this eleventh hour, is felt to be the only method of superseding conjecture by something like genuine induction. Yet it seems very doubtful whether such a measure is consistent with the genius of our common law. The neglect of the coroner to receive evidence which might easily be got, his misdirection of the jury on a point of law, and his alleged refusal to make anything but an open verdict, were grounds for questioning the original inquisition, but not for issuing a new one.

"It is certainly inexplicable how the coroner could have so misapprehended the scope of his responsibilities as to let sympathy for an afflicted family defeat the ends of justice, or how any acute and experienced man could have refused

[1] *A Mid-Victorian Pepys*—S. M. Ellis.

to follow up any of the clues which the evidence, scanty as it is, offered for his guidance. . . .

"Nothing remains but for justice laboriously to retrace its steps, availing itself of the vast and various materials already accumulated, but adopting precisely the same method which should have been followed from the first."

After hearing the Attorney-General's argument the Lord Chief Justice said that he and his associate judges were of the opinion that in this case there should be a rule calling upon the coroner to shew cause why the inquisition should not be quashed and a writ of *melius inquirendum* issued. The Attorney-General had satisfied himself as to the facts he had stated, and as to the authorities he had cited concerning the validity of the record, it being on paper instead of parchment. That left the great question open, and although they might not feel themselves called upon to quash the inquisition on the grounds of informality, yet the interests of public justice demanded that a further inquiry should take place. As the judicial conduct of the coroner was called in very serious question, and as the result of their decision must materially affect his position as coroner, they would not do justice or act in fairness to him if they were now at once to quash the inquisition without affording him the opportunity of answering matters stated in the affidavits, and therefore they could do no more than grant a rule calling on him to shew cause why the inquisition should not be quashed and a writ for a better inquiry issued.

Unfortunately that day, 26th November, happened to be the last day of term, and therefore the rule could not come up for argument before the opening of the Hilary Term on 11th January, 1861. So, by interposing yet another delay, Fortune once more favoured the guilty.

2

The case of *The Queen v. Sylvester* finally came up for hearing at the end of January 1861 before Lord Chief Justice Cockburn, Mr. Justice Hill and Mr. Justice Blackburn at the

Court of the Queen's Bench. In arguing the case for the Crown the Attorney-General said:

"The child that was murdered was a boy nearly four years of age, described as a fine, healthy, strong child. . . . The murdered child was found in a privy in the garden, wrapped in a blanket, which appeared to have been extracted from the crib in which the child slept. Below the child was a piece of flannel.[1] The child appeared to have been caught in its descent down the orifice of the privy by what was called the splashing-board . . . and he was found lying upon that board covered by a blanket, and with his throat cut in so complete a manner that every cartilage—every structure of the throat—was divided down to the vertebrae of the neck. But it did not appear that there was, either in the privy itself, or on the blanket, or upon the flannel lying beneath the child, that quantity of blood that might have been expected if death had been produced by cutting the throat whilst the circulation of the blood continued; for, as all know, if the carotid arteries of the throat are divided whilst pulsation is going on, the pump of the heart sends the blood through the arteries with such force that it would spurt out in such large streams as to cover any surrounding place within a few feet of the child. . . . Though blood was found, it was of that kind of clotted or coagulated blood which would issue out in heavy, thick drops from a wound . . . inflicted after the pulsation of the heart had ceased. On the side there was a deep stab inflicted, where a knife had penetrated through the cartilage of the ribs with such force as to have divided the diaphragm, and so forcibly was the blow inflicted that it removed the heart from its right position. But from that stab no blood appeared to have flowed. Therefore it would seem that the stab had been inflicted after the throat had been cut. . . ."

The Attorney-General then came to the inquest itself, and said that the one great object he had in troubling the Court was to satisfy their Lordships of the gross insufficiency of that inquiry and the palpable neglect of the proper subjects of inquiry exhibited by the coroner. Quoting from Elizabeth Gough's evidence he said that its most striking passage was as follows: "The impression of the body still remained on the bed,

---

[1] The breast-flannel.

G

and the bed-clothes were placed exactly as if I or his mother had done it.

"Whoever took the child," he went on, "must have restored the bed-clothes with a woman's precision and neatness in the proper order after the child was taken. But how singular and extraordinary that was! If the child was awake when it was removed, certainly the person removing him with murderous intent would hardly have remained to place the bed-clothes in order. If the child was taken by one person from the bed and held, perhaps, in the blanket, it would not have been possible for the individual, so occupied, with one hand to have replaced the bed-clothes in order. Two persons, therefore, must have been concerned; or if one person only was employed, that person must have returned to the room in order to have replaced the bed-clothes in the manner in which they were found. Yet this aspect of the matter did not appear to have induced in the mind of the coroner any feeling that it was necessary to make further inquiry. No attention whatever was given to it, nor was any attention given to the piece of flannel found beneath the body, apart from the blanket in which the child was wrapped. . . ."

After reading the depositions of the witnesses and recounting the desire of the jury, and the manner in which that desire had been met by the coroner, the Attorney-General passed on to the affidavits,[1] and ended his argument by saying:

"Their lordships would find from the evidence he had read that two things were most clearly established—that the coroner had prevented that further and fuller investigation of the facts which the jury desired to make; that the anxiety of the jury, who in that respect were better lawyers than the coroner, was directed to ascertain who had done the deed, and that the coroner shifted the inquiry by telling the jury that it was not their duty or his to make that inquiry." He argued that it followed as a rule of law that the coroner could proceed only *super visum corporis*, and also that no one but the coroner could proceed *super visum corporis*.

Sir Fitzroy Kelly, Q.C., for Mr. Sylvester, based his argument on the alleged incapacity of the jury, the members of which he described as being in an excited and bewildered state

[1] See pages 99 and 100 *supra*.

of mind, not in possession of their reason or faculties, and not —like the foreman and the coroner—men of intelligence and education. Which, as the *Journal* observed, would have been, if true, a further argument in favour of a new inquiry rather than the reverse.

In delivering judgment the Lord Chief Justice said that, if the Court were not bound by precedents to quash the inquisition, independently of any discretion to be exercised on their part, it became a question whether they ought, in the interests of justice, to do so. He then proceeded to answer the question in the negative, and to give a judgment which, though it submitted the coroner to some mild criticism, upheld the previous inquest and dismissed the plea for granting a writ for a new one. Thus, exactly seven months after the crime had been committed, the last hope of resifting the evidence from the beginning, in which seemed to lie the only possible chance of ever solving the mystery and bringing the criminals to justice, was disappointed—and disappointed by the very process of justice itself. As the *Examiner* of 7th February said, in an article entitled "The Law's Protection of the Road Murderer":

". . . The Court refused the inquiry, not because nothing would come of it, but the very contrary, lest it should lead to discovery by a process condemned by law.

'If there had been judicial misconduct of a nature to justify the Court setting aside the inquisition, *it would still be a question whether that should be done and a new inquisition issued, when it was seen what the object was, viz.—to examine those among whom the guilt of the crime necessarily rested, to ascertain from their separate depositions which of them had committed the crime.* That would not be a proper exercise of the jurisdiction of this Court, to issue such an inquisition to obtain evidence against them, for that was an object which the law could not sanction.'

"So that had the Coroner's misconduct been as gross as alleged, or worse, the Court would, nevertheless, have refused the new inquest, because it might have led to the discovery of the crime through the evidence of the parties suspected. Now the practical tendency of this decision, which makes nothing of the ends of justice and everything of abortively narrow means, is to be tested by imagining the feelings with which it will affect the murderer or murderers. Now they will breathe again and rejoice that judges stand between them and justice! . . . Murder has, indeed, a handsome share of protection under the law, and somewhere about Road they know it, and are duly thankful.''

The Court's decision did, indeed, bring to an end all hope of discovering the criminals, and although for some time to come desultory investigations continued under the direction of Mr. Hughes, chief of the Bath Police, they achieved nothing beyond confirming a few points which had hardly been in doubt before. And so the crime which had created so tremendous a sensation seemed destined to end in anti-climax and remain a mystery for ever.

CHAPTER EIGHTEEN

THE SOLUTION[1]

I

IN HIS summing-up at the trial of William Wallace on the charge of murdering his wife Mr. Justice (afterwards Lord) Wright, one of our greatest judges, gave an illuminating disquisition on the value of circumstantial evidence.

"Circumstantial evidence," he said, "may vary in value almost infinitely. *Some is as good and conclusive as the evidence of actual witnesses.* In other cases the only circumstantial evidence which anyone can present still leaves loopholes and doubts. . . . The real test of circumstantial evidence is this: *does it exclude other theories or possibilities*? If you cannot put the evidence against the accused beyond a probability; if it is a probability which is not inconsistent with there being other reasonable possibilities; then it is impossible for a jury to say, 'We are satisfied beyond a reasonable doubt that the charge is made out.' "

Let us briefly review the facts of this case, and then, assuming the role of judge and jury, decide whether they "exclude other theories or possibilities."

1. All the evidence pointed to the fact that the crime had been committed by someone in the house and that two persons were concerned in it. Of the nine adults under that roof, six occupied the top floor, all of whom were females except one, a boy of fifteen. He and his sister, aged sixteen, were the only members of that group who slept alone. All had retired to their rooms at the usual hour and before eleven o'clock.

2. On the floor below were three adults, one of whom was a man. He shared a room with his wife, but he was always the last to go to bed and his time for doing so was uncertain. The time at which he alleged he did so on the night of the crime—

[1] This is supported by the article quoted in Appendix I.

11.45—was uncorroborated by anyone but his wife. The police constable, on the other hand, testified that the gas-lamp was still burning in the hall at 1 a.m.: also that there was a light in the nursery. The door of the nursery was at right angles to that of Mr. Kent's dressing-room.

3. The lantern with which Mr. Kent lit his way about the premises at night was put out for him that evening as usual by the housemaid and was never seen again. Its loss was never explained.

4. The medical evidence asserted that the child was healthy and exceptionally large and strong for his age; that the wounds in his body must have required great strength to inflict; that the stab must have been made with a "long, strong, wide and sharp-pointed knife, like a carving-knife", of which there were three in the kitchen; that death was probably due to suffocation caused by "strong pressure of a hand holding some soft substance over the mouth for five or ten minutes"; that the child "was dead or nearly dead" when the wound in the throat was inflicted; that the stab was inflicted after death.

5. The nursery measured 18 feet by 14 feet. Its door was opposite the nurse's bed which was about 9 feet from the child's cot.

6. A night-light was always lit when the nurse went to bed: it burned for about five or six hours.

7. The deep indentation in the child's pillow and the outline of his body on the mattress shewed that pressure had been exerted. The sheet and counterpane had been smoothed together, folded down and tucked in beneath the mattress: the blanket had been removed.

The above are the main facts of the crime, and the following are the questions which naturally arise out of them:

1. Could any two members of the household have entered the nursery, suffocated the child, rearranged the bed-clothes and carried off the body without disturbing the nurse?

2. Why should they increase the risk of discovery by delaying their departure in order to rearrange the bed-clothes?

3. Why, if the child were already dead—or nearly dead—by suffocation, did they inflict two unnecessary wounds, and

so increase the chances of detection by soiling their garments with their victim's blood?

4. Why was the child—against whom none had any *animus* —killed at all?

5. Who had motive, opportunity, the physical strength to inflict the wounds, and an accomplice ready to hand?

2

"The real test of the value of circumstantial evidence is this: does it exclude other theories or possibilities?"

The following theory takes into consideration these six points:

1. In 1860 Mr. Kent's financial position was precarious: a seat on the Board of Factory Commissioners would mean a substantial increase in emoluments; further scandal in connection with his domestic life while his application was under consideration would ruin its chances of success.

2. Mrs. Kent, like the rest of the household, was accustomed to Mr. Kent's irregularity in the time he came to bed, and accustomed to hearing him moving about the house at whatever time he made his nightly round of the premises.

3. Active women, like Mrs. Kent, are apt to sleep heavily during the last few weeks of pregnancy, and most people have only the vaguest notions of time when aroused from sleep.[1] Her notion of the time when Mr. Kent came to bed would be equally vague.

4. In 1844, when Mary Pratt entered Mr. Kent's household as nursemaid, he began an intrigue with her while still cohabiting with his wife: he was, therefore, neither averse from nor unpractised in this form of deceit.

5. One of the things alleged at Mr. Slack's inquiry—probably by Kerslake and Cox whose bedroom was just above— was that Mr. Kent had formed the habit of visiting the nursery last thing at night and after his wife had gone to bed.

---

[1] E.g. Mrs. Kent herself: when she heard the drawing-room window being opened in the small hours she thought it was the servants opening up the house at 6 a.m.

6. Savile was a precocious child, and a notorious and irrepressible tale-bearer.

This, then, is the theory of how the crime took place:

On Friday, 29th June, after making his round of the premises as usual, Mr. Kent put out the gas lamp in the hall and lit his way upstairs with the dark-lantern. Assuring himself that his wife was asleep he entered the nursery where Elizabeth Gough was expecting him.

Savile was usually a heavy sleeper, but that night was made restless by the calomel pill, which was due to act within the next two or three hours. Roused by unusual sounds in the room he peered over the side of his cot. What he saw made him cry out. Mr. Kent, realizing in a flash the danger that threatened him, as is the way with a weak man when thoroughly frightened, lost his head and all his self-control. He leaped up and advanced upon the child, and as he did so Savile opened his mouth to scream. Frantic with alarm Mr. Kent snatched up the first thing to hand—the nurse's breast-flannel—and clapping it over the child's mouth bore him down backwards on his cot. The wildly kicking legs thudded loudly against the sides of the cot, and the nurse held them still while both strained their ears for any sounds of movement in the house. When, reassured at last by the prevailing silence, Mr. Kent took his hand away, the child was dead.

How to conceal their guilt, disguise the cause of death and dispose of the body was their first imperative need.

Of recent years a number of motiveless murders by throat-cutting had occurred in the neighbourhood, presumably the work of a maniac who had never been caught. If this could be made to appear such another outrage suspicion would be diverted, and it would be assumed that the killer had entered stealthily and carried off the boy while the nurse was soundly sleeping.

Time was their enemy, for at 4 a.m. the brief midsummer night gave place to dawn.

It has been suggested that the privy was chosen for the disposal of the body with the deliberate intention of casting suspicion upon Constance, since she is commonly supposed to have thrown her shorn hair into its vault before her flight to

Bath.[1] More likely it was selected simply because it was the handiest and most effective place of concealment.

It was probably the nurse who closed the child's eyes and composed his distorted features; but in the need to act quickly she overlooked the protruding tongue-tip, while neither she nor Mr. Kent realized that in death bruises would appear about the mouth. Then, as they hastily wrapped the body in the blanket, the breast-flannel, unnoticed by either, was caught up in its folds.

It is probable that they went down by the front stairs, for not only would the stair-carpet deaden the sound of their footsteps but, encumbered with such a burden, it would be easier to negotiate them than the narrow spiral back-stairs. One of them, going before with the dark-lantern, lit the gas-lamp in the hall, so that, if Mrs. Kent were to awake and become curious at her husband's prolonged absence, the sight of the lamp alight, were she to look over the banisters, would reassure her and she would imagine that he was still at work in his library.

Unlocking the door between the hall and the passage they took the game-carver from the kitchen, and opened the back door, the noise bringing a sharp spasm of barking from the dog which was quickly hushed at a word from his master.

Screened by the surrounding shrubs they entered the privy and laid the body on the floor. With his hand inside the folds of the blanket Mr. Kent severed the throat in one powerful slash. Then perhaps his nerve failed him, for he had loved the child; and it was the nurse who lifted the body from the floor. Heavier in death than in life she had to brace its weight against her thighs, the blood from the wound oozing through the blanket and staining the front of her night-shift.[2]

Either they had forgotten the splashboard, or had thought that the body would pass it. When it would not Mr. Kent, in a frantic endeavour to force it down, drove the knife deep

[1] There is no evidence that she did so; and it is related in *Road* that after the Kents left Road-hill House in 1861 a box containing her hair was dug up in what had been her garden and sold to a hairdresser in Trowbridge.

[2] Later, when she folded the garment up in the piece of brown paper, some of the blood was transferred to the back of it, though less conspicuously. As Watts said, "More blood was on the front than the back."

G*

into the body. The effort was unavailing, and as the blade was "violently twisted and wrenched in its withdrawal" it made the "transverse notch" in the wound and grazed the first and second fingers of the left hand. Then the blanket was pulled away, in the hope that without its impeding folds the body might yet go down, but only the breast-flannel fell into the vault below.

There was nothing more to be done. The blanket was thrown in on top of the body, the lid of the seat replaced, the knife wiped upon the pieces of paper which Stephen Millet picked up next day and thrust, perhaps, once or twice into the ground.

Back in the house they washed it at the scullery sink and returned it to the drawer. Then they washed themselves and took clean garments from the airing cupboard close by, Elizabeth Gough wrapping up her night-shift and thrusting it up the flue of the boiler-stove in the confident expectation that it would be consumed by the flames when Kerslake lit the stove in the morning. Lest the sound of the opening of the drawing-room window might arouse Mrs. Kent it was probably left for Elizabeth Gough to do after Mr. Kent had crept upstairs and into bed beside his wife. It was opened to lend colour to the idea that someone had entered from outside, but either the weight of the sash prevented the nurse—or the noise it made frightened her—from opening it more than the usual six inches.

Back in the nursery Elizabeth Gough rearranged the disordered cot to obliterate the signs of a struggle which must unfailingly have awoken her. But she smoothed the sheet and counterpane too carefully so that they contrasted strangely and suspiciously with the deeply indented pillow and mattress.

Mr. Kent may either have destroyed his own garments in the library fireplace,[1] or concealed them somewhere in the room, and in carrying them there allowed them to brush against the wall near the door, so making the smear of blood which Mr. Groser said he noticed. But however he rid himself of them it is

[1] The question whether any tinder was found in the library fireplace next day was asked in the Press, but there is no record that it was ever answered, or that the room was searched. Nor does any examination ever seem to have been made of the Kents' bedroom or Mr. Kent's dressing-room.

unlikely that he did so on his way to Trowbridge—the difficulty of doing so and the risks involved would have been too great. Most probably he destroyed them, together with Elizabeth Gough's night-shift, in the green-house furnace while the police were under lock and key in the kitchen. This would explain why he "left the house once or twice" that night, ostensibly to "see if the lights were out". He must also have found a means of ridding himself of the dark-lantern, which had no doubt been stained with blood while it lit that last ghastly scene in the privy.[1]

3

That Mr. Kent was a man stricken with fear and anguish is only too clear. That his nerve failed him and that, had he been produced to give evidence at the inquest, he would unfailingly have made his guilt apparent, seems almost equally clear. One can only assume that the influential friends who rallied to his side had a shrewd suspicion of the truth, but combined to shield him from the consequences of an unpremeditated act of violence in an unguarded moment against the child he loved. So the jury was packed and the inquest baulked. But when he allowed Constance to be charged with his own crime their feelings underwent a change: they fell away from him and from then on, as Dr. Stapleton says, "he stood very much alone". But by then they had become so involved that they were compelled to continue shielding him in order to shield themselves. In the matter of Constance they did their best to avert her arrest, and publicly affirmed their belief in her innocence. They even applied to the Queen's Bench to rescind the order against her—but that application failed.

4

The moment the police guard on Road-hill House was removed there were demonstrations against Mr. Kent, and the household was subjected to every form of annoyance from the

[1] Extract from an unpublished letter of 24th October, 1860 from Charles Dickens to Wilkie Collins who was abroad: "Mr. Kent intriguing with the nursemaid, poor little child awakes in crib and sits up contemplating blissful proceedings. Nursemaid strangles him then and there. Mr. Kent gashes body to mystify discoverers and disposes of same."

crowds who continued to haunt the place. A barricade had to be erected around the privy, and again and again police protection had to be reimposed. According to the *Bristol Times*, when Mr. Peacock consented to Mr. Kent's remaining after Morning Service to take Communion "on his solemn assurance of his innocence of the murder of his son" the remainder of the congregation "immediately quitted the building".

In March 1861 the Kent family left Road for Weston-super-Mare, and the contents of the house were put up for auction. The sale attracted enormous crowds, but one of the main objects of their curiosity, Savile's cot, was not included, while an offer subsequently made for it by Madame Tussaud's was likewise rejected.

Road-hill House has changed hands many times since 1861. In recent years it was the home of Sir Howard and Lady Kennard, and Lady Kennard, with rare sympathy, created on the site of the privy a garden of remembrance to Savile Kent, which centres upon a charming figure of a little boy. The drawing-room window still squeaks, and still sticks at the same point as it did when it was raised in the early hours of the morning of Saturday, 30th June, 1860. The nursery, with Elizabeth Gough's little dressing-room beyond it, is unaltered; the cottages bordering the lane are still the same, while the lane itself still ends, as it did then, abruptly at a gate into the meadows.

Ann Stokes' parlour, where Elizabeth Gough paced up and down "feeling the blood rush from one side of her body to the other" still commands an uninterrupted view across the green. Only the Temperance Hall—scene of so many emotions—is gone, and a heap of rubble alone shews where it stood.

Some fifteen miles away at East Coulston the tiny church is falling into decay;[1] the churchyard is overgrown and rank with weeds, and the stone which once covered the brick-lined grave has now fallen in upon the mingled bones of Mary Ann Kent and Savile, her supplanter's son, who, the barely decipherable inscription tells us, "was cruelly murdered at Road".

---

[1] The tiny church has now been lovingly restored and the gravestone reset.

BOOK II

THE SEQUEL

CHAPTER ONE

CONSTANCE EMILIE KENT

I

WHETHER Constance Kent were innocent or guilty, however impartially one may regard her story, it is impossible to read or write of her without admiration for the courage with which she turned her suffering and humiliation into formative channels. Nor is it possible to understand the "mystery" which the sequel presents unless one realizes that it was the outcome of spiritual forces acting upon a passionate disposition.

If Constance Kent were innocent, she could scarcely have failed to know who was guilty; if she were guilty, this school-girl of sixteen was so consummate an actress, and so utterly callous, that never for an instant did she display other than normal reactions to the crime. One thing, however, is unarguable: all who had the opportunity of studying her most closely—her school-mistresses, for instance; the staff of Devizes Gaol, and others who came into intimate contact with her during her life—found it impossible to believe in her guilt.

But whether innocent or guilty every moment of the time she spent with her family after her release must have been charged with hideous tension. Accordingly, as soon as arrangements could be made, she left home and entered as a pupil the Convent de la Sagesse at Dinant in Brittany.[1] She was received under the name of Emilie Kent, but any hope that this frail disguise would conceal her identity did not endure for long. France, as well as England, had been excited and horrified by the crime, and when, as was inevitable, it leaked out that Constance Kent was at the Convent, people gathered to point her out and stare whenever the girls went out for exercise. She bore this recurrent ordeal with compressed lips, blank expression and eyes fixed upon the ground, exerting all her powers of

[1] The letter reproduced here was written on the eve of her departure, after obtaining the permission of the authorities to leave England.

Road Hill House
Nov.ber 23rd 1860

Dear Mr Edlin—

I write to thank
you for the pretty pair of
Mittens and the scarf
which I received yesterday
they will no doubt prove
very useful and will

remind me whenever I

look at them of how much

I am indebted to the giver

Fortunately they were not

left in the train Mr

Dunn found them in

the court-house and gave

them to Poppa when he

went into Frome.

I like them exceedingly

and shall always value

them very much.

With many thanks

Believe me

Yours truly

Constance E Kent

self-control. Such stark fortitude is neither beautifying to its practitioner nor appealing to the eye of the beholder, and an Englishwoman, although she herself had never seen Constance, thus described in a letter written at this time the impression Constance made upon friends of hers who had:

> "She was neither stupid nor clever, lively nor morose, and only remarkable for one particular trait: her extreme tenderness to very young children. In the whole school in which she was a pupil she would be the one who would probably be least remarked if all were seen together."

Constance Kent's need for fortitude did not begin and end on those walks. The news of her identity soon spread through the Convent, and it speaks as much for the tact and discretion of the nuns as it does for her own stoicism that this exposure caused her no embitterment. With an instinctive faith in her and an abiding wisdom they entrusted the little children left in their charge to the care of this girl who had been accused of murdering a little child; they developed a talent for designing, which they discovered she possessed, and employed it for creating the intricate patterns used in the embroideries for which the Convent was renowned and which they taught her to stitch as exquisitely as they did themselves. To the end of her life Constance remembered these women, and the three years she spent at Dinant, with grateful affection.

2

Meanwhile events at home and abroad—the American Civil War, the Lancashire cotton famine, the Polish insurrection, the Prussian invasion of Denmark—were driving the crime at Road and Constance Kent out of the public mind. She was given a breathing space. Although she could never escape the question *"Could she have done it?"* lurking in the eyes of each new acquaintance, she gradually ceased to be an object of public curiosity. Unharassed and no longer oppressed by the will of her step-mother, encouraged to think and act for herself, to express her personality, she acquired a poise and self-confidence which she had previously lacked. It is significant that when she was nineteen she was accepted, on the same footing as the other pupils, at a finishing school kept by one Mlle de la Tour, and began to meet members of the English community and to be received in their homes.

The time had now come when the question of her crippled future must be considered. She had always possessed that longing for independence which was animating so many of her contemporaries. But few careers, except the ill-rewarded one of teaching, were open as yet to young women of good birth and education, and from this her circumstances debarred her, as they did from applying for admission to Miss Nightingale's recently established training school for nurses at St. Thomas's Hospital.

In rather less than two years she would come of age and inherit her mother's legacy of £1,000. Canada was calling to the youth of England as a land of promise, and I am persuaded that Constance Kent conceived the idea of emigrating, and that it was to discuss this plan, and the possibility of obtaining the authorities' consent to it, that first Mary Ann and Elizabeth, and later her father and William, visited her at Dinant. What seems certain is that Constance—perhaps with this idea in her mind—confided to one of her friends at Dinant her wish to obtain hospital training, particularly in the care of infants and children, and by yet another of those curious chances which regulated her destiny, this friend offered to write on her behalf to the Reverend A. D. Wagner, Perpetual Curate of St. Paul's Church, Brighton, who a few years previously had founded a convent and hospital affiliated to his church, where he might be prepared to receive her as a boarder for training. This offer Constance accepted, and the letter—which explained who she was, her wishes, and her obvious reasons for desiring to conceal her identity by dropping her first name—was despatched some time in July 1863.

Mr. Wagner replied accepting her unconditionally under the name of Emilie Kent as a paying guest at the convent and a probationer at the hospital connected with it. None but he,

Constance's family and her friend, knew anything of this arrangement.

When a couple of weeks later Constance Kent boarded the packet-boat she would have appeared to anyone who glanced at her just another of the numerous young women who returned each year to England after finishing their education in France. Neatly dressed and rather below average height, her well-proportioned figure made her seem taller than she really was. Although she had no beauty, she possessed a clear, well-modulated voice, and that pleasing manner and graceful bearing which composes an indefinable quality called by the French *gentil*. As she gazed her last upon the coast of France, then turned her eyes towards that of England, she must have been tremulous with hope for the future and touched with sadness for what she was leaving behind.

She stepped from the train at Brighton on 10th August, 1863.

CHAPTER TWO

ARTHUR DOUGLAS WAGNER

I

ARTHUR DOUGLAS WAGNER, at this time thirty-eight years
of age, was already a pillar of the Oxford Movement and
recognized as one of Dr. Pusey's most ardent disciples. Few men
were better favoured than he for promoting a Cause which,
although it was destined to have a profound influence upon the
Established Church, was then viewed with the gravest apprehension by a majority both of the clergy themselves and of the
laity on account of the approximation of its doctrines and
practices to those of the Church of Rome. In certain places,
notably London and Birmingham, the new movement had
provoked riots, and its priests were not free from the suspicion
of having deliberately invited persecution in order to gain
publicity for their Cause. As Arthur Douglas Wagner's subsequent history shews he, too, cherished ambitions to be a
martyr, but his "moments of widest publicity were doomed to
be connected with the most shocking of crimes".[1]

His family, one of great wealth and influence, had been connected with the church in Brighton since 1744 when his great-
grandfather had become vicar of the parish church of St.
Nicholas, a living to which his father, who was what would
today be called a "low churchman", succeeded in 1824. He
himself went to Cambridge with the object of taking Holy
Orders and acting as curate-in-charge of St. Paul's Church
Brighton, which his father was then building as a chapel-of-ease
to St. Nicholas. But while at the University he came under the
influence of Newman, whose secession to the Church of Rome
seemed likely to be followed by his own: however, almost at
the eleventh hour he retracted, although Newman's influence
remained and the closest ties of sympathy and friendship continued to unite him with the Cardinal.

[1] *Murder and Murder Trials*—H. M. Walbrook.

"Destined from the first for the charge of his father's new church in West Street," writes H. Hamilton Maughan in *Wagner of Brighton*, "he was not yet in Holy Orders at the date of its opening in 1848, some difficulties having arisen with regard to his ordination. . . . The difficulties, however, were soon removed and Mr. Wagner was duly ordained in 1849."

He had reached an agreement with his father that he should be allowed a free hand at St. Paul's, and he immediately began to introduce those "Puseyite practices" which were everywhere arousing such bitter controversy. The yeasty qualities which the Oxford Movement generated, and the importance it attached to symbolism, exactly suited the temperament of Arthur Douglas Wagner, in which there was much that was mediaeval: and with a true mediaeval abandon he lavished money on the decoration and embellishment of St. Paul's, employing the most famous artists and craftsmen of the day for the purpose. Soon a rood-screen with a gigantic Rood was dividing nave from chancel; soon the Stations of the Cross appeared on the walls of the aisles; tall candles in six silver-gilt candlesticks of intricate workmanship illumined the High Altar with its triptych by Burne-Jones, glowing beneath the great east window by Pugin; magnificent altar frontals and vestments of exquisite embroidery confronted the astonished gaze of his congregation; a crucifix of pre-Reformation workmanship was carried in Processions; the atmosphere grew heavy with incense, and strange innovations of which the most controversial was Confession were introduced into the conduct of the Services. It is not hard to believe the story that Wagner's father, preaching one Sunday at St. Paul's, took as his text, "Lord, have mercy on my son: for he is lunatic and sore vexed."

But his activities did not cease with St. Paul's. He embarked upon a vast programme of church-building in Brighton upon which he is estimated to have spent "three fortunes" out of his own pocket. He built St. Mary Magdalene's, the Church of the Annunciation and St. Bartholomew's. When the tenants of the houses adjoining the last complained that its towering walls created a down-draught which caused all their chimneys to smoke, Wagner's response was characteristic: he bought up the whole of the property affected and reduced the rents to a minimum.

2

In June 1855 he founded St. Mary's Convent and installed it in three or four of the little Regency houses in Queen's Square, a quiet *cul-de-sac* a stone's throw from St. Paul's. These houses backed upon a row of neo-Gothic buildings known as Wykeham Terrace, the property of the parish church; and, connecting them by passages with the Convent, he established within them a penitentiary for girls, a lying-in hospital for "fallen women", an infirmary, a dispensary and a school. In 1857 he appointed Miss Caroline Ann Greame Superior of the whole institution, responsible to no one but himself, who remained its sole director and chaplain.

When Constance Kent entered No 2 Queen's Square on the 10th August, 1863, there were thirty penitents in Wykeham Terrace, and all the beds in the lying-in hospital were occupied.

CHAPTER THREE

ST. MARY'S CONVENT

I

HUMILITY, obedience, silence: these form the foundations of convent life.

The Superior is the Mother of the community. Her will is supreme and must be obeyed without question. Everyone bows lów when she passes by, and at interviews kneels before her. A summons to her room is dreaded, and novices emerge from it looking as though their very souls have been raked over. Each individual must humbly accept whatever she is called upon to endure—no matter what suffering it entails—as God's special ordinance for her. Each individual must obey with absolute submission the rules which govern the community from the moment of waking until she is permitted to sleep. Everything she does must be done noiselessly, composedly, with lowered eyes, and in silence.

The routine at St. Mary's did not differ in any essential from the general rule. Religious instruction and devotional exercises were constant and rigorous. The food, never plentiful and always plain, was, in seasons of fast, exiguous. The nuns and novices tended the sick and the women in travail, and taught in the school: they trained the penitents, who did all the heavy domestic work of the institution, some of whom had been rescued from the streets, while others had, for one reason or another, been brought in by relatives. Situations were found for them in private service as soon as they had proved themselves fit for such employement. Meanwhile within the convent their behaviour was regulated by a system of "marks": if they failed to earn the required number in the course of a week they were deprived of butter and sugar. For more serious offences, such as "using bad language", insubordination, or trying to escape, they were placed in solitary confinement; and if they resisted, were carried off forcibly.

2

No one would have recognized in "Nurse Emilie", who took charge of the newly-born infants with such mature tenderness, the immature school-girl who had stood charged with murder at Road; and the secret of her identity had been confided only to Mr. Wagner.

While there are certain gaps in the evidence of what occurred at St. Mary's in regard to Constance Kent, enough is known to shed a revealing light upon the events which led to the sequel.

The year 1864 came in bringing the season of Lent with its forty days of fasting and prayer, the peak of devotional intensity being reached in Holy Week with the entire community entering into Retreat in a soul-searching preparation for the Easter Communion. The atmosphere was pervaded with a feeling of religious ecstasy. The solemn hush of Good Friday gave place to the triumphant joy of Easter Day, when the whole community, purified by prayer and abstinence, cleansed by confession and absolution, left St. Mary's to kneel before the High Altar at St. Paul's and receive the Elements from the hands of Mr. Wagner—all, that is, except Constance Kent, who, lying under the ban of murder, had never been confirmed.

And presently, with sickness of heart, she grew aware of covert glances; a chill crept in wherever she was; the silence in which she had once had part now shut her out. In that cloistered community, the rules of which held each individual in a relentless grip, excluding the colour and movement of life and every normal human contact, the dark cloud of her identity pressed down upon her more mercilessly, more humiliatingly than ever before.

We have learned since those days that through humiliation the worst suffering can be inflicted upon the human spirit: it can swamp the being in an all-consuming sense of iniquity and shame—it can do more: it can break the heart.

The basic principle of the Christian life is that one is not made or unmade by the circumstances which befall one, but by one's reactions to those circumstances. The Christian must open his heart to the Spirit in preparation for whatever labour, whatever sacrifice may be demanded of him: if he is confronted with two alternatives, he must not shrink from choosing the more painful—remembering the promise: *"I can do all things in Him who strengtheneth me."*

As the days grew into weeks, the weeks into months, prayer became Constance Kent's sole refuge and defence.

Her twenty-first birthday, coinciding with the beginning of another season of Lent, brought the legacy which might have saved her had it come twelve months before. Now the will to create an independent life for herself had perished. She drew £800 and begged Mr. Wagner to accept it for the charities connected with St. Mary's. He refused. Thrown back upon herself even in this, each time she went to pray at St. Paul's she took a handful of the crisp Bank of England notes and thrust them into one of the alms-boxes. Suspecting whence they came Mr. Wagner set a watch upon her, and each time after she had left the church her offering was removed and set aside until the whole £800 had been collected.[1]

On Wednesday in Holy Week she approached Mr. Wagner "on the subject of her confirmation". There can be hardly any doubt that he rejected her as a candidate, and in the state she was now in she could only see herself as the despised and rejected of mankind, eternally lost to God.

That same day—the Wednesday in Holy Week—she was summoned to that dreaded ordeal, an interview with the Superior.

This woman's personality dominated the whole institution in which she was regarded with awe. To the girl kneeling before her, whose powers of resistance were at their lowest ebb, she spoke on the subject of sin: of "the sin which could aggravate a sin in God's sight".

On the next day and the one that followed—which was Good Friday: the day of the Crucifixion; the climax of the long Lenten fast—Constance Kent was twice sent for to the Superior's room and leading questions were put to her on the manner in which the crime was committed. A leading question is not a

[1] Mr. Wagner handed it over to Mr. Rodway at a later date.

probing question: it is one framed to indicate, even induce, the reply which the questioner desires.

In the predicament in which Constance Kent now found herself two alternatives were open to her: to declare who was guilty, or to take the guilt upon herself. It is my belief that she chose the more painful one in the spirit of pure self-immolation.

His Easter duties over Mr. Wagner, having sought and obtained an interview with the Home Secretary, Sir George Grey, travelled up to London and placed in his hands the following letter:

"To Sir George Grey.
"Sir,

"It is by my own particular request that the bearer now informs you of my guilt, which it is my desire to have publicly made known.

"Yours truly,
"Constance Emilie Kent"

And what were Mr. Wagner's duties, both as a priest and as a man, towards this girl whom he had accepted in full knowledge of her history as a member of his institution, and whose secret he had nevertheless divulged? If she had made a confession of guilt to him as a priest—as a Confessor who heard confessions regularly—then by the very articles of his own faith concerning the sanctity of the Confessional he was precluded from being the instrument of bringing her to justice or of bearing witness against her. His lips were, or should have been, sealed.

But if, on the other hand, she had confessed to him in his secular capacity his responsibility was equally clear: instead of immediately hastening to make public the tidings of her guilt, it was his plain duty to insist that she should inform her father and family of her intention and earnestly entreat her to seek legal advice and aid.

As it was, almost before the ink was dry upon her letter, he was speeding to act upon the authority it gave him to inform the Home Secretary that she had confessed her guilt to him. And not until a fortnight later did her father learn of what had occurred, and then through the medium of the public Press, when the step his daughter had taken was irrevocable.

CHAPTER FOUR

BOW STREET POLICE COURT: 25TH APRIL

I

OF THE several theories which were advanced at the time to account for Constance Kent's action one was that she had come, through a process of auto-suggestion, to believe herself actually guilty of the crime. But her studied calm, which only once deserted her, the determined and clear-sighted manner in which she held to her course down to the end, all go to shew that she was putting into execution a carefully thought-out plan and was prepared for every likely contingency.

Two weeks after Mr. Wagner had seen Sir George Grey, in the early afternoon of Tuesday, 25th April, she travelled to London "to give herself up to justice". The Superior went at her side: in another compartment of the train sat Mr. Wagner.

The secret of her intention had been so carefully kept that the train was well on its way before Sir Thomas Henry, the Chief Magistrate at Bow Street, was advised while sitting in court of her impending arrival. It had almost reached its destination before Inspector Williamson[1] and Sergeant Durkin received instructions at Scotland Yard to take her in charge. They had not even arrived at Bow Street when Mr. Wagner, the Superior and herself stepped from a cab and were shewn straight into the Chief Magistrate's private office where he received them.

Constance "went forward and handed him a document saying in a low voice that she had come to give herself up".

As they seated themselves—Constance and the Superior side by side; Mr. Wagner somewhat apart—Sir Thomas submitted each to a swift, practised scrutiny: the girl sitting very still with folded hands and lowered eyes, her black dress and hat severely plain, her face behind her veil, in spite of its composure, wan and sad; the nun, her down-drawn countenance shuttered and bleak; and finally the clergyman—his shaven

[1] Formerly Sergeant Williamson, and Whicher's assistant in 1860.

face fleshy and his body already thickening with that obesity which was presently to overwhelm it; his mouth loose-lipped and disproportionately small for the heavy jowl; his eyes narrow and myopic, and set too closely to the well-cut aquiline nose; his hands carefully tended, soft and white.

The thick, stiff paper crackled as Sir Thomas spread out the document before him. To read the fifty-four words it contained, written in a large, clear hand, was the work of a moment, but he studied them carefully before he asked:

"Am I to understand, Miss Kent, that you have given yourself up of your own free act and will on this charge?"

In a "low, sad voice" she replied:

"Yes, sir."

She had not raised her eyes. He regarded her steadily, then studied the document over again.

"I, Constance Emilie Kent," it said *"alone and unaided, on the night of the 29th June 1860, murdered at Road Hill House, Wiltshire, one Francis Savile Kent. Before the deed was done no one knew of my intention, nor afterwards of my guilt. No one assisted me in the crime, nor in the evasion of discovery."*

This astonishing composition, so concise and lucid, and answering with such remarkable foresight any questions which might arise concerning accessories both before and after the fact, was now being tendered as the unaided confession of a girl of twenty-one proclaiming herself guilty of a terrible crime.

"Is this paper now produced before me," asked Sir Thomas, "in your own handwriting and written of your own free will?"

"It is, sir."

After a moment's pause he handed it to the clerk, saying:

"Then let the charge be entered in her own words."

A round-faced clock on the wall ticked stridently; the clerk's quill scratched; the door opened gently and Inspector Williamson and Sergeant Durkin entered and stood beside it.

The clerk's quill ceased scratching, and Sir Thomas held out his hand for the document.

"Have you any objection to sign that statement?" he asked. As Constance hesitated, as though unprepared for the question, he added gravely: "I must remind you that it is the most serious crime that can be committed, and your statement will be used against you at your trial. I have had the words written copied upon the charge-sheet, but I do not wish you to sign it unless you desire to do so."

"I will do so if necessary."

"It is not absolutely necessary. There is no occasion for you to sign the charge-sheet unless you wish it. I will have your statement attached to the deposition." Then, regarding her steadily, he solemnly urged her: "I will again ask you if you have máde it by your own desire and without any inducement —from any quarter whatsoever—to give yourself up?"

"Yes, sir."

With his eyes still upon her, Sir Thomas signed to the clerk, who handed the Bible to Mr. Wagner. The priest took the oath. His voice was thin and high.

"I am a Clerk in Holy Orders," he stated, "and perpetual curate of St. Paul's Church, Brighton, which is a chapel-of-ease to the Parish Church. I have known Constance Kent nearly two years—since the summer of 1863."

"In August," Constance interjected quietly.

"About twenty-one months?" queried Sir Thomas.

"Yes. As far as I can remember an English family wrote to me asking for her admission to St. Mary's Home, or Hospital, in consequence of her having no home, or of some difficulty respecting her. This Home, or rather Hospital, as it is now called, is a Home for religious ladies, and is attached to St. Paul's Church. She came about that time as a visitor, and has been there up to the present day."

"Now, Mr. Wagner, it is my duty to ask you if any inducement has been made to the prisoner in any way to make this statement?"

"None whatever hàs been made by me," he declared. "The confession is entirely her own voluntary act to the best of my belief. It was about a fortnight ago—as far as I can recollect— that the circumstances first came to my knowledge. It was entirely her own proposition that she should be taken before a

London magistrate. She herself proposed to come to London for the purpose. The nature of the confession she made to me was the same, in substance, as the statement in her writing, and copied upon the charge-sheet."[1] Sir Thomas read it aloud. "Yes, it is the same."

"She made this statement to you?"

"Yes, she did." He began to explain that in using the word "confession" he was not referring to Sacramental Confession, but to an open, public confession; but Sir Thomas cut him short.

"I will not go into that point here," he said. "It may be gone into at the trial—perhaps very fully." Then, turning once more to Constance he again solemnly reminded her, "I hope you understand that whatever you say must be entirely your own free and voluntary statement, and that no inducement that may have been held out to you is to have any effect upon your mind?"

"No inducement ever has, sir."

"I am anxious," he insisted, "that you should most seriously consider that."

"I wish to mention," said Mr. Wagner suddenly, "that many are in the habit of coming to confess to me as a religious exercise, but I have never held out any inducement to her to make a public confession."

"Did you in the first instance induce her to make a confession to you?"

"No, sir. I did not seek her out, or in any way ask her to come to confession. She herself wished to do so."

"If you think that the confession she now makes has been induced in consequence of anything which she said to you—or which you said to her—you ought to say so."

"I have never recommended it," declared the priest. "I have simply been passive. I thought she was doing right, and I did not dissuade her."

"But do you say that you did not *persuade* her?"

---

[1] In a letter to *The Times* a few weeks later Mr. Wagner was to state that he had no knowledge of the document, and the first time he became aware of its existence was when Constance handed it to Sir Thomas. Yet, *before Sir Thomas has read it aloud to him*, he is declaring that its nature is the same, in substance, as the confession made to him. How does he know this?

"I do say so. She thought of it herself without my ever suggesting it."

"That must be added to Mr. Wagner's deposition," Sir Thomas told the clerk, and holding up the document he said to Constance: "This is the paper you wish handed in as your statement, is it?"

"Yes, sir."

He laid it down; then, leaning a little forward, his eyes searching her tense face, he made one final effort on her behalf.

"It is not too late even now," he said with deep and solemn earnestness. "I wish to tell you once more that this is a very serious charge and that whatever you write, or say, may be used against you." He paused expectantly, then assured her, "You are not bound to make any statement unless you desire to do so."

She sat rigid, uttering no word and making no sign. The clock ticked on—the only sound in a silence which lay with the weight of water upon the room. At last Sir Thomas signalled to the clerk to proceed with the usual formalities.

The clerk asked Constance if the document was in her own handwriting. Her dry lips framed a barely audible assent. Sir Thomas asked Wagner if he could confirm that statement. For some reason the question seemed to disconcert him, and his reply had a note of testiness.

"I could not possibly tell. I have never seen her write. But I have no doubt the document was written by her."

The clerk read out the charge. In reply to Sir Thomas' question as to whether she had anything to add, she murmured an almost inaudible:

"No, sir."

"The offence was committed in Wiltshire, and the trial must be in that county. It will therefore be necessary to send her to be examined before the magistrates of that county."

She was delivered over for Justice to take its course.

2

The last rays of a golden April sunset were touching the smoke-grimed buildings of London to a rare beauty and burnishing the breasts of the pigeons which whirred up from under the very hooves of the horses and the wheels of the vehicles they drew in the unending stream of traffic through which a closed carriage threaded its way from Bow Street to Paddington Station. Constance Kent, with the Superior at her side and the two police officers opposite, never once lifted her eyes.

All through the long hours of the night in the swaying train, jerking to hissing stops at dim, lamp-lit stations and whistling shrilly as it gathered speed to leave them behind, the two women, with the two officers facing them, never exchanged a word and scarcely altered their positions. In just such an attitude had Constance sat all through the night on the hard bench at Bath Police Station after she had begged that William should be allowed to sleep in comfort: with just such benumbed control had she listened to the proceedings against her at Road and heard their collapse. On her way back after five years to plead guilty to that charge, did Mr. Edlin's prophetic words echo in her ears?

"If this murder be never discovered, it will never be forgotten that this young lady was dragged like a common felon to Devizes Gaol. . . . The step you have taken will be such as to ruin her life. . . . Every hope is gone with regard to this young girl. If she be innocent, as I believe, it is really terrible to contemplate the result for her."

The result was more terrible than any that day had contemplated.

Each time she had travelled over those rails—returning from her father's wedding with Mary Pratt; returning from her school in Hertfordshire after the tidings of Edward's death; and now—she had been destined for pain and suffering. But now the ordeal was to be more terrible, the anguish more profound than any she had been called on to endure.

In the chill of early morning they left the train at Chippenham and entered a waiting post-chaise. For fifteen miles they drove through peaceful country lanes, dew-drenched and flower-scented, to Trowbridge.

When the formalities at the police station were over, and the Superior's request to be allowed to stay with her had been refused, Constance Kent turned away and followed the Superintendent's wife from the room in a trance of exhaustion.

CHAPTER FIVE

TROWBRIDGE POLICE COURT: 26TH APRIL[1]

I

WHEN Society is shocked by an event its first immediate reaction is incredulity: but once the fact is established the initial incredulity with which it was received sharpens the perceptions and gives a keener edge to criticism.

The public in those days was identified with the middle-class: serious, clear-thinking and capable of forming its own opinions which were voiced through the medium of a Press that, metropolitan or provincial, adequately reflected these qualities.

In 1860 both Press and public had broadly divined the truth concerning the crime at Road: but the authorities had chosen rather to "hush the cry for justice which had reached its ears" than allow an ugly scandal to develop. Still mindful of the volume and vehemence of that cry, the authorities, when in 1865 they were confronted with Constance Kent's "confession", determined to take every precaution to prevent a repetition of it. But the suddenness with which the news came, the soil in which the "confession" had germinated, and its whole character, instantly provoked a second outcry, the original cause of which was presently swamped "in another and entirely different wave of popular passion, half political and half religious".[2]

Before Constance Kent had reached Chippenham great bales of newspapers containing detailed accounts of the proceedings at Bow Street—coupled with the erroneous information that she had been sent to Salisbury—had been loaded on to trains setting out for every part of the kingdom. While the post-chaise was carrying her along the winding lanes of Wiltshire, running newsboys were crying her name in the London streets.

[1] The quotations in this chapter, unless otherwise stated, are from the local Press.
[2] *Murder and Murder Trials*—H. M. Walbrook.

The news exploded like a bomb in Trowbridge. Before the London newspapers arrived it had passed from lip to lip with magic speed that she was in their midst and would appear before the magistrates that afternoon. When the papers came people craned over each other's shoulders and read with amazement the reports, most of which cast doubts on the spontaneity of Constance's document and hinted that it was the product of sinister influences. While the reporters, who had been on a wild-goose chase to Salisbury, were scurrying on to Trowbridge, and Mr. Wagner, better informed, was arriving by the mid-day train, every approach to the court was being blocked by excited throngs.

"Every precaution was taken by the police to keep order, but children screamed, women and strong men fought their way in, and in ten minutes every inch of standing and sitting room was occupied, while hundreds of people were unable to gain admittance. . . . Constance Kent, attired in black and closely veiled, walked into the court from the private rooms of the police station, attended by Miss Green (*sic*). . . . All eyes were turned in pity towards her. Her conduct in the dock was at first marked by great composure, though, as will be seen below, her feelings afterwards overcame all control. The past five years had wrought a considerable change in her appearance, she being taller, and more robust and womanly, than when she was previously in this neighbourhood. Miss Green, who had a most abject expression of countenance, was allowed to occupy a seat at the side of the prisoner."

When Constance Kent had entered this court five years ago, Elizabeth Gough had stood in the dock where she was standing now; the majority of those who crowded it now had crowded it then, and had cheered Mr. T. W. Saunders when he had interrupted his speech for the Crown to proclaim his faith in her innocence. They had taken every means of shewing their confidence in that innocence, and their belief in her father's guilt.

And now she had repudiated their faith in her: now she

stood before them self-accused of all the hideous violence and indecency done to her little brother.

Sunk in dark sockets by strain and fatigue her eyes stared into emptiness with an anguish so profound as to wring all hearts, and stifled sobs were heard. She got up with the movements of a blind person and stood inertly when Mr. Ludlow, the Chairman of the Bench, addressed her. She was numbed, as prisoners sometimes mercifully are by all they have endured. But when in the intense silence which had descended upon the court, the clerk read the first words of her written confession— *"I, Constance Emilie Kent, alone and unaided . . ."*—she shuddered as though they pierced through her daze like the pain of returning circulation in a frozen body; and at the words *"on the night of the 29th June* 1860 *murdered . . ."* she dropped upon her knees in a paroxysm of weeping as though mortal body and immortal soul could endure no more.

A great gasp went up; the clerk's voice ceased; the nun, weeping too, knelt beside her; "the Bench and spectators gazed at them in painful suspense and many were overcome with emotion". Amidst sounds of weeping "from all parts of the court" Constance dragged herself to her feet, dried her eyes and made an immense effort to control the convulsive sobs which shook her. A glass of water was offered her, but she refused it, and with hands gripped together stood still, staring at the floor.

Inspector Williamson gave evidence of her arrest. When Mr. Ludlow asked her whether she had any questions to put to the witness she answered in a steady voice, "No, sir." But when he asked her if she knew any reason why the magistrates should not remand her she merely shook her head.

"You will be remanded until tomorrow week, when you will again be brought up in this court at eleven o'clock in the morning."

In a tense, dramatic silence she left the dock "with unfaltering step".

The time was two o'clock.

2

About the time when Mr. Wagner was alighting from his train to attend the court that day, Mr. Kent was leaving his home at Rhydycilgwyn-isa-Llanymys, near Llanhaiadr in Denbighshire, where he had been living in seclusion since 1861, to go to Oswestry on business; he was talking to an acquaintance in the town while Constance was on her knees in the dock at Trowbridge; when she was leaving it, at two o'clock, the London train was steaming into Oswestry Station, and Mr. Kent, promising to return later, broke off his conversation to go and meet it, and buy a copy of that morning's paper.

Standing on the platform he opened it and thus "first became acquainted that his daughter had given herself up upon her own confession of guilt for the murder at Road-hill House. Temporarily paralysed his first impulse seemed to be to hide himself from human observation, and rushing up the main street he entered the Wynnstay Arms Hotel where he ordered a carriage in which he immediately started for home."

3

"In the name of all human justice," the *Standard* cried, "we must protest against any prejudiced opinion being arrived at in the case of Miss Constance Emilie Kent. This young girl has delivered herself up as the perpetrator of that terrible and mysterious Road-hill House murder which five years ago shocked all society. We have her own confession, but it came on Tuesday in a strange form before the magistrate at Bow Street. . . ."

After quoting it the article continued:

"It will be a very remarkable thing if this proves to have been the undictated language of a deliberate and independent young murderess. There is an attorney's stamp about it. At all events it bears the impress of a too zealous persuasion."

Later on the same paper added:

"Her professed confession, brief though it be, is drawn up in the form and language of an affidavit. It could not have been written undictated by herself. It is a specimen of clear and accurate composition, and all the circumstances connected with it must be searchingly investigated before we can judge Constance Emilie Kent to have been the murderess of her infant brother. . . . We attach no judicial importance to her confession drawn up at St. Mary's Home, a religious house attached to St. Paul's church, at Brighton, and we think it would have been far wiser and better, and more legal, had a private gentleman not escorted the young girl from Brighton to Bow Street, in order that she might confess herself a murderess. . . . For our own part, instead of regarding the Road-hill House murder mystery as solved, it appears to thicken. But distinct as our own sympathies must be from any man, woman or child who slew the helpless innocent at Road-hill House, it is the duty of public opinion not to consider anyone guilty who was then a child, and who is now only a young girl, and who by a mistake of law might become the victim of a second murder worse than the first."

The *London Review* said:

"No one who knows anything of women, or the way in which women write, will ever believe that the document handed to Sir Thomas Henry was the spontaneous and unaided composition of a girl of twenty-one. Nothing more comprehensive, terse and exact in language could have been drawn up by the best criminal pleader at the Bar. A confession springing directly from her own heart and shaping itself in her own words would have been at once more vague and more detailed. There are in the language of this document palpable indications of a foreign hand and a strange influence: of a hand and influence, too, upon which we look with the utmost distaste and jealousy when we see them touching the conscience of a woman. . . ."

The article went on to suggest that Mr. Wagner and his "Sisters of Mercy" might have induced the confession through a process of "filtration" and concluded with the following hypothesis: "Seclusion in a religious house may have inclined the delusion that the horrid crime, the memory of which must have been constantly present with her, was committed by herself."

The *Express* observed:

"The law does not favour the indiscriminate reception of confessions; and out of the atmosphere of religious houses girls of the age of Constance Kent have been known to accuse themselves wrongfully of terrible crimes. As a rule the public would sooner see a prisoner attended to Court by her legal than her spiritual adviser, the director of her conscience, and this is a wholesome jealousy."

4

While everywhere the case of Constance Kent was being debated; while hostile crowds—who were soon to adopt more violent means of expressing their feelings—gathered daily outside St. Paul's Church and St. Mary's Convent to scowl and mutter at all who entered and departed, the prisoner in her cell at Devizes Gaol was displaying the same calm and gentle fortitude which five years before had won the admiration and respect of those in whose charge she was. Yet, though shewing gratitude for the privileges accorded her—a bed, special food, and even the use of an adjoining cell furnished with writing materials, a table and two chairs—she nevertheless appeared as indifferent to her fate as she did to the long hours of solitude, or to the presence of the warder on guard day and night outside her cell, who could peer at her whenever he chose to do so through the grille.

H*

She had informed the governor of the gaol that she intended to plead guilty and required no legal aid; and when, presumably on instructions from her family, Mr. Rodway obtained permission to visit her "in order to offer his professional services and to prepare a defence" she refused to see him, although later she was "induced to do so". When he pointed out the seriousness of her case "she appeared to manifest the greatest indifference to her position, and again declined the professional assistance offered her".

On Monday, 1st May, without previous notification, the door of Constance's cell was thrown open and her father entered alone. No one was present during the interview which took place between them: only their meeting and parting were witnessed. She "rose to her feet, staring wordlessly at him" and holding to the edge of the table at which she had been writing. As he advanced towards her "she swayed as though she would fall and he caught her in his arms". When the door was opened for him to take his departure, it was apparent that "the interview had been of the most painful character" and "both were in a state of great emotion". As Mr. Kent was on the point of leaving, Constance, who had been "walking up and down and weeping", flung her arms about his neck and cried in a voice of anguish the only words she ever uttered in explanation of her action:

"My course is due to you and God."

Her father's visit had one practical result: she consented to accept Mr. Rodway's services, although neither that nor anything else could shake her determination to plead guilty.

CHAPTER SIX

TROWBRIDGE POLICE COURT:
THURSDAY, 3RD MAY

I

TO THE London journalists who were seeing Constance Kent for the first time, standing in the dock that day in her commonplace black dress and unbecoming hat, she looked both dull and plain: but the local reporters, like the public in that crowded court, knew her more intimately, for her personality had impressed itself upon them five years before, and they regarded her now with grief and pity.

Surely no drama, so strange and passionate, and so far-reaching in its consequences, has ever, before or since, been played out in any provincial court? For on that day and in that court another issue was in the balance besides the fate of Constance Kent: and on that day both were decided.

2

The presence of almost all of those who had played prominent parts in the proceedings of 1860 touched the atmosphere of tension which prevailed in the court with a fantastic sense that the intervening years were an illusion. Once more Constance Kent's black-clad figure held the centre of the stage; once more Mr. Ludlow presided over the Bench, and once more Dr. Stapleton joined those sitting behind it; once more Mr. Dunn was representing Mr. Kent, who "although on the premises" was once more conspicuous by his absence; once more Captain Meredith took his place: only one familiar face was missing—death had overtaken Superintendent Foley.

The uncanny sensation heightened as one familiar figure after another trooped in and out of the witness-box—Chief Inspector Whicher, Elizabeth Gough, Thomas Benger, Mrs. Holley, Sarah Cox (now Sarah Rogers), Dr. Parsons. . . . Their evidence varied in no relevant detail except in the case of Dr. Parsons, who, as he had done before, altered his testimony to suit the charge in progress.

Now he informed the Court, "In my opinion the incision in the throat was the immediate cause of death, but the appearance of the place where the body was found was such as to induce me to suppose that the throat was not cut there, or that the circulation of the child was in a great degree stopped by suffocation before that was done." But when Elizabeth Gough had been charged he had said: "*My opinion is that the cut in the throat was made after pulsation had ceased. . . . Considerable violence must have been used in suffocating the child; . . . the tongue protruded between the lips; the lips were of a very dark colour and livid. . . . My opinion is that the child was first suffocated by pressure on the mouth, and after that the throat was cut.*"

On the subject of Constance's night-dress he *now* stated: "I accompanied the late Superintendent Foley in his search of the house. . . . I examined, among other things, the night-dress of the prisoner; I made a remark to Mr. Foley that it was extremely clean. I cannot judge how long it had been worn; the starch in the frills and wrist-bands was not gone so much as it would have been if worn from Saturday or Monday. . . . I examined other night-dresses besides that of Constance Kent in the company of Mr. Foley, and I was struck by the difference in appearance of the prisoner's to those of the other night-dresses—it had less the appearance of being worn." But in the charge against her in 1860 he had said: "*I could not say whether the night-dress had on it the dirt resulting from a week's wear or not; there was nothing on it that particularly attracted my attention; I could not say if it was cleaner than the others I had seen; in my judgment it might have been worn a week, or nearly so, by a young lady sleeping alone.*"

It is not surprising that, in answer to a question from Mr. Rodway, he admitted:

"I have not the notes of my previous evidence."

Sergeant Watts then gave evidence concerning the finding of the blood-stained night-shift in the boiler-stove, but if the public hoped for any further details which might help to elucidate that mystery they were doomed to disappointment.

Then Chief Inspector Whicher entered the witness-box. With the air of a man whom time has vindicated he described the part he had taken in the investigations five years before. He was clearly convinced that the prisoner's lost night-dress and the garment discovered by Sergeant Watts were one and the same, and that in which the crime had been committed; and he ended by reminding the court that he had never been informed of its discovery. "The first I heard of it," he said, "was three months afterwards, when Mr. Saunders brought it to light. I then wrote to Mr. Ludlow telling him it was the first I had heard of it."

Mr. Ludlow: "I may say that the magistrates never heard of it at the time."

And so the two garments were accepted as identical: which the very description of them, and all the facts regarding them, rendered impossible, and which Constance Kent herself was to deny at a later date.

"Caroline Anne Greame!"

Until now the excitement had been subdued, but as the Superior took the oath, with a sound as of a wave running out over shingle all craned forward lest they missed a word she said.

She was an exceedingly bad witness. Disingenuous and piously evasive, she seemed constitutionally incapable of facing a fact or calling a spade a spade. Only a few weeks later, at Brighton, in a case against a former penitent of St. Mary's, an exasperated Counsel was driven to exclaim, "I wish to shew the Bench that but little reliance can be placed on what Miss Greame says."

Her first words were a plea that no questions should be put to her which would tend to damage the relationship of mother and daughter which existed between the prisoner and herself.

The Chairman: "The proper questions in a Court of Justice must be put to you and no more."

She then submitted to interrogation by the Clerk of the Court and informed him that the prisoner had entered St. Mary's Home on 10th August, 1863.

"Had you known her previous to then?"

"No."

"Did she come in her own name?"

"In the name of Emilie Kent."

"Had she said at any time anything to you about the Road murder?"

"I spoke to her first about it on the Wednesday in Holy Week."

"Did you say anything to induce her to make a confession to you?"

"No. I had known previously that she had spoken of it."

"Did you say anything to her?"

"I said to her that I knew of it."

"Did you say anything to induce her to tell you?"

"No."

"On the Wednesday in Holy Week you said nothing to induce her to speak about this?"

"No."

"You are quite certain that you have never said anything to induce her to confess to you?"

"Quite certain."

"What did she do then? What was the conversation when it first turned to the question of the Road murder? What did you say?"

"I cannot remember what I said—nothing to do with the murder at that time."

"What did you say?" prompted the Chairman.

"I said, 'I know about it.' I asked her if she fully realized what it involved. I said, 'I know of it.'"

"That was before she gave herself up?"

"Yes. I think I said I was sorry for it."

"By *it* you referred to the Road murder?"

"I referred to the wish to give herself up."

"Give us the exact words."

"The rest was entirely on religious subjects. I did not refer in any way, as far as I can recollect, to the act."

The Chairman intervened.

"You used the words: 'I know of it'?"

"I sent for her having been told of it. I sent for her to my room."

"You said, 'I know of it'?" the Chairman repeated.

"I cannot remember the exact words. I understood that I stated to her that I had been told of it."

"What reply did she make?"

"She said, 'Yes, she fully realized it'."

A brief consultation took place between the magistrates, and the Chairman asked:

"The magistrates understood you to say when you used these words that she—the prisoner—had said nothing to you previously to that?"

"I do not think she had."

"You had derived your information from other sources?"

"Yes."

"From whom?"

"I think I most likely said that I had heard it from Mr. Wagner—that he had told me of it. She understood."

"Were those her only words—'she fully realized it'?"

"Yes. The other conversation was religious."

"When was the next conversation on the subject?"

"The same week, I think—I cannot remember exactly. Then she spoke more fully about it."

"Tell me her exact words," the Chairman requested.

At the beginning of her examination glances had sped back and forth from the bleak face of the nun to the withdrawn one of the prisoner. But as excitement, mingled with impatience, mounted every eye became fastened upon her only, in sharp concentration; and the trifling pause she made before replying to Mr. Ludlow's last question became a moment of climax into which a feeling of hostility had crept.

"I had her up to speak to her on religious subjects. Something in the conversation made her tell me that she had carried the child downstairs; that she left the house by the drawing-room window, and that she had used a razor for the purpose."

Incredulous gasps went up. Voices cried: "No!" "Impossible!" Eyes swept over to the prisoner; she closed her own as though her senses reeled; Miss Greame's lips moved as though she were praying.

"Order! Order!"

The Chairman then asked the witness what took place next.

"I can't recollect anything else. She said nothing else about the actual deed."

"Did she say where she got the razor from?"

"From her father's dressing-case."

"Did she say anything else?"

"She spoke of the night-dress that was lost. I think she said that she had taken it out of the basket again. I don't think she told me anything else. I do not recollect."

"Did any other conversation take place?"

"Not that day, but since then I have not spoken to her of it."

"Did she assign any motive?"

"I think she said it was not dislike of the child."

"What, then?"

"But that it was revenge on the step-mother."

The tension had been steadily mounting, and this statement produced another sensation and more cries of disbelief.

"When did she say this?"

"The third time, when she told me the other. I am not quite so sure that she said it was not dislike of the child."

"You are quite sure that she said that about the step-mother?"

She hesitated, then characteristically hedged.

"My impression is that she said so. At all events words to that effect."

"Did she say anything more about the night-dress?"

"I think not. I had no other conversation about that."

A consultation then ensued between the magistrates and the Clerk of the Court; then the Chairman asked:

"In your examination you referred to '*something* in your conversation' which you had with her—what was that 'something'?"

"I think I said to her that Mr. Wagner had told me of it. I never used the word 'murder'."

The Clerk of the Court read out the relevant sentences— " 'Something in the conversation led her to tell me that she had carried the child downstairs.' "

"What was that 'something'?" asked the Chairman again.

"I cannot remember exactly what I said, but I think I said to her, '*Did the child cry to you for mercy?*' I think I said something of that sort."

Again there were exclamations and murmurs in the body of the court, necessitating another demand for order.

"What else?"

"She said it was asleep, and that she carried it downstairs asleep."

This reply provoked further expressions of disbelief.

"Did she say what she did with the razor?"

"No, she did not."

Again the Chairman intervened.

"I wish you would refresh your memory with respect to the point that 'she said *something*'. Will you try to remember the exact words that passed between you—that took place previous to the conversation?"

"There was nothing but religious conversation before that conversation."

"You said, '*Did the child cry?*'—did you say anything before that?"

"Yes, I tried to point out how a sin would be aggravated in God's sight."

"You were speaking of the murder?"

"Yes."

"Was that the third time you spoke of it?"

"Yes—in the way I mentioned."

"What words did you use?"

"I pointed out the sin that would aggravate a sin in God's sight."

"You say, 'I was pointing out the sin that would aggravate the matter'—what did you refer to?"

"I said '*aggravate the sin in God's sight*'. I did not mention the sin. I never mentioned the murder to her—she knew very well what I meant without my doing so."

Once more the magistrates whispered together, then the Chairman made a further effort to extract a plain answer out of the witness.

"We do not wish to press you unduly, but I am bound to

P

take the depositions in such a way that the judge can understand them. What does the word *sin* refer to? I have no antecedent."

"The murder."

"You are sure it was the murder?"

"Yes. I did not use the word *murder*, but the word *sin*. I said to her, as far as I can recollect, 'All sins are aggravated by circumstances in God's sight.' Then I asked the questions I have referred to."

The Clerk (quoting): " '*The sin I referred to was murder*'— is that correct?"

"Yes."

The Chairman: "At that time was there any other conversation? Have you stated all the conversation relative to the murder that took place?"

"I think there was no other conversation."

"Did the prisoner express any wish relative to the confession being made public?"

"I don't think she did. I think she said the first day that it was her wish to give herself up when I spoke to her about 'realizing'."

"Are you quite certain that, after the conversation you have given us, you never offered her any inducement to confess—to give herself up?"

"Never, never!"

The black-habited figure left the witness-box.

"*Arthur Douglas Wagner!*"

"It is difficult," writes John Rhode,[1] "to avoid the impression that Mr. Wagner, at least, was deliberately inviting persecution by his attitude in the witness-box at Trowbridge, rather in the spirit of an early Christian martyr."

Having taken the oath in what the *Journal* described as "a whining voice", he indicated a piece of paper which he held in one hand and thus addressed the court:

"Before I am examined I must ask that the Court will permit me to read a brief statement which I have committed to writing, and which I consider it essential I should read."

[1] *The Case of Constance Kent*—John Rhode.

The Chairman: "We had better have nothing until you have given your evidence."

The Clerk of the Court then read the deposition which Mr. Wagner had made before Sir Thomas Henry, asked if it were correct that the prisoner had confessed to the murder and that he had not influenced her to give herself up. Witness replied that this was true and in the course of the ensuing examination made the following statements:

"I have known the prisoner about twenty-one months; she came in the name of Emilie Kent; I was told that her name was Constance, but that it had been changed so that she should not be known; all the communications which have been made to me by Miss Constance Emilie Kent during the last seventeen or eighteen months have been made to me under the seal of confession, and therefore, she having made that confession under the seal of confession, I shall decline to divulge anything which may have passed between us which shall incriminate her."

A storm of protest broke out which it took some moments to quell; then the witness continued:

"I am quite willing to say when she authorized me to speak to the Secretary of State for the Home Department, but I must decline answering any questions which will be a breach of the secrecy of the confessional."

The air had become electric: Mr. Wagner had "suddenly become a more prominent figure in the public eye even than the young woman in the dock[1]."

The Chairman: "You must answer the questions that are put to you. You have sworn to tell the truth before God: upon the responsibility of that oath you have to answer."

"My duty to God forbids me to answer any question which shall in any way divulge anything that has been said to me in the secrecy of the confessional."

There was another outbreak of disorder accompanied by hoots and hisses, while fists were shaken in the direction of the witness-box. The prisoner closed her eyes, as though summoning all her powers of endurance, and the magistrates sternly threatened to clear the court. Plainly Mr. Wagner was trying to force the issue as to whether or not a priest is privileged to

[1] *Murder and Murder Trials*—H. M. Walbrook.

withhold evidence imparted to him in the confessional. The magistrates held a hurried consultation: they were not sure of their ground: the point had hardly arisen since the Reformation:[1] there was no judicial ruling. Mr. Ludlow's next question shewed that they had decided not to be drawn.

"When did the prisoner authorize you to speak to Sir George Grey?"

"She first authorized me to speak to Sir George Grey about three or four weeks ago—that is, on the subject under discussion."

"Had you said anything to her to induce her to do so?"

"I had not."

"Did you say anything else at the time?"

"I do not recollect."

"Who spoke about it first?"

"She did."

"What led her to telling you?"

"I cannot answer that question."

"What was the antecedent conversation?"

"I cannot tell you that without a breach of confession."

"Did she give you any reason?"

"She spoke to me first. It was her own voluntary act. I did not ask her."

"Without any inducement she spoke to you first?"

"She did."

It was over.

When the Chairman addressed the prisoner she stood up automatically. The charge was read out to her and she was asked if she had anything to say. She merely shook her head. She was committed to take her trial at the next Assizes to be held at Salisbury, and she left the dock with the set composure which she had maintained throughout.

[1] See Appendix III.

CHAPTER SEVEN

REPERCUSSIONS

I

Two quotations from the London Press will suffice to shew the general nature of the reaction to the proceedings at Trowbridge. The *Pall Mall Gazette* said:

"Miss Greame at Trowbridge stated that she had sent for Miss Kent to her room on Wednesday in Holy Week, and held a religious conversation with her, in which she got the whole story. Miss Greame also asked Miss Kent if she fully realized what it—that is, the private confession—involved, and was told by Miss Kent that she did. What did it involve, if not a public confession? This certainly looks like putting pressure upon the girl which could only lead to one result. What life was possible for Miss Kent after Mr. Wagner had begun to tell the inmates of the house that one of their number was a murderer? It seems clear from the evidence given at Trowbridge that both Mr. Wagner and Miss Greame, while careful to avoid laying any injunction on Miss Kent, were all the while forcing her into a police court; and much value cannot be attached to public confessions obtained by such means."

The *Daily News* said:

"If instead of alleging a right or a system Mr. Wagner had pleaded the confidence which Constance Kent had placed in him as a friend as a reason for not bearing witness against her, he would have placed himself on strong grounds. A claim for official immunity excites prejudice, but we can all understand the obligations of ordinary human confidence. If, however, he had wished to stand in that free condition, he should have forborne in the first place to hold himself out as a person desirous of hearing confessions, a systematic receiver of secrets, and, in the next place, he should not have presented himself as a witness at all."

The *Brighton Gazette* suggested that the "sinister effects of the Confessor's probe" upon the delicately balanced imagination of a girl who had undergone months of close confinement in the unhealthily intense atmosphere of a convent had caused her to become a victim to the delusion that she was guilty of the crime. Meanwhile Brighton became the scene of angry demonstrations, and Mr. Wagner himself "the centre of a whirling storm of execration".[1] The mob tore down the notices announcing the hours of confession outside St. Paul's, broke the windows of Wykeham Terrace, and a police guard had to be placed upon Mr. Wagner's vicarage and St. Mary's Home. The local Protestant Association, and similar bodies, called public meetings at which resolutions were passed urging the introduction of a Bill into Parliament "for the purpose of preventing such persons as the Reverend A. D. Wagner from officiating as a clergyman of the Church of England" and demands were made that "a stop be put to the conduct of affairs at St. Paul's".

"The Rev. Arthur Wagner," said the *Brighton Gazette*, "alone holds the key to the difficulty, but the key would unlock the secrets of the confessional and would violate the priestly conscience. . . . It is not enough to convict a person of a crime that the Court of Justice should know the truth, it must be acquainted with the *whole* truth and that is only to be obtained from the Rev. A. Wagner, who shields himself by saying 'My duty to God forbids me to answer any question which will in any way divulge anything that has been said to me in the secrecy of the Confessional'! The statement is positively astonishing, the consequences terrible. . . . Is the Confessional of the Anglican Church sealed against the law of the land?"

This question was the vital one; and although in the House of Lords the Lord Chancellor, in answer to a question put by

[1] *Wagner of Brighton*—H. Hamilton Maughan.

the Marquess of Westmeath, gave a decisive reply to it, there was none of the unanimity he seemed to indicate among the Judges.

"There can be no doubt," he said, "that in a suit of criminal proceedings a clergyman of the Church of England is not privileged to decline to answer a question put to him for the purpose of justice. . . . He is compelled to answer such a question, and the law of England does not allow even a Roman Catholic in dealing with a Roman Catholic to refuse to give evidence. . . . It is a matter of regret that the magistrates did not insist upon an answer."

When the matter was raised in the House of Commons by Mr. Whalley, M.P. for Brighton, asking whether the magistrates "were justified in allowing the Rev. A. D. Wagner to refuse to give evidence on the ground that the same had become known to him under the seal of the Confession", the Home Secretary's reply carefully evaded a definite statement. He said that the case in question had come before a full Bench of Magistrates and he "was not aware that they had allowed any person to refuse to give evidence", adding that "at the trial all necessary evidence would, no doubt, be forthcoming".

The Times commented as follows:

"The discussion in the House of Lords on Mr. Wagner's case has thrown little light upon the matter except that the Lord Chancellor has assured us that the law of England does not permit anyone to refuse to answer a question in a Court of Justice on the ground that the information sought to be elicited was imparted in Confession.

"Lord Granville tells us that the Bishops have no remedy, and the Bishop of London declares that he and his Right Reverend brethren will not be deterred 'from bringing an offender to justice when there is a distinct violation of the law'! Seeing that Mr. Wagner did what the Lord Chancellor tells us the law of England does not permit, these conflicting statements are very suggestive."

In point of fact, in spite of divided opinions and lack of precedents, this very question had recently been put to the test twice. In the first case an Anglican clergyman had yielded and given evidence under the threat of commitment for Contempt of Court, while in the second a Roman Catholic priest had actually been sent to prison on that count. But as John Rhode points out,[1]

"it became increasingly difficult to understand why Mr. Wagner had ever mentioned this most controversial question at all, unless it was to bring himself and his convictions into the limelight, to strike a blow, as it were, for the High Church point of view. In a letter to *The Times* he makes it quite clear that his evidence could be, and actually was, given without any reference to the matter."

Mr. Wagner's letter to *The Times* was as follows:

"As I have been most unjustly charged by a portion of the public Press with committing the grave offence of betraying Miss Kent's sacramental confession, you, I am sure, will allow me to contradict that assertion in the most public manner possible. It was at Miss Kent's own request, and by her authority, that I communicated to two persons only the fact of her guilt. These two were Sir George Grey and Miss Greame, and the following document, written by Miss Kent herself and given me a few days before Easter, proves that I have only acted in all I have done in accordance with her instructions. The note, which is entirely her own composition, is as follows: 'Sir, it is by my particular request that the bearer now informs you of my guilt, which it is my desire to have publicly made known. Constance E. Kent to Sir G. Grey.' I may add that the written paper which Miss Kent gave to Sir Thomas Henry at Bow Street was also, to the best of my belief, her own composition. I never saw it, nor was I aware of her having written any paper at all until she herself produced it in Court."[2]

---

[1] *The Case of Constance Kent*—John Rhode.
[2] See Footnote, page 208.

2

Miss Greame's allegation at Trowbridge that Constance had confessed to revenge against her step-mother as her motive for the crime revived those stories of ill-treatment which had caused the children to run away from home. Whether Constance on learning of these acted on her own initiative or whether she was persuaded to do so by others is not known, but on 18th May she wrote the following letter to Mr. Rodway:

"Sir,

"It has been stated that my feelings of revenge were excited in consequence of cruel treatment. This is entirely false. I have received the greatest kindness from both the persons accused of subjecting me to it. I have never had any ill-will towards either of them on account of their behaviour to me, which has been very kind. I shall be obliged if you will make use of this statement in order that the public may be undeceived on this point.

"I remain, Sir,

"Yours truly,
"Constance E. Kent."

But Mr. Rodway took no immediate steps to undeceive the public by publishing this letter, probably because it raised a new doubt: while it was conceivable that, goaded by a step-mother's ill-treatment, a girl of sixteen might have revenged herself by murdering that step-mother's favourite child, with the stimulus of ill-treatment removed the motive had still to be found. He decided therefore to explore the possibility of entering a plea of insanity, in which he was no doubt influenced by the rumours which had circulated concerning Constance's mother. He obtained the Lord Chancellor's sanction to have her examined by a well-known specialist in mental diseases, Dr. Bucknill, of Rugby; who, however, after a searching examination, "found himself compelled to advise the Defence to abandon the plea of insanity of which he could find no trace".

Meanwhile the greatest pressure was being exercised to induce Constance to withdraw her plea of Guilty and enter a defence, but she steadily refused; and it was only when it was pointed out to her that the judge might reject such a plea and insist upon a trial that she consented to be represented by Counsel. Mr. J. D. Coleridge, Q.C. (afterwards Lord Chief Justice), was briefed accordingly, but "before taking the very unusual course of acquiescing in a plea of Guilty he desired to have his instructions direct from his client",[1] and advised her: "If you plead Not Guilty, then whatever I can do shall be done for your acquittal. If you plead Guilty, anything I can say to set others right shall be said. But I advise you against any intermediate course."[2] Constance replied as follows:

"Sir,

"I announced my determination yesterday to Mr. Rodway to plead guilty, and then if the judge should consider that a trial would conduce to clear those who are unjustly suspected, I would consent to leave the case in the hands of my Counsel for that purpose.

"If the case is not gone into it will not be believed that my confession is a true one, and I am persuaded that nothing will tend to clear the innocent so completely as my conviction.

"Yours truly,
"Constance Kent."

---

[1] *The Road Murder*—J. B. Atlay.
[2] *Life and Correspondence of John Duke, Lord Coleridge.*

CHAPTER EIGHT

SALISBURY[1]

I

As THE day of the Assizes drew near public excitement mounted.

> "It was more than hinted," writes J. B. Atlay, "that the confession had been extorted, and was said that the Court would not accept the plea of guilty, but insist on trying out the case, and that incidentally the question whether the law recognizes as privileged statements made in confession would have to be set at rest once and for all."[2]

Late in the evening of Tuesday, 18th July—ten weeks and three days after she had been committed to Devizes Gaol—Constance Kent was removed to Salisbury. The gates of Salisbury Gaol opened to admit her and were quickly shut: once more she heard the formal delivery of her person to the authorities and was conducted along stone corridors to her cell.

The city was filled to overflowing, for, although no announcement had been made, "it was generally understood that the trial of Constance Kent for the murder of her step-brother would commence on 21st July at nine o'clock". Lodgings were at a premium; yet visitors continued to arrive and the streets teemed with people who discussed the case all day and far into the night.

Early next morning—Wednesday, 19th—"workmen began erecting barriers in front of the Council Chamber to keep back the immense crowd which was expected to press into Court for the trial". While these preparations were going on outside it, within it a Grand Jury of twenty-four county magistrates with

---

[1] Quotations unless otherwise stated are from the local Press.
[2] *The Road Murder*—J. B. Atlay.

Lord Henry Thynne as foreman was being sworn in before Mr. Justice Willes.

"After they had been sworn the Judge charged them in reference to the case and entered into a narrative dwelling on the fact that the missing night-dress was a material factor in the case.

"The inquiries of 1860, being fruitless, the family left the neighbourhood and Miss Kent was sent abroad. Afterwards she was placed in St. Mary's Hospital, Brighton, and in consequence of several conversations with Miss Greame, the Lady Superior, Mr. Wagner was communicated with, and the prisoner confessed that she murdered her brother out of spite for her step-mother. Subsequently a confession in writing was signed by her, and in consequence the prisoner was taken before Sir Thomas Henry and by him sent to the Wiltshire magistrates, where, on being asked with the usual caution whether she had anything to add, she had said she did it of her own free will.

"The Judge cautioned the jury that such a confession should be closely watched, but that the confession of the prisoner, coupled with the concurrent circumstances, warranted him in advising them that it was their duty to find a True Bill against her. The True Bill was returned."

That the Judge should have accepted the missing night-dress as "a material factor in the case" is curious in view of the evidence given in 1860; while the details of his narrative as to how Constance had made her confession is at variance both with the evidence given at Trowbridge[1] and with Mr. Wagner's letter to *The Times* already quoted.

Friday, 21st, dawned, and with its dawning a crowd began to collect which, as it grew in size and excitement, swept aside the barriers and the police who manned them, and fought its

[1] See Miss Greame's evidence, page 223.
"You had derived your information from other sources?"
"Yes."
"From whom?"
"I think it most likely that I heard it from Mr. Wagner—that he told me of it."

way up to the very doors of the "trumpery little Crown Court"
At 8.30 reinforcements of police had to be called out.

The building presented a blank and silent façade to the
eyes of those outside it, but within its walls one of the strangest
and most dramatic scenes in the long history of British justice
was already beginning. The prisoner had been conveyed to the
Court very early and secretly; Mr. Kent and Mary Ann had
also been smuggled in and conducted to a room where they
remained; thirty-five witnesses were already on the premises;
the Press and about a hundred privileged spectators had been
admitted; Mr. Karslake, Q.C., for the Crown, Mr. Coleridge,
Q.C., and Mr. Rodway had taken their places.

At 8.45 the Judge entered. "As soon as Mr. Justice Willes
had taken his seat the prisoner was placed at the Bar, and the
eyes of all who had been fortunate enough to obtain ingress
were fixed upon her." Dressed as she had been at Trowbridge,
but with her veil thrown back from her face, she "appeared in
good bodily health" and her "air of composure was even more
remarkable".

The indictment was read out in an intense silence.

"Constance Emilie Kent, you stand charged with having
wilfully murdered Francis Savile Kent at Road-hill House on
30th June, 1860. How say you: are you Guilty or Not Guilty?"

The words fell with dreadful distinctness into that strained
hush. The prisoner neither moved nor spoke.

The Judge: "Are you aware that you are charged with
having wifully, intentionally, and with malice killed your
brother?"

"Yes."

The Judge: "And do you plead guilty to that?"

Again the prisoner made no reply. The atmosphere was
taut with strain. Were her youth and the cherished hopes of
future achievement, for which she had striven so long against
the relentless tide of her destiny, assailing her with a last-
minute temptation to vindicate herself? In that fearful and
most solemn moment did she find it beyond her power to utter
that fatal word for which the Court and the scarlet-robed judge
were waiting—*because it was not true?*

The Judge: "What is your answer?"

Silence.

The Judge: "I must repeat to you that you are charged with having wilfully, intentionally and with malice killed and murdered your brother: Are you Guilty or Not Guilty?"

"Guilty."

He regarded her for a moment intently, then said heavily, as though the words cost him an effort:

"The plea must be recorded."

Mr. Coleridge then rose "amid the most painful silence and stated to his lordship that the prisoner wished to inform the Court that she alone was guilty of the murder; and that she wished to make her guilt known and atone for the crime, with a view to clearing the character of her father and others who had suffered most unjust and cruel suspicion. It afforded him pleasure to have the melancholy duty of stating that there was no truth whatever in the assertion that the prisoner was induced to perpetrate the crime because of harsh treatment at the hands of her step-mother, for she had always received the most uniform kindness from that lady, and on his honour he believed that to be true."

The Clerk: "Constance Emilie Kent, you have confessed yourself guilty of the murder of Francis Savile Kent; have you anything to say why sentence of death should not be passed upon you?"

"No."

The black square was placed on the judge's head. His face was set and pale.

"Constance Emilie Kent, you have pleaded guilty to an indictment charging you with the wilful murder of your brother Francis Savile Kent on 30th June, 1860. It is my duty to receive that plea which you have deliberately put forward, and it is a satisfaction to me to know that it was not done until after having had the advice of Counsel which would have freed you from this dreadful charge, if you could have been freed.

"I can entertain no doubt, after having read the evidence in the depositions, and considering this is your third confession of the crime, that your plea is the plea of a guilty person.

"The murder was committed under circumstances of great deliberation and cruelty. You appear to have allowed your feelings of jealousy and anger to have worked in your breast until at last they assumed over you the power of the Evil One."

Until then the prisoner had kept her eyes lowered: now she raised them to the Judge's face; they filled with tears of mortal sadness. Her lips moved; then she turned her head away.

"Whether Her Majesty with whom alone the prerogative of mercy rests may be advised to consider the fact of your youth at the time when the murder was committed, and the fact that you were convicted chiefly upon your own confession which removes suspicion from others, is a question which it would be presumption for me to answer here.

"It well behoves you to live what is left of your life as one who is about to die, and to seek a more enduring mercy, by sincere and deep contrition, and by reliance upon the only redemption and satisfaction for all the sins of the world. It only remains for me to discharge the duty which the law imposes upon the Court without alternative, and that is to pass upon you the sentence which the law adjudges for wilful murder. . . ."

A sob suddenly choked his voice: ("the greater part of the assembly as well as the jury were in tears".) Controlling his emotion with an effort the Judge then began, slowly and painfully, to pass sentence of death.

". . . That you be taken from this place where you now stand to the place whence you came, and that you be hanged by the neck until your body be dead . . ." (Again sobs forced him to stop, "and it was a minute or longer before he was able amidst great manifestations of feeling to conclude the pronouncement") ". . . that when your body be dead it be buried within the precincts of the gaol in which you were last confined. And may God have mercy on your soul."

2

So, as the clocks were striking nine, while the crowd roared for admittance to the court and the thirty-five witnesses waited to be called, Constance Kent was condemned to death at "proceedings which lasted only a few minutes . . . and was being conveyed in a prison van to the county gaol".

J. B. Atlay, Barrister-at-Law, writes: "Sentence of death was passed amidst a scene unexampled in our judicial annals. Mr. Justice Willes broke down in tears, the prisoner's fortitude gave way and there was not a dry eye in Court."

All who witnessed that scene were haunted by it. *Why?* The prisoner had stood in the dock self-accused of planning in cold blood and committing with consummate craft a deliberate and most revolting crime. She had stood there in a dowdy black dress and hat, with set face and lowered eyes, devoid of any of the beauty or allurement which can make so poignant an appeal to the senses. No defending Counsel, gifted with eloquence and skilled in the art of playing upon the Court's emotions, had lifted his voice on her behalf: on the contrary Mr. Coleridge had taken pains to point out that he believed Constance Kent, without the slightest provocation, had cut the throat of her defenceless brother out of spite towards his mother from whom "she had always received the most uniform kindness".

How to explain this paradox? There is no explanation unless it be that the personality of the silent girl impressed itself upon those who beheld her with such a profound sense of innocence that they knew instinctively "a judicial murder of a scarcely less obnoxious character" was taking place before their eyes.

That evening Constance Kent saw her father, William and her sisters at "a short but painful interview". Later Mr. Wagner and the Superior were, separately, admitted to her cell, and "she appeared much pleased with these visits, especially that of Miss Greame".

Constance asked that the £800 which Mr. Wagner had forwarded to Mr. Rodway should be handed over to her father "for the benefit of the family". As soon as the trial was over Mr. Kent returned to Rhydycilgwyn where he died of "a disease of the liver" on 5th February, 1872.

CHAPTER NINE

THE "DETAILED CONFESSION"

I

IT HAD been argued that it was not sufficient under British law that a person should avow a crime: a jury must be satisfied by means of corroborative evidence and circumstances that such an avowal was proved against the person making it. But the case of Constance Kent had never been submitted to a jury's consideration: she had been condemned to death without the usual process of a criminal trial.

"Constance Kent," said the *Observer*, "has been convicted and sentenced to death for murder. The crime has been most cruel and most deadly. Mr. Justice Willes—although not given to the melting mood—was seriously affected when he passed sentence of death. But although he could hold out no hope of mercy himself, he yet suggested some points which perhaps might weigh with those who have to advise the interposition of the prerogative for mercy. In the first place there was no trial. This is always unsatisfactory. But it could not be avoided for Counsel was cognizant and approving of the plea. In the second place she was convicted on her own confession, which is also unsatisfactory. All the more so since the former charge had failed for want of evidence."

But there were more positive grounds than this for the misgiving which was generally felt. In the first place the Court had failed to seek any explanation as to how Constance Kent "alone and unaided" had committed a crime which every authority in 1860, from the Attorney-General downwards, had declared "could only have been done by two persons". Secondly there was the question of the weapon: the medical evidence had stated categorically that the wound in the chest could only have been inflicted by a "long, strong, sharp-pointed knife like a carving-knife"; yet the judge had accepted without question, or any demand for elaboration, Constance's only reference to the weapon—given in conversation with Miss Greame—which was that "she had used a razor for the purpose".

> "Many conjectures," said the *Daily Telegraph*, "have been hazarded respecting the weapon which the murderer used, from the fact that the child had its throat cut and also a stab in the heart. . . . It is not easy to understand how a stab could be inflicted with a razor . . . and it is hardly probable that the perpetrator would take a razor . . . to cut the throat, and a sharp-pointed instrument to stab with."

In fact the public conscience was seriously disturbed; and although the announcement made on 26th July that Constance Kent's sentence had been commuted to penal servitude for life afforded some measure of relief, this was diminished by the thought of the horrors of prison life at that date—which included an initial period of nine months' solitary confinement for long-term offenders—so that many felt that even death itself might have been more merciful.

The only thing which could allay the general uneasiness would be a detailed confession from the condemned girl explaining exactly how she had committed the crime; and on 30th August what purported to be such a statement appeared in the Press in the form of a letter from Dr. Bucknill.

> "Sir," he wrote,[1]
>
> "I am requested by Miss Constance Kent to communicate to you the following details of the crime, which she confessed to Mr. Rodway, her solicitor, and myself, and which she now desires to be made public.
>
> "Constance Kent first gave an account of the circumstances of her crime to Mr. Rodway, and she afterwards

---

[1] The numbers and italics which appear in this letter have been inserted for the purpose of drawing particular attention to points which will be examined later.

acknowledged to me the correctness of that account when I recapitulated it to her. The explanation of her motive she gave to me, when, with the permission of the Lord Chancellor, I examined her for the purpose of ascertaining whether there were any grounds for supposing that she was labouring under mental disease. Both Mr. Rodway and I are convinced of the truthfulness and good faith of what she said to us.

"A few days before the crime she obtained possession of a razor from a green case in her father's wardrobe and secreted it. *This was the sole instrument she used* (1). She also secreted a candle with matches by placing them in a corner of the closet in the garden, where the murder was committed. On the night of the murder she undressed herself and went to bed because she expected that her sisters would visit her room.

"She lay awake watching until she thought that the household were all asleep, and *soon after midnight she left her bedroom and went downstairs and opened the drawing-room door and shutters* (2). She then went up into the nursery, withdrew the blanket from between the sheet and the counterpane and placed it on the side of the cot. *She took the child from his bed and carried him downstairs* (3) through the drawing-room.

"She had on her night-clothes and in the drawing-room put on her goloshes. *Having the child on one arm she raised the drawing-room window with the other hand, went round the house and into the closet* (4), *lighted the candle and placed it on the seat of the closet, the child being wrapped in the blanket and still sleeping* (5). *While the child was in this position she inflicted the wound in the throat* (6). She said she thought the blood would never come, and that the child was not killed, so *she thrust the razor into the left side* (7) and put the body with the blanket round it into the vault. *The light burned out* (8).

"*The piece of flannel which she had with her was torn from an old flannel garment placed in the waste-bag and which she had taken some time before and sewn it to use in washing herself* (9).

"She went back to her room, examined her dress and

found only two spots of blood on it (10). These she washed out
in the basin, and threw the water, which was but little
discoloured, into the foot-pan in which she had washed her
feet overnight.

"She took another of her night-dresses and got into bed.
In the morning her night-dress had become dry where it had
been washed. *She folded it up and put it into the drawer. Her
three night-dresses were examined by Mr. Foley and she
believed also by Dr. Parsons* (11), the medical attendant of
the family.

"She thought the bloodstains had been effectively
washed out, but on holding the dress up to the light *a day
or two afterwards she found the stains were still visible* (12).
*She secreted the dress, moving it from place to place, and she
eventually burned it in her own bedroom and put the ashes into
the kitchen grate.*

"*It was about five or six days after the child's death that
she burned the night-dress* (13). On Saturday morning, having
cleaned the razor, she took an opportunity of replacing it
unobserved in the case in the wardrobe.

"She abstracted her night-dress from the clothes-basket
when the housemaid went to fetch a glass of water. *The
stained garment found in the boiler-hole had no connection
whatsoever with the crime* (14).

"As regards the motive for her crime, it seems that
although she entertained at one time a great regard for the
present Mrs. Kent, yet if any remark was at any time made
which in her opinion was disparaging to any member of the
first family, she treasured it up and determined to revenge it.

"She had no ill-will against the little boy except as one
of the children of her step-mother. She declared that both
her father and her step-mother had always been kind to her
personally, and the following is a copy of a letter which she
addressed on this point while in prison before her trial. . . ."[1]

---

[1] I.e. the letter quoted on page 233. The rest of Dr. Bucknill's letter is
mainly concerned with the question of Constance Kent's sanity. He states that
"she evinced no symptoms" of insanity, but alludes to the possibility of her
becoming insane if subjected to solitary confinement. She was then still in
Salisbury Gaol and his observations may have been intended to influence the
authorities on her behalf.

2

"It will be a relief," said *The Times*, "to be offered a detailed confession from Constance Kent. So far as her confession had previously gone it amounted simply to acknowledgement of the fact, and it contained no explanation of the motive or of the manner in which it was committed. In this respect it was certainly very unsatisfactory, and although it was impossible not to feel with the judge that the confession had every appearance of truth, yet it is equally impossible not to be anxious that it should be made complete by the addition of the circumstances of the murder. . . ."

But in point of fact this "detailed confession" affords no relief, for it will not bear examination. Let us consider those points to which particular attention has already been drawn.

1. *The sole instrument used was her father's razor.* Attention has already been drawn to this point on page 242 and it will be necessary to refer to it again (see section 7).

2. "*Soon after midnight she left her bedroom and . . . opened the drawing-room door and shutters.*" But it was 12.45 when P.C. Urch saw the gas-lamp alight in the hall and a light burning behind the nursery curtains; and when Mrs. Kent heard the shutters being opened (and thought it was the servants) "*it was just light*".

3. "*She took the child from his bed and carried him downstairs.*" Let anyone try removing a boy of four from his bed at midnight without arousing him to vigorous protest: let them try carrying even an infant downstairs *in the dark*, unerringly!

4. "*Having the child on one arm she raised the drawing-room window with the other hand, went round the house and into the closet.*" Firstly; no child so "exceptionally heavy" as Savile could be carried on one arm like an infant: secondly; would anyone familiar with the house deliberately choose so complicated and circuitous a route, involving so many unnecessary

risks of attracting attention, when the backdoor offered the obvious exit?

5. She "lighted the candle and placed it on the seat of the closet, the child being wrapped in the blanket and still sleeping". That the child should have slept through all the movement to which it had been subjected since being taken from its bed, and still be asleep, is inconceivable.

6. "While the child was in this position" (i.e. lying on her arm) "she inflicted the wound in the throat." That the throat could be "severed in one clean cut to the very vertebrae" by someone unaccustomed to handling a razor, and while the child lay in such an awkward position, is exceedingly improbable.

7. "She thrust the razor into the left side." The medical evidence was clear as to the nature of the weapon which must have inflicted this wound—"it could not have been inflicted by a razor". This is obvious, for it is impossible to stab with a razor. If anyone should doubt this let him try the following experiment suggested by John Rhode: "Wrap a loaf of bread in a blanket and endeavour to inflict such a wound as is described upon it with an ordinary razor. It is difficult enough to make a long cut in the loaf, but to stab it, as the child was undoubtedly stabbed, is utterly impossible."

8. "The light burned out." Yet none of the innumerable searchers and investigators reported finding a pool of candle-grease on the seat of the privy next morning.

9. "The piece of flannel which she had with her was torn from an old flannel garment . . . which she had taken some time before and sewn it to use in washing herself." Foley in evidence described it as "a new article, shaped to fit a woman's bust". His description was corroborated by Mrs. Dallimore, who tried it on various members of the household. Had it been what Constance alleged, the maids must have seen it in her room, yet they denied all knowledge of it. In any case, for what purpose did she take it with her to commit a murder?

10. She "found only two spots of blood on" her night-dress. After cutting the child's throat while it lay on her arm, and stabbing it in the side? Comment is superfluous.

11 and 12. "She folded" her night-dress "up and put it into the drawer. Her three night-dresses were examined by Mr. Foley and

. . . *also by Dr. Parsons.* . . . *A day or two afterwards she found the stains were still visible.*" The night-dresses were also examined by Mrs. Dallimore. Yet none of the three noticed that one of the night-dresses in the drawer was soiled by a week's wear: all were expressly looking for stains, yet none noticed any mark on the garments!

13. *She secreted the night-dress, moving it from place to place, and eventually burned it in her own bedroom five or six days later.* Cox stated in evidence, "On Saturday, 30th, I took one of Miss Constance's night-dresses down to air as usual; one was in her drawer, and the third on her bed." Furthermore during these "five or six days" the house was in the hands of the police and for at least the last two of them they were searching specifically for the missing night-dress.

14. *"The stained garment found in the boiler-hole had no connection whatsoever with the deed."* That a blood-stained garment found the day after a murder in a place where it had obviously been concealed with the object of contriving its secret destruction should have no connection with the murder is not credible.

How, may one ask, did the child come by its bruised mouth and other unmistakable signs of suffocation? And how and when was the cot remade with that "practised neatness" which required *two hands*?

The "confession" bears the stamp of an exhausted young woman's responses to questions put to her by an Attorney chiefly concerned in pacifying public agitation. Had it been presented as a case for the Prosecution, it would have been demolished in five minutes by Counsel for the Defence.

Constance Kent failed to prove the case against herself.

CHAPTER TEN

EPILOGUE

I

MUCH has been written about the "amazing psychology" of Constance Kent. But it is only when one tries to regard her as the perpetrator of an abominable crime that she appears in any way abnormal, and this solely because of her complete normality. Search as one may there is no hint in her character of vindictiveness, jealousy or that vanity which marks the criminal, just as there is no trace, either in her brothers, her sisters or herself, of that insanity from which it was sought to establish that her mother suffered; while of her good-nature, unselfishness and tenderness, especially towards little children, there is ample evidence. On the other hand, not only within his household but beyond it, many were familiar with Mr. Kent's intemperate habits and violent temper which together might make him liable to just such an action as that which resulted in Savile's suffocation.

2

It is practically certain that Constance Kent, encouraged by her friends, had left Dinant for Brighton with the intention of equipping herself at St. Mary's—the only channel available to her—for service overseas in midwifery and child-welfare. She had surmounted her appalling handicap at Dinant; what made her rush upon her doom at Brighton when achievement lay before her? Why, after nearly two years—and just when she came of age—did Mr. Wagner betray the secret of her identity to Miss Greame? And why did they hasten with such speed to make her self-accusation irrevocable? Was it in order to conceal evidence of moral, material and spiritual pressure applied by them? The very pains they took to rebut the suggestion serve only to point to it the more emphatically.

Was spiritual pressure exerted by refusing her admission to

the Sacraments; moral pressure by disclosing her identity to the other inmates of the Institution; and material pressure by threatening her with expulsion? Finally, what benefit was derived by forcing her into the Courts?

Perhaps the answers to these questions—particularly the last—lie in the following extract from Canon Hutchinson's foreword to H. Hamilton Maughan's booklet *Wagner of Brighton*:

> "I am especially grateful to the author for the information he gives of the case of Constance Kent, and the almost nation-wide stir it made, and the prominence given by it to the integral place of the confessional in the economy of the English Church. All the great guns were brought up and trained on Wagner of Brighton in that connection.
>
> "He stood his ground, and a great—a really great— victory was won. One might almost say that from that time the confessional in the Church of England remained unchallenged."

The case of Constance Kent made history.

3

This girl, whose life was to be a saga of suffering, had been born of her mother's piety and her father's passion into an age of intense religious revival. She had spent her childhood in a part of England through which Wesley's evangelism had flamed, and her adolescence within close range of the Oxford Movement through one of its most ardent exponents, the Reverend W. I. E. Bennett, of Frome. I am persuaded that, with the failure of her flight with William, during the long hours alone in the charge-room of Bath Police Station, she began to construct for herself a philosophy based on the purgation of emotion through submission to the will of Providence—which alone could arm her against her step-mother's tyranny—and to register the determination to gain her independence by earning her own livelihood.

The results can be seen in her application to her studies,

I*

and the composure she maintained through all her ordeals. But these related to the mind and body: at St. Mary's she was subjected to a spiritual onslaught as well.

I am convinced that she was innocent of the crime; but that the measures taken at St. Mary's induced in her the belief that only by taking its guilt upon herself could she escape from it; that only through the process of self-annihilation could she attain spiritual rebirth.

I am convinced that the greatest obstacle she had to overcome was acting the lie of guilt, and that she could only bring her conscience to it by regarding it as the means to an end which justified it—the absolving of her father's guilt and the attaining through love of the Kingdom of Love. *Pietas*.

"My course," she had cried to him, "is due to you and God."

4

From Salisbury she was sent to Millbank Prison, which stood close to the Houses of Parliament. She was not subjected to the nine months' solitary confinement which was the usual lot of long-term offenders in those days, and she was given a cell to herself. A silent figure with her cropped hair and in her hideous prison garb, never speaking unless spoken to, she unobtrusively carried out the duties allotted to her, her greatest tribulation being those visitors who obtained a ghoulish thrill from having her pointed out to them.

"Constance Kent," writes Major Arthur Griffith, "who I remember at Millbank, was first employed in the laundry and afterwards in the infirmary. A small, mouse-like creature, with much of the promptitude of the mouse or the lizard, surprised, in disappearing when alarmed. The approach of any strange or unknown face whom she feared might come to spy her out and stare constituted a real alarm for Constance Kent. When anyone went the length of asking, 'Which is Constance?' she had already concealed herself somewhere with wonderful rapidity and cleverness. She was a mystery in every way. It was almost impossible to believe that this insignificant, inoffensive little person could have cut her infant brother's throat in circumstances of peculiar atrocity. No doubt there were features in her face which the criminal anthropologist would have seized upon as being suggestive of instinctive criminality—high cheek bones, a lowering, overhanging brow, and deep-set, small eyes; but yet her manner was prepossessing, and her intelligence was of a high order, while nothing could exceed the devoted attention she gave the sick under her charge as a nurse."[1]

Later, at Parkhurst, her artistic talents were discovered and put to use in executing the mosaics which adorn the chapel in the Bishop's Palace at Chichester, the sanctuary of East Grinstead Church, and that in St. Paul's Cathedral. In penal servitude she found an outlet for her abilities and attained the peace of mind she had so long sought.

She was released from Fulham Prison on 18th July, 1885, and was met by members of a Community affiliated with St. Mary's which Mr. Wagner[2] had established at Buxted—some twenty miles from Brighton—where he had a house. The end of her story was related to me by one of this sisterhood who was twenty-two years of age at the time.

"All the sisters were full of fear when they were told that a convicted murderess was to live in their midst, but our chaplain pointed out that she had made full atonement for her sin, and he asked us," she said with a little smile, "how many of us could say the same?"

When Constance Kent—who now called herself Emilie King—had left Dinant she had looked what she was, a well-educated young lady who had learned "deportment" at a finishing school in France. Looking into the clear, bright eyes of my informant—eyes which had looked into Constance's own—I learned with compassion of the changes which twenty years of penal servitude had wrought in her.

[1] *Secrets of the Prison House*—Arthur Griffith, H.M. Inspector of Prisons.
[2] Mr. Wagner died in 1902; he left estate to the value of £50,000

"She walked like a convict—flatly. Her hands were rough and hard, and she had forgotten how to sit at table and how to use a knife and fork. . . . She wore dark spectacles, and she had to report to the police at Brighton every month. . . ."

"She had lovely auburn hair," I said, "soft and wavy."

"They had cropped it short. Things had been put on it in the prison—for insects, you know. It was harsh, and almost black. . . . I was with her more than anyone else—except for a friend she had: a wealthy and influential lady who took a great interest in her. At first she was very silent, but when I got to know her better she used to talk about her time in France, and the nuns there and the fine embroidery they taught her to do—and the little children: she loved little children. She liked to talk of her mosaics, too, especially the one in St. Paul's Cathedral—have you seen it? . . . No, she never spoke of her family."

"It has been stated," I said, "that she joined an Anglican sisterhood and went abroad."

"Oh no, she never joined a sisterhood. But she did go abroad —to Canada. The lady I spoke of used her influence to get her there. She stayed with us until all the arrangements had been made. Before she went she gave me a little book as a keepsake —excerpts from the Gospels."

"She got work in Canada?" I asked.

"She was trained in nursing. Her work was arranged before she left. She corresponded regularly with the lady I spoke of right up to the time of her death. The lady herself told me of it—she too died not so many years ago." There was a pause, then my informant added softly: "Miss King was well content. We always prayed for her. We remember her still in our prayers."

5

There is reason to believe that "Miss King" through the influence of her friend obtained employment after her own heart, accompanying to Canada one of those batches of child emigrants which were leaving England periodically, and that the remainder of her life was devoted to their welfare.

POSTSCRIPT

I

WHEN this book was already in the hands of the publishers I heard from Mr. John Rhode that, subsequent to the publication of *The Case of Constance Kent*, he had written another account of the crime in a volume, now out of print, entitled *The Anatomy of Murder*, in which he had incorporated some fresh material. He very kindly sent me the book in question.

The new material to which he referred consists of an unsigned document he received soon after *The Case of Constance Kent* appeared. This had been posted from Sydney, New South Wales, and was dated February 1929. Unfortunately it has since been destroyed, Mr. Rhode tells me, by enemy action, so it is only possible to comment upon those quotations which are given in *The Anatomy of Murder*.

On the subject of the first Mrs. Kent's reputed madness, the Sydney document says:

"Was Mrs. Kent insane? Her two elder daughters always vehemently denied it. No act has ever been mentioned to prove it. The second governess[1] who was employed for the education of the two elder daughters, arrived about the time of John's birth in 1842. She was a pretty, very capable woman. Considering Mrs. Kent's frequent confinements, also several miscarriages, and that servants took advantage of the circumstances, was it anything out of the way that Mr. Kent was only too glad to find someone willing and able to superintend the *ménage*? Many wives are incompetent or unwilling housekeepers, but they are not therefore deemed insane. As Mr. Kent only ceased to live with her about two years later, did he then consider her so?"

This passage confirms my own contention that the first Mrs. Kent was perfectly sane, and the confirmation is all the more striking in view of the fact that hitherto her insanity has

[1] I.e. Mary Pratt.

been taken so much for granted that in 1865 articles were contributed to *The Lancet* and the *British Medical Journal* suggesting that Constance had committed the murder in a frenzy of hereditary madness.

On Constance's relations with "the governess" the document has this to say:

"The governess had made a great pet of Constance and was very fond of her, but soon trouble began. The governess had a theory that once a child said a letter or spelt a word right it could not forget it, and she conscientiously believed that it was her duty to treat any lapse as obstinacy. The letter H gave Constance many hours of confinement in a room where she listened longingly to the music and sights on the lawn outside. When words were to be mastered punishments became more severe. Days were spent shut up in a room with dry bread and milk and water for tea. At other times she would be stood in a corner of the hall sobbing 'I want to be good, I do, I do', till she came to the conclusion that goodness was impossible for a child and that she could only hope to grow up quickly as grown-ups were never naughty. At times she gave way to furious fits of temper and was locked away in a distant room and sometimes in a cellar that her noise might not annoy people.

"Constance did not take her punishments very seriously, but generally managed to get some amusement out of them. Once, after being particularly provocative and passionate, the governess put her down in a dark wine cellar. She fell on a heap of straw and fancied herself in the dungeon of a great castle, a prisoner taken in a battle fighting for Bonnie Prince Charlie and to be taken to the block next morning. When the governess unlocked the door and told her to come up she was looking rather pleased with her fancies. The governess asked her what she was smiling over 'Oh', she said, 'only the funny rats.'

" 'What rats?' asked the governess, who did not know there were any there.

" 'They do not hurt me. Only dance and play about.'

"After that, to her disappointment she was shut in the

beer cellar, a light room but with a window too high to look out of. She managed to pull the spigot out of a cask of beer. After that she was locked up in one of the two spare rooms at the end of the vestibule, shut off by double doors. She liked the big room, for it had a large four-poster bed she could climb about, but the little room was dreary. The rooms had a legend attached to them and were said to be haunted on a certain day when a blue fire burned in the fireplace.

"At one time at Baynton House Constance's place of punishment was in one of the empty garrets. The house was built in the shape of an E, and there was a parapet round the best part of the house. She used to climb out of the window and up the bend on the top of the roof and slide down the other side. She tied an old fur across her chest to act the monkey and called it playing Cromwell. To return she got through the window of another garret. The governess was puzzled at always finding the door unlocked with the key left in. The servants were questioned but of course knew nothing. One day she found Constance and her brother out on the ledge and told them not to do it as it was dangerous. Next time when she did climb out she found the window fastened. She could not climb back the way she came, but just where the parapet ended was the window of a room where the groom slept. She reached across and climbed through, and though she upset and broke a jug on the washstand, the cat got the credit for this. Afterwards she heard that her father did not approve of the window being fastened to trap her, and said when unruly she could be shut in the study, the room where her father wrote and kept his papers. Being on the ground floor she easily got out of the window and passed her time climbing the trees in the shrubbery, also displaying a very cruel disposition by impaling slugs and snails on sticks in trees, calling these crucifixions. The affection between Constance and the governess no longer existed."

Mr. Rhode comments that all this throws light upon "the strange character of Constance Kent". But does it? Does it not rather throw a lurid light upon the strange character of her step-mother? To me it seems to reveal that Constance endured a malignant persecution with remarkable pluck and fortitude. The punishments described were so obviously devised by a pitiless woman in the determination to break that spirit in the child which led her to quell with flights of make-believe her natural terror of a haunted room, of rats in the dark cellar and crawling spiders in the stuffy attic. It is not surprising that her health was in consequence seriously affected as related in Chapter Four, Part I.

That the punishments were out of all proportion to the misdeeds is clear when we are told that for merely watching some children at play beyond the grounds of the house, whose games they longed, but were forbidden, to join, Constance's and William's little gardens were uprooted and despoiled. For none of the first family were allowed either friends or play-mates; nor were they permitted pets, and a pair of little birds sent to them from the West Indies by Edward were consigned to a sunless, disused room where they perished of cold.

As for the "crucifixion" of the slugs and snails what evidence is this of "a very cruel disposition"? Constance would have seen the gardener scores of times, impaling them on his fork as destructive pests, and, as children will, copied his example. There is no record anywhere of her causing a moment's pain to any more sentient creature.

The picture of this thwarted, ill-used little girl condemned to stand for long hours in a corner of the hall of her home, on legs becoming inflamed and soon to cripple her, sobbing with pain and hunger while her family took their meals in the adjoining room, is one to wring the heart.

And of this woman who ordained all this the worst Constance had to say, even in the confidences of school-friends, were those trifling utterances which Helen Moody repeated in the witness-box; while in return for it all—and for the far greater evil done to her after the crime—Constance wrote from her cell in Devizes Gaol in 1865 that at the hands of her step-mother she had never received anything but kindness.

The document goes on to confirm the nature of the relation-ship between "the governess" and Samuel Kent.

"Why did the mother when speaking to her" (i.e. Constance) "often call herself, your poor Mamma, which the governess said was silly? Why was the governess taken out for drives and her mother never? Why was her father in the library with the governess while the rest of the family was with her mother? She remembered many little incidents which seemed strange. One was during a thunderstorm, when the governess acted as though frightened and rushed over to her father who drew her down on his knee and kissed her. The governess exclaimed, 'Oh, not before the child.' Though her mother seemed to feel being placed in the background, why did she not resent it and assert herself?"

These were the questions everyone was asking; this was the situation which caused the Kents to be socially boycotted by their neighbours and led to those awkward interviews between Mr. Kent and Mr. Howell, of the Board of Factory Commissioners.

At school, the document alleges, Constance was perpetually in trouble. We know little about her schooldays, but what we do know indicates the precise opposite; at least we possess the positive evidence that she was well-liked by both her schoolmistresses and fellow pupils at Beckington, and was awarded a prize for good conduct.

On the subject of her confession, and of her motives for the crime, the document has nothing new to say, but follows in the well-worn track.

2

In *The Anatomy of Murder* Mr. Rhode suggests that this anonymous document might have been written by Constance herself, but in a recent letter he has informed me that a handwriting expert, Dr. C. Ainsworth Mitchell, has compared the document with Constance's letter reproduced on pages 192-4, and "in spite of the interval between the two gave it as his opinion that it was unlikely that the writings were by the same hand".

This gives me satisfaction for it coincides with my own opinion, based upon all I know of Constance Kent, that, apart from what she may have said to Mr. Wagner and Miss Greame, never at any time did she allude to the crime—not even to the intimate friend whom I mention in the final chapter of this book.

Who, then, was the author of the Sydney document?

It must be remembered that the Kent *ménage* had been focussing attention upon itself for years before the crime, and that at Mr. Slack's inquiry—among a host of other people— some thirty of their former servants were examined. In 1860 Road and its neighbourhood were humming with the case; accounts of such incidents as those related in the document were passing from lip to lip, and many of them are current there today. It only needed someone on the spot to collect and arrange them—perhaps through the medium of those voluminous letters or diaries in which the Victorians took so much delight—for all the material of the document to be available to its anonymous author in 1929.

APPENDIX I

THE following theory to account for the crime appeared in the *Bath Chronicle* in 1860:

". . . It appears to be irrefutably proved that the murder of this unhappy child was committed by someone in the house. Now, was that person an habitual dweller in the house or a stealthy visitor, whose visits were made possible and safe by another person? In either case, suppose that those visits were made with impure objects. Suppose that the girl Gough was the object of these visits, and that no greater crime attaches to her in the first instance than that she was not stronger than thousands of her sex to resist temptation. Now we proceed to the supposition, no very violent one, that a menial servant might have an intrigue. We do not, of course, assert that such was the case, as in the absence of proof no one has the right to make such an assertion, but . . . in whose house has such an incident not taken place, during any long period of housekeeping?

We now come to the graver question. If this girl had an intrigue, who was the *particeps criminis*? Was he a person to whom exposure would have been so terrible that it seemed to him worth while to prevent it by the most hideous of all crimes? . . . Were he a labourer, or any similar chance connection, the worst that he could expect from exposure would be the loss of a place or some disagreeable treatment from his superiors or employers. . . . It is not such a disgrace, or punishment, that falls upon such an offender, that would drive him to a horrible crime. . . .

If this hypothesis that the girl had an illicit intrigue and that the other party preferred murder to exposure be well founded, we must unhappily endeavour to find someone to whom such exposure would have been ruin, or at all events would have produced a state of things so terrible to himself that in a moment of wild terror he seized the most dreadful means of avoiding it. Who is there to whom such terms would at all apply? . . . Let us suppose him to have paid a nocturnal visit to the partner in the wrong; . . . that the dawning of a June morning revealed him to the wondering eyes of an awakened child; that the mingled feelings of the moment rushed upon him at a time when we are all prone to give way to foolish promptings . . . when we have all the power of thought, almost painfully vivid, but are without the will and wise resolution which comes when we buckle ourselves to the duties of the day. . . . Roused in sudden action by a painful necessity at such a moment . . . what would the effect of that hour be to a man who was guilty, meanly guilty, and was convinced that in an hour or two an innocent voice that could not be silenced would proclaim him guilty? *That could not be silenced*. A weak, bad, terrified, violent man sees a child between him and ruin—and the fearful deed is madly done.

There is an hypothesis, and it is at least more tenable than many of the solutions that have yet been proposed. Let it be thought over . . . in connection with the stages at which these subsequent points fasten upon the following questions:

How the statement of the nurse that she supposed the child cried, and therefore that his mother moved him, can be received as worth anything? Is a mother at a distance more likely to hear a child cry than the nurse at its side? Is this an excuse which would have occurred to an experienced nursemaid, except in the flurry of having to concoct a story at short notice?—and if we shrink from placing the case in the plainest of words on paper, it is not because we have the least doubt as to its being most meet and right to do so. . . . Has due thought been given to the conduct of the only person to whom as it seems to us the hypothesis we have shadowed could apply?

A child is lost from its bedroom . . . in the *penetralia* of the mansion . . . and a man to whom the child should have been most dear . . . who should have been most intense and practical in his researches after it, adopts the frivolous idea that the child has been stolen by gypsies! Had he said that it had been flown away with by the angels, the suggestion, under the circumstances, could not have been more ridiculous. But with this folly in hand he rushes to Trowbridge. Is it irrational to suppose that . . . the scouring away from the scene, the avoiding of being present at the discovery, the obtaining time to prepare a manifestation of surprise and grief, might have been demonstrations easily connecting themselves with the other symptoms of this case . . . ?"

APPENDIX II

THE following communication appeared anonymously in certain organs of the Press soon after Constance Kent had been condemned to death at Salisbury:

"Mrs. Kent was never a mill girl, nor in any way connected with a mill. She was born at Tiverton, Devon, and was the daughter of one of the most respected tradesmen in the town. She was educated in a first-class school under the charge of a lady of superior attainments. In fact she received a superior education to qualify her completely to fulfil the situation of governess and such a position she had occupied before her engagement in the family of Mr. Kent.

The statement of ill-treatment by her of Mr. Kent's children has not even the shadow of truth about it. What Constance Kent instructed her Counsel to say was literally the fact—that she had been treated by her step-mother with 'kind and forbearing love'. Mrs. Kent was brought up as a lady and has always conducted herself as such. I must observe that Mrs. Kent's first child was born ten months after her marriage."

APPENDIX III

The Rt. Hon. the Lord Coleridge to the Rt. Hon. W. E. Gladstone

"Hotel Bellevue,
The Hague,
Easter Day (6th April) 1890.

My dear Mr. Gladstone,

Your letter reached me here in (I think) perhaps the most beautiful capital city I was ever in. I should not bore you, but I think it will interest you to know what Willes (Sir James) once told me he thought as to confession.

He was on the whole the greatest and *largest* lawyer I ever knew, and I knew Jessel, Cairns and Campbell. I defended Constance Kent, John Karslake prosecuted her, and Willes tried her at Salisbury. Wagner was to have been a witness and Willes had made up his mind that he should have to *hold* one way or the other as to the sanctity of confession. He took infinite pains to be right, and he was much interested because the point since the Reformation had never been decided. There were strong dicta of strong Judges —Lord Ellenborough, Lord Wynford and Alderson—that they would never allow Counsel to ask a clergyman the question. On the other hand Hill, a great lawyer and good man, *but* a strong Ulster protestant, had said that there was no *legal* privilege in a clergyman. The thing did not come to a decision for Constance Kent pleaded guilty, and Karslake told me he should never have thought of putting the question to Wagner, and I had resolved *if* he did (but I knew he was a gentleman) that as an advocate I would not object but use it in my speech. Willes, however, I suppose did not know us quite so well as we knew each other; and he had prepared himself to *uphold* my objection if I made it. He said he had satisfied himself that there was a *legal* privilege in a priest to withhold what passed in confession. Confession, he said, is made for the purpose of absolution. Absolution is a judicial act, the priest in absolving acts as a Judge, and no Judge is ever obliged to state the reasons for his judicial determination. . . . Whether the English Judges would have upheld Willes's law I own I doubt—but I thought it might interest you to know the opinion and the grounds of it of so great a lawyer and so really considerable a man.

. . . .

Always most truly and gratefully yours,

Coleridge."

APPENDIX IV

The Reverend A. D. Wagner to the Rt. Hon. W. E. Gladstone

"Vicarage,
Brighton,
July 24, 1865.

My dear Sir,

You will not, I hope, think me guilty of any impropriety if I write a note to you at the present moment of anxiety to beseech you that if you can do anything in behalf of Constance Kent, you would kindly do it.

She has acted so honourably ever since she has been in prison in refusing to plead not guilty—tho' great pressure has been laid upon her to induce her to do so—that I trust mercy will be shewn her by those in whose hands the decision of her case lies.

What I could most wish for her would be that if her sentence could be commuted she might be handed over to my custody at St. Mary's Hospital, where she would be almost as much shut out of the world as in a prison, but could be at the same time in enjoyment of those religious privileges to which she has been accustomed, and which, under God, have mainly led her to repentance.

Hoping that you will forgive me the liberty I have taken in thus writing to you,

Believe me,
Yours very faithfully,
A. D. Wagner."

The Rt. Hon. W. E. Gladstone to the Rev. A. D. Wagner

"July 25, '65.

My dear Sir,

I am so entirely unacquainted with the rules which guide the Executive in matters of criminal jurisprudence that I feel a great difficulty in interfering with respect to the custody of Constance Kent. I will gladly forward to Sir Geo: Grey any statement you may send me for the purpose, and will state to him anything that may occur to me as likely to support it.

I must take this opportunity of recording my sense of the

extraordinary injustice with which you have recently been treated
in regard to this case. Having conferred a real service on society,
you have been dealt with by a large portion of the Press as if you
were yourself a criminal. You have borne and will bear this by a
strength proceeding from within and from above. But society is not
intentionally unjust, and commonly comes round after a while in
such cases. After a while I think it must come to be recognized that
in the faithful discharge of your pastoral office you have conferred
a service on your country.

W. E. G."

The Reverend A. D. Wagner to the Rt. Hon. W. E. Gladstone

"Vicarage,
Brighton,
August 16th, 1865.

My dear Sir,

As I fear from Mr. Gladstone's reply to my last note that
I may have no opportunity for some time to come of speaking to
you, by word of mouth, on the subject of Constance Kent, and as
I am anxious to lose no opportunity, thro' any unnecessary delay
on my part, of giving her what help I can, I venture to write another
note to you, in continuation of my former one, the purport of which
is to ask you whether you think anything can be done to get the
sentence passed on her somewhat modified.

I cannot of course but feel very thankful, for her friends' sake,
that Her Majesty has been pleased to commute C. Kent's sentence
to penal servitude for life, yet that commuted sentence is in her
case—who was, I trust, well prepared for death and possessed of
great courage—almost a worse punishment than the original one,
not so much because it involves a life-long penance, as because it
cuts her off from some of the means of Grace to which she has been
accustomed, and from the use of many spiritual books which may
be of great benefit to her soul, exposed as she is likely to be as life
advances, and with such sad antecedents, to great internal
temptations.

The particular boon, therefore, which I earnestly pray for on
her behalf, and which, tho' it would bring with it little else but
trouble, anxiety and expense on myself, I would do almost anything
to accomplish would be this, that after a certain period of imprisonment, longer or shorter, she might be handed over to my custody

and confined in St. Mary's Hospital either with a ticket of leave or in any other way that the proper authorities might approve of. She might thus be kept almost as secluded from the world as in a prison, and I would willingly make myself responsible for her good conduct, and for the observance on her part of any conditions which it might be thought proper by authority to impose.

Her conduct during the 21 months she lived at St. Mary's was so uniformly good—she was always so truthful and ready to do anything I told her—she has acted so honourably in coming forward at the probable sacrifice of her own life to establish the innocence of others, and lastly she has so manfully resisted the temptations offered her by the lawyers to plead not guilty that I cannot but feel that her case is a very different one from that of an ordinary criminal, who has been condemned simply because he could not help it, and that, tho' she ought not altogether to escape temporal punishment, yet perhaps that punishment might be modified without injustice in some such merciful way as I have suggested. Indeed to be confined for life in a religious house, and in an involuntary way, would be thought by many no small punishment in itself, and hardly less than confinement in a prison.

If you think anything can be done in the matter I should be most grateful. You will not, I am sure, be surprised at my feeling anxious about her, because tho' I did not suggest to her the propriety of giving herself up to justice, I concurred in it when she proposed it and so have to a certain extent incurred some responsibility in the matter. It would be a great sorrow to me if the result of what she has done were in any way prejudicial to her soul. I care comparatively little for the temporal part of her punishment, believing that it will do her no harm, nay, that patiently borne, it will deepen the grace of repentance in her heart.

With many apologies for bothering you in the matter,

Believe me,
Yours very faithfully,
A. D. Wagner."

The Rt. Hon. W. E. Gladstone to the Reverend A. D. Wagner

"Aug. 17, '65.

My dear Sir,

I transmit to you herewith a letter and enclosure which Mr. Waddington[1] has kindly sent me. I am afraid it offers no

---

[1] Permanent Under-Secretary, Home Office.

present or early prospect of compliance with your wishes, the rules in criminal cases being, I apprehend, very rigid.

W. E. G."

The Rt. Hon. W. E. Gladstone to the Rt. Hon. Sir William Harcourt

"Oct. 14, 1880.

My dear Harcourt,

    I have not the knowledge which would be necessary to warrant an opinion or even a suggestion on the inclosed letter of Mr. Wagner which recommend the release of Constance Kent.

    But I can speak to the merits of Mr. Wagner in connection with this particular case, which, availing himself of a slight personal acquaintance, he originally submitted to Sir George Grey through me.

    Mr. Wagner is a well-known High Church clergyman at Brighton who as the pastor of Constance Kent received her confession of her crime, and induced her to make the confession to the ministers of public justice. He thus conferred a service to society by bringing to light a terrible crime, which the police of the country had vainly laboured for years and years to discover.

    I give this not as a reason which should bias your judgement against general rules, but as one which governs me in bringing the case before you. This I will simply tell him I have done.

. . . .

Yours sincerely,
W. E. G."

The Rt. Hon. W. E. Gladstone to the Reverend A. D. Wagner

"Oct. 14th, 1880.

My dear Sir,

    I am unable, of course, to pronounce upon the course which ought to be taken with regard to your request on behalf of Constance Kent. But I have a lively recollection of the occasion to which you refer, and I feel that I cannot do less (I regret I cannot do more) than bring your request before Sir William Harcourt and set forth the ground of your personal title to be heard with respect and attention in the matter.

I remain,
Faithfully yours,
W. E. G."

The Rt. Hon. Sir William Harcourt to the Rt. Hon. W. E. Gladstone

"Oban,
Oct. 20, 1880.

Dear Mr. Gladstone,

Your letter of the 14th on the subject of Constance Kent only reached me to-day. I will have the matter carefully considered. It seems strange to me to have to deal with this case when I recollect in the early days of my married life the pain and trouble the case caused Sir C. Lewis who was greatly blamed, I remember, for not being convinced the guilty person was the father.

. . . .

Yours sincerely,
W. V. Harcourt."

INDEX